Intimate Solutions
A 21st Century Guide to Managing Your Relationship

Intimate Solutions

A 21st Century Guide
to Managing Your
Relationship

Dr Andrew Stanway

Vermilion
LONDON

1 3 5 7 9 10 8 6 4 2

First published in the United Kingdom in 2004 by Vermilion,
an imprint of Ebury Press
Random House UK Ltd
Random House
20 Vauxhall Bridge Road
London SW1V 2SA

Random House Australia (Pty) Limited
20 Alfred Street, Milsons Point, Sydney
New South Wales 2061, Australia

Random House New Zealand Limited
18 Poland Road, Glenfield
Auckland 10, New Zealand

Random House (Pty) Limited
Endulini, 5A Jubilee Road, Parktown 2193, South Africa

Random House UK Limited Reg. No. 954009
www.randomhouse.co.uk
Papers used by Vermilion are natural, recyclable products
made from wood grown in sustainable forests.

A CIP catalogue record is available for this book from the British Library.

ISBN: 0091891590

Typeset by seagulls

Printed and bound in Great Britain by
Mackays of Chatham plc, Chatham, Kent

I would like to thank the many patients whose wisdom and experience have enriched my understanding and enabled me to extend my professional insights. My wife, Penny, has helped me put into practice the things I preach. Without her this book would not have been possible.

Contents

Top Ten Myths About Bad Relationships

People in a bad relationship often say:

PART TWO

**Sixty-four Things That Can Destroy Relationships
and What You Can Do About Them**

Contents

Introduction

In nearly thirty years of working with couples with problems, I have learned one major lesson: relationships can be managed, just like other areas of our lives. Most people have lost sight of this or have never known it to be true. They are influenced by a number of cultural myths; have all kinds of irrational agendas from their pasts; would rather see themselves or their relationship as 'broken' so it's someone else's responsibility to mend it; or sincerely believe that there is some kind of 'magic' to making a success of man-woman relationships. There is not.

Relating to one another is a skill that some people alight on more easily than do others. But it is learnable, and without a doubt, those who appear to possess it 'naturally' have, in fact, learned it from the cradle.

The beauty of all this is that such skills can be acquired by anyone who cares to take the time. There are no mysteries – only realities for those who are prepared to take the trouble.

This book is about managing yourself. It is not about managing your partner. The only person you can change is yourself.

RELATIONSHIP BUSINESS

Today's woman is actively involved in the management of her work life, her family and friends, her leisure time, and even, sometimes, her partner. Yet strangely, she often fails to believe that her intimate emotional life can be positively managed in the same way.

I have spent literally thousands of hours listening to individuals and couples talking about their problems. Many feel hopeless and helpless, fear that nothing can be done and certainly never imagine they could creatively manage their way out of things. That this is not only possible but desirable is the basis of my marital work with couples. I can only be a 'management trainer'; they have to direct their own lives. No outsider, however skilled, can manage anyone else's relationship business for them. And they shouldn't even try.

I start off on this journey by asking couples to think of their relationship as a real business. Like any company it has resources, a brand image, a management team, a past, a current trading position, a bank account, and, hopefully, a future. All of these need managing on a daily basis. The two key members of staff are, of course, the couple themselves but in the realities of life their business has all kinds of ancillary 'staff' that include their parents, other relatives, their children, their work colleagues and friends, and indeed everyone who plays a part in their life together. A boss at work, a new baby, someone of the opposite sex, and much more can, unwittingly, have a profound impact on the way a couple's relationship business works. Some 'staff' even have profound effects after they are dead! As in any other business, their legacy lives on after them.

BRANDING

We live in a world dominated by universally recognized brands such as Nike, Coca-Cola, McDonald's, and so on. Branding is about being focused and communicating what's different about your product to the outside world. Now think of yourself as a brand. Your relationship is the 'marketplace' in which you function. Ask yourself these questions:

▶ What qualities do I have that I'm most proud of?
▶ What do I want to be 'famous' for in my relationship?
▶ What am I best at?
▶ What do I have that adds measurable, distinctive value?

Identifying these attributes of your brand is a great start on your journey to building a thriving relationship 'business'. As with any branding exercise you'll need to assess every day-by-day decision against whether it will enhance or detract from delivering the values you want to associate with your brand. Positive branding ensures that every communication, spoken or unspoken, is upbeat and a clear 'next step'. The main job of all brands is to develop a relationship with their customers. The Nikes and BMWs of the world leave us feeling we'd like to do business with them again. It's a pleasure being associated with them and what they stand for. How good does your brand make you or your partner feel?

It's obvious, then, that brands are measured not only by their financial and sales successes, but by the feel-good factors they generate. When you're developing your 'me' brand, be sure to monitor how effectively you are building your brand values. What perceptions are you creating in your customer's (partner's) eyes? Do they fit with where you want your brand to be? Brands stand for a particular attitude. Nike sponsors certain sports stars but not others. Häagen-Dazs ice cream isn't just about 'food' or 'nutrition'. A brand delivers its message straight to the heart, or even the soul, of its customers, often without them realizing it. A great brand makes us feel comfortable, part of something valuable, loved and 'at home'.

MANAGING YOUR RELATIONSHIP

Now you've thought about your personal brand, it's time to look at how this fits your marketplace – your relationship. The thing with markets is that they're forever on the move. You can't pin the devils down. Just when you think you've got to the heart of your market and pitched your brand accordingly, a new product comes into the field, the 'technology' changes, or the market is turned on its head by uncontrollable factors. In any one-to-one relationship these variables make it hard, or impossible, to be complacent about how your brand is performing. I always tell couples that if they are standing still in their relationship development, just as in the world of business, they're actually falling behind. Complacency and inertia are at the heart of more failed relationships than any other factors.

If you were to have all your worldly wealth invested in a real-life business you'd take a lot of trouble to monitor its progress, take a serious interest in the competition and see what the company's plans were for the future. I tell couples to remind themselves regularly that their partner (the customer) always has a choice. This means that however popular your brand has been in the past, things can easily change and you need to be fleet of foot to re-position it if necessary. This, together with the goal of always striving for improvement, ensures you'll manage your life together as a couple in a way that guarantees your relationship business will flourish no matter how the world marketplace performs.

Many of the couples I see whine on about how tough life is, what a curse things are when they go wrong, and so on. As a result of years of digging at this coalface I have a very different view. I work on the assump-tion that, by definition, life's a bitch. No one has the right to an enchanted life; no one has a direct line to God; no one finds everything easy all the time; changes in society stand everything we think we know on its head with monotonous regularity, and so on. The couple that wants not only to survive but thrive works constantly at managing these changes to their advantage rather than wishing things would stay the same in themselves, their partner or the world around them.

This book is about managing your personal brand in a fast-moving marketplace. And by doing this, you will grow and enhance your life skills and personality development in a way that benefits your whole life, not just that with your partner.

PART ONE

Read This If You Read Nothing Else

Anyone who has dealt with me professionally knows that I'm pretty straight-talking, no bullshit, and believe that psychobabble gets no one anywhere. A lot of well-meaning relationship counsellors produce very poor results and even unwittingly collude with couples in their pathology. It's a sobering fact that, according to research, about two thirds of couples in counselling are worse, or no better, after one year. In spite of the millions spent on therapy of all sorts, divorce rates are rising everywhere and sexual encounters among the married are falling. This cannot make sense. What many professional so-called helpers are doing clearly isn't working.

If this is the sort of thing you're looking for — feel-good, cosy, 'we-can-work-it-out-by-being-nicer-to-one-another' stuff — you've bought the wrong book. And if, as the partner of the person who bought the book, you read only this part, be prepared for some hard times because things are going to change in your life whether you like it or not. This book isn't about cosy, feel-good answers.

It will mean getting real and honest about yourself and your relation-ship in a way you have never done before. This will be tough. We've spent a lifetime learning to be the way we are. And we've probably spent years in our relationship reinforcing our negative behaviours. Sorting these out won't happen overnight.

The good news is that it *can* happen but for this to occur you'll need to be aware of several things.

AIM HIGH

You must stop thinking about mediocrity and start thinking excellence. Most of us settle for way too little when it comes to our relationships. This is foolish and shoots the whole process in the foot right from the start. If you aim low, be sure you will achieve even lower. Aim for the stars and, with luck, you'll end up somewhere close to where you should be.

DON'T STOP BEING YOU

Nowhere in this book do I expect you to change your personality, to become someone you are not. Many people, especially women, ask me if their personality could be seriously flawed. Perhaps this is why they can't make relationships work, they argue. They kind of want to be told they need major psychological or emotional 'surgery' before anything can happen. This is nonsense – and a cop-out. There's almost certainly nothing wrong with your personality. It's just that you don't get the best out of yourself, and so cannot hope to get the best out of your relationship.

IT'LL MEAN REAL WORK

This journey will require commitment. If you think reading a few sections and poking about in this book will magically transform your life, throw it away right now. It will work only if you sincerely want, and intend to devote time and effort to making, real changes. As we see on page 32, many people say they can't see how their relationship can be any good if they have to work too hard at it. This is also nonsense. Anyway, it's not the relationship they should be working at, it's themselves. And that's a life-time's job.

LOVE-WORK, WORTHWHILE WORK

Work, however, doesn't have to mean hardship. Try to get rid of the Protestant work ethic notion. The work I'm asking for is the sort you'd happily put into a hobby and not think twice about it. Yet I'd bet you've never invested a hundredth of this level of 'work' in your most important relationship. The effort you put into this, though, is an investment that will

7

pay huge dividends for your whole life. Remember, you aren't doing any of this for your partner, so there should be no sense of hardship. You must, however, be selfish and focused. Your partner will inevitably win out if you get things more right than you do now. But that's just a pleasant side effect, not your goal. You are not trying to rescue or reform your partner. The job in hand is working on yourself. (See also pages 9 and 220.)

YOU'RE NOT A RELATIONSHIP CRIPPLE

However you feel at this moment, remember you aren't some sort of relationship cripple, whatever anybody, including your partner, tells you. It's not your fault that things are bad in your relationship. After all, no one trained you for it; you didn't take a test to get married; you've probably seen mainly bad models of how it should (not) be done; modern culture makes it hard to get it right; there are no classes in selecting the right person in the first place; no one ever tells you what to do when things go wrong, even if you could define what 'wrong' was. Don't lose sight of how wonderful you are. I know that if you've bought a book like this you're probably feeling pretty rubbish about yourself, and thinking it's entirely your fault somehow. It is not. I am not blaming you and you shouldn't blame yourself. If your partner is blaming you, use it as an opportunity to look with complete, bleeding-knuckles honesty at yourself but don't immediately become a victim.

THE BUCK STOPS WITH YOU

Stop being passive and start taking responsibility for your relationship's status the way it is today. It is the way it is, good, bad or indifferent, because of the way you've lived your life. Your entire lifestyle, beliefs, family background, and so on have set you up for how things are and this is the way it is. Lots of people I see moan about their terrible upbringing; their drunken, abusive father; their bad luck in business; their poor health; and many other things. But none of these produces predictable, universal outcomes in us all.

What makes the difference when it comes to life's setbacks is not *that* they occur – shit happens – but how you handle them when they do. This is all part of the 'life's a bitch' syndrome I mentioned in the Introduction.

IT'S YOUR JOB

Although this book might appear to be about the two of you, in reality it isn't. As I've said, there's only one person you can change and that's you. You will have to travel on your journey whatever your partner thinks or feels, whatever they threaten, or whatever they do. This will mean staying single-minded and focused because, paradoxically, the more they kick, the better the job you'll know you are doing.

You cannot control your partner. This is at the heart of the whole book. I don't want you to read this book with your partner, or, until you are very advanced, even talk about it with them except when doing the exercises. Frankly, I don't care if your partner even knows you have it. Hide it away if you like. Your only job is to control yourself better. Anything else that comes about as a result of this achievement is a bonus. What you'll find actually happens is that as you change for the better, your elevated spirit, your self-knowledge and insight, your love, tolerance, forgiveness, graciousness, and patience will all so shine through into your daily life that your partner will inevitably change even if you never say a word about what you are up to. This might sound fanciful but it's true. I have taken on individuals in marital therapy who experienced wonderful results even though they never told their partner they were coming.

Stop feeling bad about your partner not being involved. That's their business, not yours. Whilst you may not think it fair that you have to 'do all the work' –and you're right, it's not – life itself isn't fair, but you can complain about it or get on and do something. It's up to you.

Actually, by not doing this valuable sort of work on himself or herself, your partner is the one who is missing out. Fortunately, however much they struggle against 'taking part', they won't miss out entirely because changes in you will effect positive changes in them whether they want it or not.

STOP KIDDING YOURSELF

Get humble. Most people I see with problems seem very resistant to believing that what they are currently doing with their lives isn't working. We are all guilty of this to some degree. Because something's familiar and 'sort of works', we argue to ourselves, maybe tinkering with the existing system a little might just get us where we want to be. It won't. You need to get down and dirty with yourself – to walk the talk. What you are currently up to isn't any good. It's that simple. It has to change, and maybe very dramatically.

A CHANGED YOU

The really challenging bit about this book is that it calls for serious changes. And most of us are pretty scared of change. By this I don't mean fiddling with the edges of how you think, feel, and behave, but getting to the very core of these things. This could mean some total re-thinks about basic things you've taken for granted for years – possibly for the whole of your life. These tablets of stone, as I call them, are hung around your neck, with old messages carved into them. What I'll be looking for isn't just re-writing the inscriptions, it's about getting rid of the very stones themselves.

Note that I'm saying *think*, *feel*, and *behave*. Any one of these three drives the other two. Altering the way you think about something, for example, will alter your feelings about it and how you then subsequently behave. People often ask me if they need to start their journey by 'getting their thinking right'. Of course they can. Others, more often women than men, ask if they should start by sorting out their feelings. Certainly they could. Many men ask if they could start off the process by altering their behaviour. Yes, absolutely.

I don't mind where you start, but wherever you begin you'll start thinking, feeling, or behaving differently depending on the area of life that needs attention. Be gentle on yourself with this. Allow yourself to be flexible. It's a paradox that you might be able to create real change by behaving differently way ahead of being able to understand the issue intellectually, or even to be able to feel differently about it. Be reassured that wherever in this think-feel-do triangle you start, you'll get a result.

KEEP HOPE ALIVE

One of the commonest things couples say when first meeting a relationship therapist is that it's all probably too late. It's certainly true that many people leave things until they're pretty dire before seeking professional help but that said, it's *never* too late. You'll probably feel a failure, that you've tried everything known to mankind; you are no doubt feeling physically, spiritually, and emotionally exhausted by it all, perhaps even hopeless and defeated. But I don't mind how bad things *seem* at the time, it's all an illusion. As I say to people repeatedly, 'For goodness' sake, don't trust your emotions!' Psychobabble since the 1970s has had us believe that we should listen to our emotions. My personal and clinical experience is that this is very dangerous when the emotions are negative ones. Such feelings can all too easily overwhelm us and be so compelling that they appear to be true even when they are not.

Things are never that bad, believe me. All I ask is that there is enough goodwill remaining, some small spark somewhere, for you to want to make something happen. As I say to my patients, '*You* don't have to know what to do. It's not your job. That's what you're paying me for. If you knew what to do you wouldn't be here.' I say the same to you. Please stop blaming yourself for not knowing what to do. I don't know how to do your job and I don't feel at all bad about it!

If you've stayed with me this far, and you think you'll enjoy the challenge, let's start by looking at some common myths that plague modern thinking about relationships.

Top Ten Myths About Good Relationships

people in a good relationship:

HAVE VERY SIMILAR PERSONALITIES

This common myth asserts that in order to get on well the individuals in a relationship have to be very similar. In fact, exactly the reverse is true.

Of course, it's true that at a superficial level we choose someone who suits us in obvious ways. This so-called 'homogamy' ensures that on an everyday basis we can actually co-exist. This is why we deliberately choose someone of roughly the same age; who's roughly as good-looking as we are; from somewhat the same cultural background, social class and education level; and who appears to share our outlook on life. It is comfortable.

At a much deeper level, though, we unconsciously seek out a mate who has a near-exact mirror image of the dark part of our personality. This so-called 'shadow side' is that part of our personality we'd rather not own up to, that we're afraid of and need to integrate into ourself if we are to be a whole human being. It is easy to acknowledge the sunny side of our personality but it is far harder to accept the dark. It is, however, a lot easier to perceive exactly the same psychological 'stuff' in someone else!

People who are very like us make good friends. We seem to have affairs with those who are like us and to marry those who are not. When we meet someone who is like us we unconsciously project fantasies about ourselves onto them and see things we like about ourselves in them. This works well for a short fling but isn't any good for long-term development. For this we need a partner who won't simply mirror the 'nice' bits of us back to ourselves.

If we are to stand a chance of doing any deeper 'emotional business' on ourselves we have to find someone who'll facilitate our struggle with our inner devils and enable us to come out the other end a better person.

It is from this basic, but unconscious, decision that many of us choose a partner who is very different from ourselves. In fact, many people ask therapists like me, 'What on earth is it that I saw in him/her?' This all starts from the assumption that we are normal. But when we live with someone who believes themselves to be normal yet is so obviously different from us, it makes us think. For many couples this is as far as they get. They see this difference as a cause for disagreements, fights, rows, and worse. They claim they are mis-matched and often part. For others, though, such differences give them pause for thought. 'How is it that someone who thinks, behaves, and feels so differently from me about X can be so nice to be around/so lovable/so sexy (or whatever)? Perhaps I'm not the only one who is right. Could it be that there are other ways to be "right"?'

Now you can start to ask, 'Are there ways of looking at this subject other than my way?' 'What have you learned that I have yet to learn?' 'How come you can so easily cope with X when I can't?' And so on.

Whenever we make damming, or even accusatory statements about our partner we are often really talking about ourselves. The part of their personality that we paired with (unwittingly) that so annoys us is really that very part of us we haven't even recognized, let alone healed.

But our task in life is to discover and work on ourselves, not to try to reform our partner. Examining our criticisms of our partner can often give us insights into what's really wrong with us. It's also very useful to remember that what our lover says about us might just be right, even though we'd much rather deny it. But by denying things we don't just deny what we think is going on, we deny ourselves the chance of learning from the situation, even if, at the time, it looks highly unlikely there is anything *to* learn.

Given that our partner usually has our best interests at heart – to be cynical for a moment, because our best interests are so bound up with theirs – it's a crying shame not to listen to what they have to say, or more to the point to consider it an honour that he or she takes the trouble to try to get us to heal ourself. Most people wouldn't bother.

I hope you'll agree that by turning the concept of difference on its head like this the myth of similarity falls apart. Apart from the obvious similarities I've mentioned already, the couple that does really well over a long time together has many differences from which they grow. When patients yell in frustration at me, 'Why can't s/he be more like me?' I reply that to be married to our clone would probably destroy us. Imagine liking the same foods, holidays, music, art, pets, or food. Imagine knowing that what your partner was thinking and feeling was exactly what you were thinking and feeling at that moment. Imagine, in short, being married to an opposite-sex version of yourself. It would be hell. And you'd never grow. You'd simply reinforce all your worst bits and justify them till the day you died.

This is no recipe for success in life. To become the person we really can and need to be, we require someone with lots of differences we can kick and scream against as we deal with our inner demons and grow in the safety of knowing that we are loved, not in spite of, but because of this struggle. If there were no differences this simply couldn't happen.

BASE THEIR RELATIONSHIP ON ROMANCE

Far be it from me to deny the importance of romance. I believe that to be successful a couple needs to retain and grow the remnants of romantic love they experienced when they first met. But romance isn't the *basis* for a long-term relationship. At least not the Hollywood model of romance. This asserts that not only is such love the be-all-and-end-all of love, but that if it is 'real' it should last for ever and ever, preferably without any effort. Sadly, or perhaps happily, it never does.

Romantic love is, in fact, a rather dangerous version of the real thing. When we are romantically in love we are almost ill with the sensations and beliefs that engulf us. We see only our lover's positive side, we actively ignore their negatives, we walk on air. It is, in our secular world, the nearest we get to heaven. Even though most people rationally understand that this isn't in fact true they still go on believing it.

What it is that makes us fall in love so desperately isn't perfectly understood. But it has a lot to do with our need for idealization, to believe that somewhere out there is someone who is just perfect for us, someone who won't let us down, who will answer all our needs. Perhaps because we have all experienced flawed parenting and other negative early life experiences we are vulnerable to hoping that sometime, somewhere we'll find our 'other half' and be whole. Because such unconscious stereotypes are so powerful, Hollywood and other sources of fiction have capitalized on this deep-seated need. Just as images in men's magazines and porn films leave men longing for the unattainable in women, so this 'emotional porn' of women's magazines and romantic fiction, which can never be satisfied, leaves women with fundamental problems in their love lives.

It should come as no surprise, then, that when we think, or rather feel, we have met our perfect individual, we go completely haywire and behave in a very strange way. The power of believing that at last our world is complete is so great that it literally shuts everything else out at the time. Even other people can see there's something odd about us. The Japanese send one another Get Well cards at this stage of love! But this isn't 'true' love. It is self-love. Our beloved makes us feel great, and our mutual admiration society feeds on itself.

True love isn't about such delusions, it's about the reality of the other person's essential self, not our projected needs of what they should be for us, or parts of us we'd like to see reflected in them. We know we are experiencing true love when we see our beloved for what they are, warts and all, and love them for all of it. This is the love that lasts, that can withstand adversity, and that we can teach our children.

KNOW THE 'RIGHT' WAY TO BEHAVE

We look at 'Being "Right"' on page 70. Here, I'll say something about the 'right' way to be in a relationship.

Very few couples know the right way to behave. At least, not with any certainty. And this is because there is no universally accepted, correct way to run a relationship. Of course, there are basic rules such as being courteous, thoughtful, considerate, loving, caring, empathic, and so on. But these could equally apply to any human interpersonal relationship.

Couples who get on well with one another have learned, perhaps organically by trial and error, lots of the things in this book. Yet perhaps all they can truly claim is that they have found ways of dealing with one another and the world in a way that works for much of the time. For them. This doesn't mean it would work for you or me. I have often sat with couples married fifty years and wondered how I would cope for one minute living in their relationship. Yet they, to the outside world in general, seem to have 'got it right'. And indeed, for them, they have.

Many patients over the years have tried to get me to tell them what it is about my relationship with my wife that is so good. After all, they exclaim, you've been together for over thirty-five years, you must have some jewels to share. The truth is that, apart from the obvious things I've mentioned above, there probably aren't many things I could transpose from my relationship to theirs. After all, by definition, I am not married to them and the way I/we manage things interpersonally might not apply or appeal to them at all. There simply is no magic key. If there were, the state of man-woman relationships would be a lot healthier than it is today.

It's both a false comfort and an unnecessary weapon to believe that successful couples somehow have all the answers. They certainly don't. They do, however, have more answers than unsuccessful couples. And it's these answers that I'm sharing with you in this book. I have learned most of them from working with people over many years. They aren't necessarily things that would or could work for me. But this is the lesson to be learned here. The struggle to discover the way that's right for you two as a couple is half the fun/hell of being together. If someone were able to wave a magic wand over us on our wedding day and make it 'all right' we'd miss out on a lot.

HAVE LOTS OF COMMON INTERESTS

Remember what I said about difference? Then this point will already mean something to you. The truth is that you need only as many interests in common as are necessary to keep you basically interested in and interesting to one another.

Okay, it's great to share a hobby. Of course it's pleasant to do things together. But it is emphatically not good to do everything together so there's no seed corn coming in from the outside world.

We all need our own spheres of interest, areas of expertise, personal space, and opportunities for self-fulfilment, so we can import them to refresh and grow our relationship. By doing this we run our relationship business with the very best economy. If my partner enjoys and is passionate about something outside my personal experience, or even taste, she opens up a whole new world to me. I don't need to do the thing to get vicarious pleasure from her enjoyment of it ... or even to learn quite a lot about it myself. Our total relationship pool of resources is increased and I am the better for it. At first this could simply open a window on something I'd never otherwise have thought of. But eventually it could lead to me becoming fascinated with the subject ... which could then form another shared part of our life jigsaw.

But it might not. And this could be important. Many people today fear becoming their partner. Many individuals see this as a major barrier to making a commitment in the first place. And lots of well-meaning, lovey-dovey marital advice in the past focused on doing things together, spending time together, and so on. People today are more independent than ever. This particularly applies to women. Today's woman of almost every age no longer validates herself in the context of her partner. She wants autonomy in her life, and not just at work. Yet even today many men fear this autonomy and see it as a threat rather than a way they can grow together and grow 'together'.

NEVER ROW OR DISAGREE

Oh yes they do! Because there is difference, there will always be rows and disagreements. Whenever I see a couple that tell me they never row I sigh inwardly because I know I'll soon have my hands full with denial, unreality, and what I call 'stuck-ness'. Couples, or individuals, who'll do anything to keep the peace easily find themselves in trouble. As one woman put it to me, 'My marriage is a very peaceful one. As peaceful as the grave!'

Of course, there are more effective ways of rowing and dealing with conflict than many 'failing' couples use. And this is why they avoid conflict – they haven't discovered or learned a way of obtaining a positive outcome. So they back off. Unfortunately, the underlying issues that should have been rowed over or argued about don't go away – they just emerge some-where else.

EXPRESS THEIR 'TRUE' FEELINGS ALL THE TIME

This is an appealing myth because we have all been taught that it is right to express our feelings, especially to those who love us.

As with all such myths, there's a grain of truth in it. But successful couples certainly don't let everything hang out all the time. Quite the contrary. They know when to talk and when to remain silent; when to inter-vene and when to keep their own counsel. They know that just because they are feeling something, even if it's quite big to them at the time, it might not be appropriate to let it gush out all over their partner. In short, they have learned when and how it is appropriate to express their true feel-ings. This doesn't mean that they deny their feelings but that they are emotionally intelligent enough to be selective in how and when they express them. A hurting little baby can't do this. Hopefully, a mature adult can. Unfortunately for most of us, there's a hurting little baby inside that craves instant satisfaction and healing of its painful emotions. It's when he or she starts demanding attention that we get into really big trouble with our partner.

A lot of the let-it-all-hang-out theory of modern relationships is simply abusive. Just because I am in a relationship with you doesn't mean that I have permission to give full rein to everything I feel, whenever I feel it. 'Getting it off my chest' means dumping it on to yours and you may not be able to deal with it at the time I feel I need to do this. What have I achieved? I may feel better for a while but only at the price of having forced you to contain my stuff in a way you may find uncomfortable at the very least. You may even feel very bad indeed about my doing this. If you have any 'victim-ness' about you (see page 290) you could feel tyrannized or even actually abused. Now we're both in trouble because I feel abused by my feelings and you feel abused by my dumping them on you.

HAVE GREAT SEX

Quite the contrary. Research over several decades has found that couples that have 'a great marriage', as defined by them, have more sex problems than do others. In contrast, couples with bad relationships often claim to have great sex. Why should this be?

When I discuss this with couples that say they have a good relationship they clear the matter up quickly. They may have all manner of sexual mishaps and perhaps even disasters but see them as trivial in comparison to the rest of their relationship – which is good. Such couples tolerate the man's occasional impotence, the woman's PMS putting her off sex, don't freak out because sex is off the agenda for several weeks after a baby, and so on. Many such couples don't even see such setbacks as 'problems' in their sexual lives, even if others do. They are also realistic about what sex can actually deliver. I work on the basis that for the average couple sex is great about three times out of ten; a 'failure' about another three times; and okay about four times. Emotionally mature couples know this and tolerate even quite long periods of unsatisfactory sex – or even no sex at all – because they have so much else going for them.

Couples who have unsatisfactory relationships, on the other hand, can often have great sex because they are working to a different agenda. They wouldn't even stay together if they had the experiences I've just outlined for the 'successful' couples. To them sex *is* the relationship. And its powerful 'medicine' is used to 'treat' all kinds of other relationship 'illness'. Their problems start when sex itself goes wrong, or is off the agenda for some reason.

WANT THE SAME THINGS FROM LIFE

At some level this is, of course, true. None of us would get together, let alone stay together, unless we wanted somewhat the same things from life. But exactly what these are and how they are to be achieved can be very difficult indeed to work out.

Everyone says they want to be happy, healthy, have enough money, have friends, an interesting job, and so on. But dig even slightly below the surface and what this actually means can be very different indeed within any one couple. Everyone I've met professionally says they want to have a satisfying sex life. Yet on even scant consideration it becomes clear that each partner thinks rather differently about what this means in practice. At one extreme, 'satisfactory' in this context may mean none! And so it goes on.

What I think is fair to say is that successful couples want the same sorts of *outcomes* from life. They are, however, emotionally bright enough to realize that they may have to achieve these outcomes in ways that are very different from those of their partner. And even then, given their intrinsic differences, they will have to achieve these 'wants' in ways that may not involve their partner. The couple that can negotiate such stormy seas is successful indeed.

ARE SOMEHOW 'LUCKY'

It appears that some people are luckier than others. But I don't believe they are in reality. My personal and professional experience is that most people make their good luck. People who are said by others to be lucky often take more risks, make an effort when others do not, constantly work on their relationships, and see life as a continuous journey of growth and learning.

Outsiders don't see all this going on — all they see are the results, which are, of course, impressive.

Finding the 'right' person in the first instance could be said to be lucky but I personally don't think luck has much to do with this either. Few people we meet at the time we are looking for a partner actually fit the bill at a conscious or, more importantly, unconscious level. Whether you believe finding your special person is a matter of luck or the result of your efforts, personality, style, and so on, will be up to you. The numbers of individuals with whom we could create our one-to-one partnership is actually very small indeed. If you think back to when you met your partner there were probably very few serious candidates available to you at the time. Most of us have a fairly small window of opportunity and make the most of what is available. For example, if we live in London, we don't usually go searching in Sydney for a partner, even though, logically, Mr or Ms Right could well be waiting there!

Following on from this is what I see as the main danger of talking about luck in relationships. If everything were indeed down to luck then no one would ever have to work at their life together as a couple, the lucky ones would simply be okay and get with it. But I have never met anyone, let alone a couple, like this. Where luck may come in is in the sort of parenting someone has that makes them more likely than others to choose well and to create the sort of relationship they want and need. This is true luck because we can't choose our parents.

But most couples that do well together don't do so because they are lucky. They do so because they have relationship management skills. This book will, by increasing your skills, make you appear lucky to others. You, of course, will know different. It wasn't luck that bought you this book!

COME FROM HAPPY FAMILIES

As I've just pointed out, coming from a happy family where intimate relationships were dealt with well certainly helps when trying to make a one-to-one partnership work. However, it is no guarantee of success if only

21

because however 'lucky' you may have been with your family of origin, your partner may not have been (remember you'll have chosen them because of your shadow side – and they because of yours) and anyway life changes all the time, so however well you were brought up and however loving your early role models were, you may still have lots to learn about making things work effectively in your current environment.

It is also undeniably true that many people who had a very unhappy upbringing actually do rather well in adult relationships because they've learned many a lesson in childhood and adolescence and have seen what they don't want to perpetuate in their own relationships. Those who were raised in charmed households, if there are any such things, can be blissfully unaware of what it takes to succeed in this difficult area of life and may not have the tools to do the job. Someone whose own upbringing was stressful and less than ideal may also be much more in touch, not only with their own shadow side, but also that of others. Paradoxically, this can make for a better partner than someone who has taken such matters for granted all their life.

The trouble with all these myths is that they sort of give permission to the believer that if only they had had the advantages certain other couples had, they too could be happy. This just isn't the case. Such beliefs simply set you back on your own journey, as you feel somehow disadvantaged in the game of love. But we are all equally disadvantaged in reality. We all have to find our way, and make things work.

Top Ten Myths About Bad Relationships

people in a bad relationship often say:

MY PARTNER IS INTRINSICALLY FLAWED

Some people I see try to convince me that the reason their relationship isn't working is because their partner is a 'nutcase', a 'neurotic', or whatever. The trouble is that when someone says something like this it's hard to know exactly what they're complaining about. Often they simply mean their partner is different from them (therefore 'mad'?). This comes about because none of us can truly say we know what 'normal' is. And, of course, normal isn't a point, it's a huge range.

Clearly, certain sorts of abusive behaviour are completely unacceptable, or even criminal, and if you're involved in this it makes sense to seek professional help and probably to leave. If you seriously believe your partner has a mental illness, you will, of course, out of love for them, want to get medical help.

But the overwhelming majority of the time this is not what most people mean when they claim their partner is flawed. What I usually find is that the complainer is really saying their partner's behaviour is hard or impossible to understand ... and that, almost by definition, this makes them 'mad'.

This is clearly an unsound argument because we all go through stages of life when we 'lose the plot', if only for a few hours or days. But it doesn't make us impossible to relate to in general. Unfortunately, many men fear that all women are somehow 'impossible' – that being a woman is an intrinsically flawed state. Such men talk a lot about hormones, PMS, post-natal depression, and so on, and genuinely believe that they are some sort of saint putting up with the weirdness of females. Sad though this is, you don't have to scratch very far beneath the surface to uncover a variant of this in many men.

Of course, women aren't 'impossible', but they are different from men in certain ways. Interestingly, very few women claim that their man is mentally flawed. It is a sad fact that Western culture tends to encourage the notion of 'batty women' but shields men with equally difficult behaviour from such labels. To be fair, men tend to get labelled 'bad' rather than 'mad' and this doesn't much help either.

I know it can be very hard at times to accept what seems irrational, or even 'mad' behaviour in your lover, but stay with it and try not to label them. People have a tendency to listen to those they love and may feel trapped in the relationship anyway. If you tell someone frequently enough that their mental state or personality is intrinsically flawed they can just come to believe it ... and then do you the honour of acting like it. You'll have produced your own monster. And you'll deserve it!

This does neither of you any favours. Your partner now has to live down this label and you sort of have to live up to what you have created. This is bad news and can only harm your life together.

When you feel like labelling your partner — unless it's in the height of an argument — take time out to seriously consider what you are really saying. If it means that you can't understand them, or that you fear something about them or their behaviour might harm you, get professional help in case the person who's really in trouble is you. Remember that when a man accuses his lover of being 'mad', he usually means 'You make *me* feel mad (insane)'. This often has nothing whatever to do with her!

MEN AND WOMEN ARE SO DIFFERENT, IT'S HOPELESS

I have a lot of trouble with the Mars and Venus concept. It just doesn't resonate with my experience professionally, or indeed personally. I have found men and women to be vastly more similar than they are different. I believe that focusing on gender differences is of limited value, tends to excuse bad behaviours, and makes us lazy.

A man can go into a bar in any town in any Western country and say, 'Bloody women' and get an instant audience. I think this is tragic. Anything that automatically damns half the human race must be crazy nonsense.

No, the Mars and Venus stuff simply helps people reinforce their irrational beliefs that men and women are so intrinsically dissimilar that it's hopeless trying to understand one another. But I see far more intra-sex than inter-sex difference. And why make so much of it anyway?

Okay, it's a measurable fact that most women aren't that great at reading maps. So what? They can get someone else to help them. It doesn't make them fatally flawed in some way. Okay, men in general aren't very good at being naturally empathic, but I can show you hundreds of highly empathic men who can outshine most women at this so-called feminine skill after only a few days' 'training'. It can't be all that much of an intrinsic failing of men in general if such huge transformations can be brought about in a few days. Hardly sounds as if it's rooted in their genes, does it? And, of course, most women can learn perfectly well how to read maps!

And so it goes on. I always tell people they have to be sinking pretty low to put their troubles down to the gender of their lover. We owe it to ourselves to do better than this.

I CHOSE THE WRONG PARTNER FOR ME

Whilst of course this could be true – after all, we all make mistakes – it usually isn't. I tell people that the chances are that, unless their partner is obviously dangerous or abusive, or an un-reformable addict or criminal, the partner they have is probably just about as good as they're going to get.

Individuals are capable of such massive transformations, given the right encouragement and skills, I find clinically there's no sense dumping what we have to try again with someone else. Certainly many people do have a better life with someone new but that's not to say they couldn't have made their first relationship work perfectly well, given the same amount of effort and goodwill. And many millions of people are doing just this every day of their lives.

We are seduced in the Western world with the notion of the new. Our throw-away, materialistic culture almost worships disposability. Unfortunately, this has come to infect our relationships too. We are so used to taking in our TV, for instance, to be repaired only to be told it would be easier to junk it and buy a new one that we have come to believe this is true of relationships. Minor faults and glitches thus become 'hardly worth the bother' and we unwittingly look for a dumpster for our mate.

Problems arise when we find it so hard to make the changes necessary to get the best out of our existing relationship that starting afresh looks attractive. I have no answer for this. We all have such different levels of tolerance, different abilities to work at something until it gets better, a variety of basic moral and ethical stances about commitments we think we've made and ties that bind us. And so on. These variables make it impossible to create absolute rules for how any one individual 'should' behave in their unique situation. I know people who have stayed together for decades in far from satisfactory marriages and yet have brought up a wonderful family, had a rewarding career, and a pleasant social life. They take the view that even if their one-to-one relationship isn't that great, it's not the end of the world either, and that where there's life, there's hope. They also feel, with some reason, that millions of people live alone and that what they have is way less attractive than living in a less-than-perfect marriage. In this, as in so much to do with man-woman relationships, it's helpful to remember not to make perfection the enemy of the good.

Some people who fear they've chosen the wrong partner consider their life worthless unless at its core there's a meaningful, soul-to-soul relationship. Their need for connection, for intimacy and love is so focused on someone of the opposite sex they can't obtain these rewards and feelings from anywhere else in life. Such individuals can't be talked out of their quest for the 'perfect mate' and some spend a lifetime trying to find one.

I'M NOT SUITED TO BEING WITH ANYONE AT ALL

Increasing numbers of individuals claim that the pressures and demands of working at a relationship simply don't seem worth the trouble. Whatever they do, however hard they try, they just don't get the results they want. A few such people are, consciously or unconsciously, confused about their gender identity, others about their sexual orientation. Many gay men who find themselves in unhappy marriages fall into this category. When they complain that they're not suited to anyone, therapy can show that they'd be very well off with a man, and that they'd simply made the wrong gender choice in their partner. The same can, of course, apply to a woman.

Some people aren't suited to marriage or any form of one-to-one committed relationship, so for them this isn't a myth. The percentage of people remaining single is increasing all the time as social changes make it more acceptable and more workable. Without a doubt, many people got married in the past because it was the only practical social and economic model, especially if they wanted to have a family. But things are changing dramatically and millions are finding that one-to-one relationships aren't worth the trouble. Just what will happen over the next few decades I don't know but I think it's a temporary social fashion, which, like all fashions, will change. There's a limit to how much social and interpersonal isolation and self-centredness we can tolerate as a culture and when the pendulum has swung in one direction I think things will once again favour one-to-one relationships. My theory is that once modern life becomes unacceptably alienating, people will start to form deep, lasting pair bonds again.

I'M SO HURT, IT'LL NEVER WORK

This is the cry of the individual who feels desperate, hopeless, disadvantaged, or angry, yet needy. When I hear someone saying this I start by getting them to identify what they actually mean by saying they are 'hurt'. Dealing with whatever's at the heart of this can often provide answers, usually by empowering them in what seems, to them, a hopeless situation.

Unfortunately, as we live in a fairy-tale world based on Hollywood notions of romantic love, so we can feel sorry for ourselves if we're not getting our share of the romantic cake. Of course, there is no such cake and we're not missing out on anything nearly so impressive as we fear we are. This 'poor little me' syndrome is at the heart of many people who fear they're so hurt things can't ever get better. They may also come from a family where idealization, romance, and wishful thinking were rife. In such families unless things are going really well, they're a disaster. If we have unconscious needs to have a wonderful relationship to counteract our parents' terrible one, or if we're trying desperately to create a good new one after a disastrous previous experience of our own, then certain personality types will tend to despair when things go even moderately wrong.

As with everything to do with man-woman relationships, this attitude is coloured by our conditioning from childhood, our current experiences, and other societal pressures that come to bear at the time. If everyone around us in our social circle seems to be having a great time with their partners or 'happy families', our less-than-perfect situation can seem irretrievably awful when, in fact, it's not that bad at all and could easily be mended. Making comparisons with the relationships of others is a complete waste of time.

Lastly, be careful when using the word 'never' in the context of your relationship. It might well *seem* that never is the right word to use about yourself, your partner, or the relationship. Believe me, you are likely to be terribly wrong. I have numerous experiences of people coming to me with the 'You'll never get us right' challenge. Within a few weeks, not years, things are so much better they can hardly believe it. This doesn't make me some sort of miracle worker. What it does say is that when it comes to such deep, personal matters our underlying unconscious fears and beliefs so dominate our current feelings that we really do believe things are impossible. The further back such feelings originate in our very early childhood, the worse they appear to be. And the more desperate we feel things are. Sort out the 'hurt' and you could surprise yourself.

IT'S BEEN LIKE THIS FOR SO LONG, IT'LL NEVER CHANGE

This myth is a very understandable one. But it is still a myth. Just because a situation has been ongoing for a long time doesn't mean it can't be changed. We may fear it can't but this doesn't make it a fact.

When people say this to me, I agree that in their position I too would feel helpless and hopeless and unable to change things. In other spheres of life I also feel equally incapable of making things better. But I am wrong.

Just because you've persistently been working to the wrong agenda for years doesn't mean that trying something new won't work. Take heart from the experience of therapists like me who see people who've been unhappily together for forty years or more and who, given the right motivation and effort, can turn things round brilliantly. We all tend to believe our own efforts are all that there is. The trouble is that by trying the same (inappropriate) thing time and again without success, we dig ourselves deeper into our crazy beliefs and sense of failure. Hopefully, once you know which direction to take, you'll be able to use your experience and wisdom from other fields of life to make real changes, even if matters have been apparently hopeless for years. The thing is not to get dispirited, but simply to admit that you don't know what to do in this particular situation. With luck, someone else *will* know and you'll be able to get things sorted out.

I'M ALL ALONE IN THIS, IT'S HOPELESS

When the going gets really tough and we feel hopeless, most of us also feel desperately alone. Even if our partner could and would be helpful, we regress in an instant to our babyhood experiences of existential loneliness and shut them out. Of course, we're most likely to do this if we actually experienced such 'alone-ness' as a baby or very young child. Our 'computer programme' kicks in and we become that little baby left to cry – hungry, abandoned, and feeling like death. Just as we didn't stand a chance of influencing how our mother behaved or cared for us then, our unconscious argues, we're equally helpless now as our current source of love seems to be producing a similar kind of hell. Old anger and rage prevents us from turning to the very person who could most help us. In that moment our 'awful partner' becomes our 'wicked mother'.

But this, whilst compelling at the time we're feeling so low, doesn't stack up in adult life. As an adult we're not trapped in a cot helplessly waiting for someone to make the world happen for us. We can take ourselves off to get the help we need. Many people are terribly lonely and alone in their one-to-one relationship, but I find some such individuals create this situation as an unconscious way of acting out their old infantile pains. Their partner is often highly capable of being there for them, of holding them both metaphorically and literally while they regain their self-confidence. But they aren't given the chance. When you're hurting as much as this, it's hard to let anyone comfort you, for fear that, as your programming suggests, you'll just be dumped again, so why bother? We all try to protect ourselves from being hurt in familiar ways and, as a result, get mixed up between loved ones in the here-and-now and those from the past.

All this means trying, however alone and horrid you feel, to let your partner in, if only to hold and love you. Many couples get things wrong at this stage and try to talk at a time when the pained one is experiencing things at a raw, pre-verbal level. Talk is not what they need or want. Their needs are far more primitive.

None of this has to be done by your partner, of course. You may not even have a partner. Given the issues are so profound and pre-verbal, other loving, caring people can 'hold' you when you feel like this. I have spent thousands of hours simply holding people, saying nothing. The results are formidable yet people understandably find it impossible to say why. A good friend, your closest girlfriend, someone of the opposite sex who loves you but has no sexual agenda to act on, a parent, or a grandparent, can all perform this role when you need it most. So long as they don't talk, don't do any 'therapy' on you and are just there for you, you'll get exactly what you need ... or enough of it to be able to think again like an adult once you are emotionally stable.

I'D BE BETTER OFF OUT OF IT

I doubt it. As I've said, unless you're in a relationship that is abusive or completely irretrievable because your partner is addicted or criminal in some way, you're probably better off staying and trying to grow what you have.

But you're right in saying that you're better off out of it unless things change dramatically from where they are now. If you feel like getting out, you certainly can't stay unless matters change a lot. And this will take time, energy and knowledge. I hope this book will enable you to act on this fear of having to get out. Getting out is never the only way.

THERE'S NOTHING WRONG WITH ME

It's a common feature of human behaviour that when the going gets tough we tend to blame others. After all, we argue, we're a pretty decent sort of person who seems to get on well with most people. We're holding down a job and family, are good to our friends, and play our part in society. In other words, 'Given that *I'm* basically okay, it must be my partner who's the schmuck.'

Unfortunately, however 'right' we might be on all this (see also 'Being "Right"', page 70), it's never safe to assert that there's 'nothing' wrong with us in any troubled situation. We have to take responsibility for our role in the drama, or accept that we aren't in the play at all. To continue the analogy: when a scene in a play in which I am acting goes wrong, I can't blame the other players, the director, the lighting man, or the stage manager. The whole thing comes together as a piece and if I am happy to claim my part in its success I must also be able to look at myself and accept that I might just be responsible when things go wrong. Most people want it both ways in their relationships. They are happy enough to bask in the praise when people say what a wonderful marriage they have, but when things go wrong it's never their fault. This isn't honest. On the basis of statistical averages alone it's got to be your 'fault' about half the time.

I know it'll sound preposterous to some readers but I believe that the best starting point when a relationship gets into trouble is to assume that it's your 'fault' right from the start. Given that the only person we can change is ourselves, this is a wise beginning. Instead of spending valuable time and energy calculating the numerous ways in which your partner could be at fault, you could have made some significant changes in yourself (over which you have control) and got things back on to an even keel.

This said, I don't mean that any of us should say, 'Just because it isn't my partner's fault, it's all my fault.' It isn't. But successful couples don't spend much time worrying about whose fault anything is, they get things back to a stable state by doing what they can, rather than fussing themselves with what their partner should be doing. This isn't as selfless or 'doormat-like' as it might seem. I find it's far more empowering and gracious, even if you do it day after day, month after month, than doing anything else. You don't have to seek justice in such situations, simply something you know works. You're not trying to reform your partner or teach them some eternal truth, simply to recreate an even balance and to re-start living and loving again as quickly as possible.

YOU SHOULDN'T HAVE TO WORK THIS HARD TO BE HAPPY

I mentioned the notion of 'relationship work' above. Hollywood myths would have us believe that true love means we don't have to make an effort to create or maintain a loving relationship, that it just sort of happens and lasts for ever, whatever we do.

Of course, this is a fantasy – and it's an evil one because it creates expectations that cannot be fulfilled by normal people however hard they try. To set people up for failure like this is nothing short of wicked.

Okay, the couple that love and respect one another, and whose sexual life cements their souls, have a great start over most other relationships but this is only a start. When life is changing so fast, when we as individuals change so frequently, when our expectations of one another are so high, only a wishful-thinking fool imagines all this could be accommodated with little or no effort.

The problem in our culture is that work has become a four-letter word.

But love-work is a joy and an honour. We owe everything to our partner if he or she can facilitate this kind of learning and growth by standing by us as we falter and stumble on our journey through life. Certainly this 'work' can be done alone, but not nearly so effectively nor so quickly, in my experience. And by doing it alongside our lover they too have an opportunity to grow. I have learned more from my patients as they have struggled with their stuff over the years than I have learned from any number of textbooks.

At the risk of annoying some readers I'd like to suggest that our greatest goal in life shouldn't be to be happy. Numerous people tell me, 'All I want is to be happy.' Yet this is an elusive commodity that most people find it hard, or even impossible, to define. Philosophers have spent decades and written book after book seeking answers on happiness, so I won't say much here. Suffice it to say that true happiness has little to do with how we are feeling at any one moment. Our feelings come and go like autumn leaves and cannot be trusted in any absolute sense. The deep joy of knowing that we are doing the right thing by ourselves and our partner is far more valuable. I know it sounds corny but it is a profound truth that by looking to the growth of our partner as our first priority we ourselves can grow. We can't do this work *for* them, of course, but by taking responsibility for ourselves and our own 'work' we can give them the very best opportunity of finding their own path to fulfilment.

This kind of happiness infects all our relationships, makes us better friends, members of society, and parents, and enriches everyone with whom we come into contact.

PART TWO

Sixty-four Things That Can
Destroy Relationships and
What You Can Do About Them

Introduction

In this section I look at sixty-four common areas of contention that make it hard, or impossible, for us to create and sustain healthy relationships. These are the hurdles that will almost inevitably get in our way, no matter how hard we try. We all experience them, if only from time to time, or with different partners. However well you think you have succeeded thus far with your relationship, be sure some of these little devils will eventually find you out. There is no room for complacency in one-to-one relationships. The task is an on-going and never-ending one. And thank goodness it is.

First, I briefly define each topic, drawing on my clinical experience. This should, I hope, open a few doors for you to start thinking differently about your relationship 'business'. This is the first stage of managing things differently. Suggestions for things to do and how to change your thinking will start to kick in here.

The second step to managing your relationship takes the form of some simple 'market research'. These short lists of questions, entitled 'Ask Yourself', should help highlight problems and trigger thinking that could be of special interest or value to you. They are meant to be provocative and to get you working on your relationship challenges. There are no right or wrong answers. Some of them you'll want to address alone and some could involve your partner, if you have one. If you don't, or don't want to involve him or her, don't worry, you'll still get lots out of this part of the book. However simple these questions appear, rest assured you'll answer them in the still quiet of your heart in very different ways as time goes by. What might appear simple, or even naive, today could have profound significance as you progress on your journey.

Lastly, there are Action Plans that could help. Again, involve your partner if you want to. Some could be done with a trusted relative or a close friend. When you feel the time is right, talking through or even practising some of these exercises together as a couple will move your relationship on in a very powerful way.

This book is rather like a large, complex jigsaw. It has no beginning and no end. Start anywhere you feel comfortable, or interested, and slowly, perhaps over some weeks, put other pieces of the picture in place. As your understanding, feelings, and behaviour grow and change, you'll find that what you started with will itself soon change. In other words, each new insight will inevitably change every piece of the jigsaw, however subtly. This, in turn, will alter the whole picture.

How and when, if ever, you include your partner in any of this will be up to you. Some people like to keep their personal journey private. Others claim that if their lover were to know they were involved in such a journey they'd feel threatened, or worse. Yet others say it's a joy to have some sort of structure they can talk about together and even perhaps work on as a team. It's an entirely personal thing. And all this will change as you work on yourself and your relationship over the weeks, months, and years.

Finally, this book isn't about problem-solving in a 'quick fix' kind of way. It's about enabling you to build your relationship business, organically, day by day, year by year. As you become a more effective 'relationship manager' you'll find your emotional 'business' will not only thrive but provide you with the rewards you've always wanted.

Good luck.

Addictions and Co-dependency

Addictions of various kinds can play havoc with relationships and are the death of many. An addicted partner appears to become something he or she never used to be, and coping with all this can drive us to despair as we feel helpless and hopeless in our inability to change things. There are many ways of coping with an addicted partner but one which has caught the public's imagination in recent decades is the concept of co-dependency.

According to one of the main 'experts' in this field, the condition is defined as: 'the tendency to put others' needs before your own. You accommodate others to such a degree that you tend to discount or ignore your own feelings, desires, and basic needs. Your self-esteem depends largely on how you please, take care of, and/or solve problems for someone else (or many others).'

According to the co-dependency movement, the condition is common in those raised in dysfunctional families and eventually causes a huge number of emotional and physical symptoms from depression, anxiety, colitis, ulcers, migraines, and high blood pressure, to sleep disorders and much more.

This said, I fundamentally disagree with many claims of co-dependency experts. The subject started in the context of dealing with alcoholic marriages. And for that it had some purpose and validity. The problem today is that from a promising start the co-dependency movement has become a beast that plays into the worst of many people's fears and actually make matters worse for them. Millions of books have been sold on the subject, which is almost devoid of empirical, scientific research. In my opinion, a lot of it is dangerous psychobabble.

When the theory was originally created it was suggested that the behaviour of wives (and families) made it easier for the addicted man to continue drinking or using drugs. The proposition was that their caring behaviour 'enabled' the addict to continue using. But from this, albeit flawed, start, things have gone from bad to worse. Today, many people believe that *any* care they show is pathological and that any compromising of their personal needs to help their partner is a sign of some kind of disease – a relationship addiction – when, in fact, it is a perfectly healthy desire to be of service to one's beloved.

The notion of co-dependency is seductive. Many people want to be told they have a 'disease' because by having one they are in control. This plays into the hands of those who find an all-inclusive diagnosis helps absolve them from maladaptive habits, skills shortcomings, or distorted principles and thinking styles. Being accountable for our happiness can be frightening. Co-dependency lets us off the hook by relinquishing responsibility for our frustrating lifestyles. If we can at the same time blame our parents for everything that's going wrong with us today, then so much the better, the argument goes.

But much of this is at odds with normal social experience throughout the history of being human. Caring for someone, addicted or not, isn't a sign of weakness, or worse, pathology. Co-dependency counsellors tell people to throw out their addicted son, or alcoholic husband in order to 'help' them. Only by such complete detachment ('tough love'), it is argued, can their loved ones be helped. But much of this simply panders to our modern obsession with ourselves and being selfish. This is one reason why the co-dependency movement is so popular and the books sell in their millions. In a self-centred world many of us want to hear that we shouldn't be caring or self-sacrificing. But empathy and caring are good human characteristics that we should nurture. To suggest that either of these qualities makes us somehow 'ill' is sad, or worse, and leads to more alienation in an already alienating society.

There's also a rather sick attitude at the heart of the co-dependency movement that suggests addictive families should be broken up on the, unproven, supposition that addictions are 'family diseases'. They are not. Just listen to any parent who has one child affected by an addiction while the others are fine. No one individual, or set of parenting/relationship behaviours, causes another's addictive behaviours. They are learned habits that the owner believes, however unconsciously, will bring about comfort, ease, or a reduction in pain of some sort. It's also indisputable that caring isn't necessarily some kind of pathological 'enabling'. Quite the contrary. Lots of research shows that a high level of social support is the very best thing for those who have psychiatric ailments.

The co-dependency notion is attractive – even compelling – because it offers quick relief in an age that is 'addicted' to quick relief. What a paradox! By going through your life to the age of twenty and listing all the 'abusive' events that have shaped you, by refusing to make any excuses for the offenders, by doing 'grief work', and so on, you are supposed, according to co-dependency theory, to be able to get to know what happened and then blame your past for it. Yet this makes co-dependency 'consumers' victims of their original family life rather than self-determining participants who can still make their lives work well in the here-and-now. When you blame some-one else for having written a rotten life-script for you it's easy to become self-indulgent, lazy, helpless, 'victim-like', and self-righteous.

Of course, true physical, emotional, or sexual abuse is hell to live through and can have damaging effects in later life. I'm not excusing it. Talking things through, and persuading the victim that he or she was not responsible for their misfortunes are vital building blocks to mental health. But the co-dependency movement has so re-defined things that almost everyone is 'abused' according to their definitions. This is nonsense and makes loving, well-meaning parents despair that they can ever be good enough, when they very clearly can be and are.

Even when things are obviously bad, such as when a girl is sexually abused by her father or a close relative, the outcome isn't totally without redemption. A study of adults who were sexually abused as children asked if there was anything at all that they had found of benefit from their experience. Forty-seven per cent said they had benefited – from 'growing stronger as a person', 'feeling more adept at protecting their children from abuse', and 'an increased knowledge of sexual abuse', to 'a belief in their ability to be more self-protective as an adult'. Also, regardless of the duration or nature of the abuse, those who saw some benefit – nearly half, remember – scored higher than normal on a number of personality adjustment scales.

So what's the answer? First, use the term co-dependency only in the context of addictions. If you aren't dealing with a family member who is addicted to food, drugs, alcohol, cigarettes, gambling, sex, or whatever, don't even let the word pass your lips. The notion is simply too big a sledge-hammer for way too small a nut.

Second, stop creating victims and blaming others. (See also 'Blaming and Scapegoating', page 84, and 'Victims, Rescuers and Tyrants', page 290.) There is no evidence that our past 'negative' experiences build up to create a huge collection of emotional pus that has to be lanced. What *is* true is that focusing on this 'pus' makes us feel more helpless and hopeless. The way we function as adults isn't about *what* happened to us in years gone by, but how we interpret what happened. Rather than seeing ourselves as a 'poor little me', hurt child trying to function in the 'rotten adult world', we need to turn this round and try to attribute new meaning to past events with the wisdom and perspective of our adult experience. After all, you have survived and grown, not *in spite* of your so-called abusive childhood but *because* of it. To do anything less than this is to devalue all you have achieved since you were a child – and this is unfair to yourself and those who have helped you grow in the intervening years.

ASK YOURSELF

▶ When you see your partner persisting with his or her addictive behaviour, how do you feel?

▶ In what ways do you think your partner's addiction has altered your life?

▶ If your partner is addicted to something, how do you behave?

▶ In what ways do you believe you have contributed to your partner's addiction?

▶ Are there ways that you could behave to make your partner's addiction less likely to continue?

▶ To what lengths are you prepared to go to rescue your partner from his or her addiction?

YOUR ACTION PLAN

How could you help? Bearing in mind what I said above, you can be of help and support without becoming co-dependent. Ask your partner what it is that he or she would like or need you most to be or do to help them. Try to do this with a good grace. Make it plain that you'll do it only if you see it producing results. Give a timescale over which you expect to see these results. Be sure to make your partner understand that you'll stick to this timescale and won't be emotionally seduced into letting it slip time and again as they fall short of their promises.

Making your speech. I think partners in this difficult situation need to have a prepared speech that they'll use when everything else fails. This summarizes my belief that there's a healthy alternative to seeing caring behaviour as a 'problem', even in a relationship plagued by an addiction.

I get people in this situation to say something like this to their partner: 'Look, I am in no way responsible for your drinking/over-eating/smoking/gambling (or whatever). All I can do in life is change myself. I love you and want the best for you and I will continue to love you for yourself even though I hate your behaviour. I am happy to support you and make your life comfortable, though I won't support your habit and make that more comfortable for you. I know that loving you and being there for you will do more good than dumping you, but I need you to take responsibility for your habit and stop expecting me to make things better/happier/less painful for you, because I can't and I'm not a self-sacrificing "victim" who'll spend my life trying to do so. Lots about you and your pains are what attracted me to you in the first place, though I didn't realize it at the time. Those things are still there, even if they are hidden much of the time. I know you can be a better person than you are being right now and I will do what I reasonably can to help you get back to that "better you" so long as it doesn't destroy me. If I destroy myself, we both suffer, and that can't be good. I won't do it.'

Affairs

Affairs are remarkably common. It's impossible to know just how common because they are under-reported in surveys and because people define what they mean by an affair so differently. For example, I often hear men claim that a woman giving them oral sex doesn't count as an affair because no 'real intercourse' took place. Clinical experience suggests that about three-quarters of all people, by the age of fifty-five, will have had at least one, even if it didn't end in actual intercourse. Most surveys don't report such a high figure because people lie when asked about affairs.

Given that almost everyone has had an affair 'in the mind', if not in reality, adultery, however defined, is clearly extremely common. Perhaps affairs are even more widespread today, with internet sex chat rooms and other forms of 'virtual affairs' being very common.

A few individuals find sexual refuge in marriage and, once married, have little practical interest in other members of the opposite sex. Some have very high moral standards and hardly ever even fantasize about sex with someone other than their partner. But for most, being married or in a long-term stable relationship doesn't make other people of the opposite sex go away.

This attraction may be expressed in fantasy, friendship, or flirtation with limited sexual aims, but it is still there. Some people, by divorcing and re-marrying several times, sort of legitimize their affairs in a way that was only rarely available in past generations.

A few couples that feel they can't stand the restrictions imposed by marriage reach an agreement, which accepts sexual relationships with others within strict, pre-agreed limits. Sometimes the agreement involves not telling their partner. This can work for those who want to remain in their relationship but for whom monogamy is unacceptable. This can, perhaps surprisingly, suit the partners of such individuals. They may not much care for sex and some people like this that I see will hold on to their relationship regardless of the conditions imposed by their partner. This scenario doesn't suit many but it can work.

Marriage used to last only about twenty years until two centuries or so ago. Most couples were divorced by death, especially with many women succumbing in childbirth. 'Till Death Us Do Part' is now more than half a century for those who stay married, and many people find such fidelity something of a burden. All this is made the more difficult compared with one or two generations ago because sex is forced upon us commercially and in all manner of subtle ways. It is hard to avoid sexual influences and 'pressures' in today's Western culture. Women have also dramatically changed their behaviour over the last forty years to become more sexually adventurous. Indeed it is alleged that most affairs are now initiated by women. My clinical experience is that this was probably always the case. Today's woman is simply more open about it.

The great problem with affairs, according to most people, is the deception and loss of trust involved. These behaviours destroy something in the partnership. A culturally accepted system of lovers and mistresses, such as exists in France, would be healthier than this. However, I see no signs of such a social revolution occurring in the near future in Anglo-Saxon countries. Unfortunately, we seem doomed as a society to handling the attractions of the opposite sex much the same today as we did fifty years ago. And there are those who claim we live in a sexually liberated and even enlightened age. I don't think so.

For most people an affair is an adventure, a break from routine, or a solution to their need for novelty. Most people tell me they never intend the affair to replace their marriage. They want both the new individual *and* their long-term partner. Of course, there are exceptions to this rule but they are few. There will always be those who are using an affair to find a new partner because they are dissatisfied with their existing relationship, and are unwittingly looking for a way out, but this isn't common.

This puts the finger on the real difficulty with marriage as a modern institution. In an age where people in long-term relationships no longer see one another as their 'property' and with increasingly efficient contraception being so universally available, the historical reasons for staying married and for remaining faithful seem to have lost much of their hold. I say 'much' because most couples today would rather their partner were faithful to them – even if they themselves would like to have a dalliance! The trouble is that however much we might theorize about being freer with our relationships, and even being open enough to allow our partner to express their true selves, very few couples run their marriages like this because they feel too insecure, jealous, afraid of catching a sexually transmitted disease, or whatever.

Preventing affairs calls for an in-depth knowledge and understanding of why they come about in the first place. Most couples I see have never thought much about prevention. They appear to believe an affair couldn't happen to them, so even *thinking* about prevention is a waste of time! This sort of arrogance – that it's only others who have affairs – is dangerous in any long-term relationship. I try to get couples to see entirely the opposite side of the coin. Given that you find/found your partner so sexy/lovable/interesting/fun, how come others don't see this? This taking one another for granted as if you were locked away in a glass cage to which only you have the key is at the heart of many a failed relationship. It makes us lazy, uncaring, and arrogant.

So what are the common reasons for affairs? They include: the search for ideal love, sex, or romance; curiosity, especially among those who had a very limited sexual experience before settling down; confirmation of one's attractiveness or sexual prowess; poor sexual self-esteem; sexual boredom; experimentation; the need for adventure; to unconsciously get revenge on our partner; the sudden opportunity to fulfil a fantasy; and testing ourselves sexually to see if what's wrong in our relationship is caused by us or our partner. There are, of course, many more.

The greatest problem with affairs is that though started for sex they can all too easily turn into a full-blown love affair. This is much more dangerous to the original relationship. I find that most women, even today, go into an affair seeking love and finding sex, and that most men seek sex and find love. Of course, younger women today feel easier about an affair for sex alone, although all but the most hard-nosed soon find this unsatisfactory and want more. Many people find that having destroyed their original relationship with an affair they are little or no better off than they were – and many are worse off. One way round this is to be honest right from the start about what you think you want from the affair. Many men display more emotion than they feel in order to get a woman into bed and many women display more sexually encouraging behaviours than they otherwise would, to engage a man emotionally.

Most affairs are kept secret, unless they are discovered. Indeed, secrecy is the main attraction for many errant partners. This satisfies their need for 'naughty' sex, which they find more exciting than sex with their long-term lover. For some people sex with a stranger is much more satisfying because they can allow themselves to be more uninhibited. I am no longer surprised to listen to women, especially, talking about how they behave in an affair, compared with how things are in their marriage. When the husband is there he can hardly believe it's his wife talking!

Perhaps the biggest single dilemma facing the person who is having the affair is whether or not to tell. There are no easy answers but I always ask people to err on the side of not telling. 'Coming clean' may make you feel good – or even self-righteous – but it almost always makes your partner feel terrible, especially if it comes as a surprise. Some people react very dramatically as it threatens their whole world. Some individuals tell to get revenge on their partner, but this sort of relationship is probably doomed anyway. There is little doubt that keeping everything to yourself is the best policy, but this puts huge stresses on the errant partner that can make 'telling' seem an attractive option. This said, few people want to hear their partner has had an affair, however it is done, and most can't accept the situation with equanimity because to do so would make it appear the relationship didn't matter to them. A massive reaction, with talk of divorce or suicide, is not uncommon and this alone can permanently damage the relationship.

Discretion, lying, subterfuge, and deceit are the prices one has to pay to keep an affair from one's partner. For many these negatives outweigh the positives of the affair, yet few people know this when they embark on it. Indeed, when talking with those about to start an affair, few ever believe me when I say that this negative scenario will unfold. They are sure they'll remain untouched by such horrible emotions and behaviours. Of course, they are not.

The discovery that one's partner has had an affair is usually a shattering blow – often to one's self-esteem. Frank discussion can help discover why they wandered and many couples can indeed grow from such talks, especially if the 'innocent one' listens and acts on suggestions that arise. Some couples use an affair to seek professional help about all kinds of relationship issues, and in such cases the affair really can trigger a better life together.

The 'costs' of an affair are many, including suspiciousness, loss of trust, jealousy, anger, divorce, broken homes, money, unwanted pregnancies, and much more, but for many the danger of catching a sexually transmitted disease comes high on their list. In an age of HIV/AIDS, and with less dramatic diseases causing long-term problems, including loss of fertility, it's an unwise individual that doesn't take these considerations into account at the outset. Many think that STDs are easily cured today and can be treated as a kind of genital 'common cold' but this is increasingly not the case. I have sat with distraught individuals whose main regret over their affair was giving their 'innocent' partner something awful, especially if it changed their lives somehow.

For all of these disastrous side effects, affairs are still common and show no signs of going away. With people marrying later, having more partners before settling down, and then being open to serial monogamy, it remains to be seen how affairs will evolve in the future. The way things are at the moment in the Western world there is no satisfactory way of dealing with the needs many of us have for more than one sexual partner over a very long period of time. Perhaps more enlightened people in the future will come up with a way of squaring this circle but I doubt it.

ASK YOURSELF

▶ In what ways do you imagine having an affair would/could enrich your relationship?

▶ How would having an affair hurt your relationship?

▶ If you've had an affair, how did it actually affect your relationship – in the long term and the short term?

▶ Would you advise someone you cared about to have an affair? If so, how would you 'sell' the idea to them?

▶ How do you think long-term, committed relationships should/could manage the attractiveness of others?

▶ How do you think your relationship should/could manage it?

▶ How do you and your partner deal with the issue of affairs?

YOUR ACTION PLAN

Thinking of having an affair? Attractive though this might appear, if you want your one-to-one relationship to remain unsullied and you want to avoid disaster, how about going through some of the sections of this book and thinking hard before you start anything? Topics that may help you pause include: 'When Love Dies' (page 294); 'Stress' (page 273); 'Flirting' (page 143); 'Jealousy and Envy' (page 176); 'Lack of Respect' (page 199); 'Conflict and Rows' (page 106); 'Unplanned Pregnancy' (page 278); 'Lack of Trust' (page 205); 'Lack of Friendship' (page 184); 'Letting Your Past Rule You' (page 209).

After an affair. Although you may be feeling aggrieved, for example, at having to give up your lover, try really hard to show your partner you still want to be with them. They'll need a lot of listening to – and reassurance. Remember what they have just been through may have brought up all kinds of difficult and painful stuff from their past to do with rejection, jealousy, anger, fear of abandonment, sibling rivalry, and much more. This could all take a long time to heal, and some say it never does. Both parties find they are grieving and mourning their separate – and joint – losses. As you let your lover go, try to focus on your relationship and use the affair as a way of growing. No one ever has an affair 'for no reason'. There's always *a* reason, however difficult it is to find. If you need professional help to do this, please seek it. Many couples find that with insight, an affair can be a wonderful source of growth.

Anger and Rage

Living, as we do, in an imperfect world, there are bound to be things that make us angry. Much of this arises from obvious and conscious issues. For example, if you drive into my car when drunk, I have every right to be angry. Sometimes we get more angry than we can easily explain but even then there's usually some sort of perceivable trigger, even if it's not all that obvious at the time.

For instance, if you see a public official and get treated like a pathetic child rather than an adult you might feel angry because, although you hadn't made the immediate connection, it reminded you of how your mother treated you from time to time. A little discussion with your partner could unravel this sort of causal link.

Rage, though, is rather different. If I respond to you crashing your car into mine by throwing you to the ground and throttling you nearly to death – this is rage. It is driven by the unconscious and originates from pains and wounds much older than the event that triggers them. It is a primitive response beyond reason. Even the most loving and insightful partner may not be able to understand or explain the origins of such emotions.

There's no doubt that people differ greatly in how angry they are. Some individuals have a very low tolerance of frustration and feel they just shouldn't be subjected to such 'nonsense', becoming exceptionally angry when wrongly accused, or when something seems unjust. Typically, people who are easily angered come from families that are disruptive, chaotic, and unskilled at communicating. There's also little doubt that some babies are born touchy, irritable, and angry.

Much anger is only superficially 'negative', though, because it can be transformed into positive outcomes, for example, as passionate personal or social concerns. These are just some of many ways we can transform anger into positive behaviours. In the same way, some couples say they have their best sex when they are angry.

Most of the time we can't express our anger as we'd like because it would be inappropriate. For example, if our boss makes us cross, we can't shout and rant at him, so we take this suppressed anger back home and jump on any tiny, annoying thing our partner does or says and vent it there. We very soon realize this over-reaction has nothing to do with them but there is pus in the boil, so to speak, and it must, we argue, come out somewhere. Unfortunately, letting all our pus out over our partner does us and our relationship great harm. We have to find other outlets if we want to make the relationship work. (See also 'Using Your Partner As An Emotional Punchbag', page 286.)

Many people who seem 'nice' and 'passive' are in fact angry, hiding behind their smiling face and sunny demeanour. Most such people discover in therapy that their 'sickness' comes from deep within their soul. They aren't neurotic and they certainly aren't 'mad' in any sense, except that which arises from their anger. It's interesting that American English uses the two words interchangeably. To be mad at someone is to express anger.

Unrecognized anger is often at the heart of: much compulsive behaviour; many addictions; many a smiling depressive; many passive-aggressives (see page 244); many acting-out behaviours; a lot of 'emotional behaviour' (as in, 'She's very emotional'); much inexplicable crying; many longstanding physical conditions that take people to doctors time and again; many an abuser or abused; many rescuers (see page 290); some sex problems; a lot of criminal and anti-social behaviour; and much more. Therapists are used to finding serious, deep-seated anger whenever they deal with such conditions.

Unfortunately, it can be hard expressing anger directly in our partner's presence because they so often feel it has something to do with them, even if it does not. Dealing with other people's anger can be difficult, especially if you come from a family where anger was running down the walls. As a child we feel so helpless in the presence of huge adult emotions that we shut down and then continue in adult life to be incapable of dealing with them. It all seems too frightening.

Even if we have done something to make our lover angry it is still their responsibility to respond proportionately. After all, we could have done exactly the same thing to a hundred other people and they wouldn't have responded in the same way. Although we might feel justified in blowing up with anger or rage, we owe it to our relationship to try really hard to curb it. Few people can withstand such a battering, even if the anger isn't aimed directly at them. In such circumstances it's probably wise to vent the anger somewhere else, provided it doesn't make us feel self-destructive being 'alone' with the anger. Any other approach can damage a relationship and, if repeated, easily becomes self-indulgent.

And this is why anger, let alone rage, is so hard to deal with in loving relationships. It appears to be aimed at us, yet our beloved may feel safe enough to let such stuff go only in our presence. This can be hard for the listener but in a way it's an honour – even if it doesn't much feel like it at the time! The issue here is one of threshold. Some people are very much better at 'holding' their partner's anger while it subsides, or even just ignoring it, in ways that aren't obvious, until the storm passes. This can be all that's needed for many angry people. They certainly don't want psychoanalysing in this angry state.

Many angry people feel helpless and hopeless at the time and may simply need loving care so they can return to their stable state quickly. Responding in anger never works. Given that most angry people say they were never heard in the past when they had such big feelings, the gentle presence of their partner can prove that however 'impossible' things appear at that moment, at least someone else in their world isn't overwhelmed by their feelings. Over time many such people learn from their partner how to be calm in the face of anger. If you're feeling very angry it isn't necessary, inevitable, or desirable to lash out physically or verbally, to cry, scream, sulk, or rush to the bottle, food, cigarette, or whatever. There are other ways of dealing with even high levels of anger.

ASK YOURSELF

▶ How do your rage and anger show themselves in daily life?
▶ How would you say your partner expressed his or her anger in daily life?

▶ How do you feel about this?

▶ What is your family history of people being angry?

▶ How do you feel about the way your partner responds to you expressing your anger?

▶ How would you like to be able to handle anger better, a) in yourself? and b) in others?

YOUR ACTION PLAN

People use all kinds of conscious and unconscious ways of dealing with their anger. The law, what's socially acceptable, and simple common sense regulate how we express it – an assertive but not aggressive manner is probably the best way to handle things. When I am aggressive, you end up feeling bad about having dealt with me. When I am assertive, I get what I want but *you* feel good about it!

Anger can be suppressed, converted, or redirected. Suppressed anger can, especially in the long term, create its own problems. Such people may become passive-aggressive (see page 244), or even make themselves physically ill. Certain individuals convert their unexpressed rage into cynicism and hostility, and others put other people down and criticize everything. Some people re-direct their anger into safer areas, at the simplest level by actually hitting out at a pillow, a golf ball, or a football, for example. As I have already mentioned, there are positive ways of converting anger into life-enhancing passions.

Managing Your Own Anger

Alter the way you think. Angry people tend to react very strongly, to use big language, and to behave and think in dramatic and exaggerated ways. When you find yourself doing this, try to replace such thoughts with more rational ones. Instead of saying, 'This is hell, everything's wrecked. Why is this happening to *me*?', calm down and tell yourself it's not the end of the world and that getting angry won't produce the outcome you want anyway.

Steer clear of 'never', 'always', and other such generalizations, either with yourself or others. They make your anger appear justified, which it usually isn't! They also fool you into believing it will solve the problem. It won't! If your anger has to do with your relationship, try to find a way of clearly stating the problem and then finding an answer to it. Most of us get angry when we feel out of control – at the mercy of a problem that can't be solved. With a little thought, most problems can be solved. Get your partner to help with this.

Relax. I look on page 276 at various de-stressing manoeuvres. In addition to these you might consider using a calming word or phrase that helps. While breathing deeply, try repeating something such as 'Relax' or 'Just calm down' to yourself. Simple though this seems, it can work for many people, especially in the early stages of rising anger.

Take time out. I'm a great fan of 'time outs'. When we get really angry, we're no good to anyone, especially ourselves. We can also be dangerous to others, be it verbally or physically. The answer is to get out for a while and calm down. I suggest that couples for whom anger is a common problem agree on a pre-prepared script in which one or other calls for a time out by simply saying something like: 'When I get really mad in your presence (whether it's about you or not) I'll take some time out rather than hurt us both any more. I'll try to say something like: "This doesn't feel constructive and I can't listen to you now, I'm just too cross. I need some time out and I'll be back in X minutes. Then we'll try to talk things through more rationally."'

By doing this in a prepared, rather formal way, you'll do far better than simply storming out. One study found that 80 per cent of men attending anger groups had been arrested for an incident involving someone leaving the room on them. Obviously, someone who already feels rejected or abandoned is likely to behave very badly indeed if such behaviour is repeated when they're in distress.

Solve your problems. On many occasions anger is caused by an all too real problem. Indeed, many of us get angry because we can't find an instant solution to such a problem. My answer is not even to bother trying! Focus instead on how to cope *in that moment* and put off dealing with the underlying problem till another time. Okay, you may not come up with an answer straight away but be gentle on yourself, you'll do so another day.

Communicate better. When you get angry, let alone full of rage, clear thinking tends to go out of the window. You now jump to conclusions and some of these can be seriously off-beam. This is the very time you need to listen to yourself and your partner. I know it's almost impossible to listen empathically (see page 167) when you're furious, but it's worth trying very hard to do so. Most of us get so tied up with our own feelings when we're angry or aggrieved we sometimes fail even to register that our partner is speaking! Listen to yourself, too. Slow down, take some deep breaths, and try to think through your responses. We all tend to go into self-righteous mode when angry but it's no good for us.

Use humour. I personally find this very unhelpful, but professionally I know many who use humour to get themselves out of their anger cycles. Some people claim that visualizing their 'adversary' as a cartoon character, or creating some sort of silly name for them helps defuse their anger. You may find this can be all that's needed to unhook your anger cycle. It can also be a good way of showing yourself how silly most of the things are that make you angry.

However, 'laughing off' your anger rather than using humour constructively, or turning it into harsh, sarcastic, or even black humour aimed at your partner, can be very dangerous.

Change your environment. Many of us get angry in particular situations at home or at work. Try to identify what these are and then change them. Most of us feel angry when trapped but in reality we can often find a way out of the trap with a little thought. This might mean giving yourself some personal space during the day, or creating vacations and time outs from work.

Make simple, common sense changes. For example, many couples say they have their worst fights at a particular time of day, night, or month. Look at when you tend to get most angry – it might be only when you're tired, distracted, or doing a particular thing – and then avoid these situations or times. Agree to discuss difficult matters with your partner only at times of the day you know you are both able to cope.

Avoidance is also well worth considering. You don't have to engage with every possible thing you know makes you angry. If the state of your partner's car infuriates you because it's so messy, use your own, or travel some other way.

Lastly, use your intelligence to find alternatives to situations that anger you. Perhaps leaving home for work half an hour earlier could get round the traffic problems that so irritate you.

These sorts of changes can be made after talking things through with your partner as they'll often be able to come up with the simple answer you are overlooking in your 'this shouldn't be happening to me' state of mind.

Managing Another Person's Anger

Responding when someone's angry with you. This can be hard because if you've had bad experiences of people being cross with you in childhood you'll have learned a way of dealing with it that may not help you today. For example, many children, feeling overwhelmed by their parents' anger, turn off and retreat into a secret world. Becoming this removed from your one-to-one relationship isn't a healthy solution, however. The only way I know of dealing with this is to listen to the angry person empathically. Most people, when angry, are not at their best and are feeling powerless and helpless. They don't need telling off or punishing, they need love. I know this will probably be the very last thing you'll feel like offering but it's the only effective thing to do.

'I can see you're feeling really upset about X, darling, what can I do to help?' is a good start. Remember that just because they are angry with you doesn't mean you are wrong, or in the wrong! They may be projecting anger from some other situation. Empathic listening will soon seek this out, if it's the case. Even if you *are* in the wrong, there are other – more effective – ways your partner should be dealing with it than being angry with you.

It's especially important to do stage two of empathic listening well. In this (see page 168) you need to identify your partner's main emotion at the time. Okay, they're cross. You'll get no prizes for working that out! But what else are they feeling? Are they: lonely; sexually frustrated; feeling abandoned; tired; drunk; self-indulgent; arrogant; or feeling worthless? Offer this back to them in a loving way: 'I can see you're shattered after that long drive. Could it be you're feeling so exhausted you're taking it out on me?' Whatever you do, don't rise to the bait, or a whole war will start.

Let me say here at once that this type of response isn't about being a doormat. With this sort of empathy you listen to someone who's in obvious pain but you absolutely *do not* take responsibility for their pain and don't take it on as your own. Stay calm, stay reasonable, and if all else fails, take some time out (see above). Frankly, if you're listening empathically this should almost never be necessary.

Responding when someone is angry about something other than you in your presence. Once again, listen empathically. This should be a lot easier than when the subject of the anger is you! Go through the above list of exercises and strategies with your partner and see how you could help him or her cope better with their anger. Make it a task you both embark on as a project. Most of us get rather self-indulgent when it comes to anger and it can take a loving partner to help us out of long-held patterns. Of course, it's in our own personal best interest to make this happen as it's so hard living alongside someone who's angry much of the time. If you think this is all beyond you, then how about suggesting your partner gets professional help? Anger, in all its forms, is probably the commonest reason people go to therapists.

Anxiety and Fear

Almost all of us are afraid of something. At one end of the scale this is a natural, self-preservatory, biological mechanism that we need in order to survive. At the other are those people who feel anxious and afraid of most things around them.

Like guilt (see page 156), anxiety and fear get in the way of our loving relationship and especially our sex lives. But whereas guilt makes us *feel* bad (immoral, deserving punishment, and so on) anxiety produces more *physical* symptoms. These usually take the form of: a fast pulse; a pounding heart; muscle tension; panic; excessive sweating; fast breathing; an extreme awareness of what's going on around us; an inability to relax; feelings of going nearly mad; poor sexual arousal; and much more.

Some of the commonest fears in relationships have to do with: being abandoned; feeling criticized; feeling unworthy; loss of any kind; being intimate; revealing our innermost parts; not being good enough in general – but especially not being good enough in bed; being truly oneself; body image problems; being a poor parent; failing (at anything); having a really great orgasm; anything new; how to behave without looking or feeling silly; and much more. Of course, any one of us can be afraid of almost anything – the list is endless.

Fear and anxiety have one main negative effect on our personal relationships – they prevent us from having fun and experiencing pleasure. Many people are so afraid of their feared situations that they stay stuck where they are and never confront them. This can often be because they unconsciously fear pleasure and will go to almost any lengths, however irrational, to avoid it. This fear of pleasure and success is a huge paradox that many people at first find hard to accept. But it is all too real.

Confronting any sort of fear means finding the motivation to do so. And this can be hard. If, for example, you are anxious about walking around naked in your partner's presence because a previous lover had ridiculed your body, it could take a lot of motivation even to want to over-come the fear. In fact, you may never bother, for a whole lifetime. This applies especially to many sexual fears and anxieties, particularly if the bad experiences occurred as part of childhood abuse, or in some sort of violent setting later in life.

In a one-to-one relationship there are two major areas where most of us feel especially vulnerable to fears and anxieties – sex and intimacy.

Being intimate with someone we love would, at first sight, appear to be highly attractive. But the very subject strikes fear into the hearts of many. This common paradox is worth thinking about.

A substantial proportion of people say they fear failure almost more than anything else. Some such individuals claim they had a childhood where intimacy was almost absent, either between themselves and their parents and relatives, or between their parents as partners. Such people tell me they'd rather not set themselves up for failure by even trying for intimacy. These individuals are intimacy avoiders.

Others, paradoxically, fear success, as I mentioned just now. They know, deep down, that true intimacy will alter their lives but, unable to fore-tell exactly what form these changes might take, they back off, scared. Some men tell me they fear becoming 'feminine', or even 'gay', when I talk about improving their levels of emotional intelligence. Some women say they too fear their man could become less 'manly' if he were to have more emotional insight, or other intimacy skills they'd normally associate with their girlfriends.

Peer pressure and opinions can also play a part. Some men fear how they'll appear to their friends if they were to become empathic, reflect emotions, be less ego-centred, or whatever. They fear not being 'one of the boys', whatever the provable advantages in their one-to-one relationship.

Most of us fear loss so, we argue, if we don't have that great an intimate relationship, we won't have much to lose! The more we invest, the more there is to lose. And if we come from a family where the loss of loved ones is a feature, this can be a real barrier.

Building an intimate life also involves time and effort – and some quite hard emotional work. Not a few people tell me they're afraid of this. Building a better life together means letting go of familiar, however unhelpful, attitudes and behaviours, and this can cause anxiety in the best of us.

The second big area that causes anxiety for many couples is a fear of sex.

At first sight this seems strange, as sex is supposed to be fun and pleasurable. The truth is that almost all of us have some sexual fears and anxieties, even if they raise their heads only rarely. So what are the commonest?

Fear of letting go comes very near the top of the list. Holding back, and an anxiety about being truly open and vulnerable are the greatest enemies of good sex. And when I say 'good sex' in this context I mean pleasurable, uninhibited sex.

Many people rein in their sexual behaviour and responses, such as shouting, moaning, or crying, because they *fear looking or sounding silly*. Yet there are few bigger turn-offs than a silent, unresponsive partner. Many women say they fear appearing like a whore if they were to really let themselves go and be seen really to enjoy sex. Unfortunately, their partners have long known this and often feel despairing for years. It is no coincidence that the women in men's magazine stories are always ready for sex, overtly excited, noisy when they have (preferably multiple) orgasms, and so on. In other words, the average man's fantasy partner enters into the spirit of her sexual arousal with abandon and delight. This is a huge turn-on for most men and is clearly not what most experience most of the time or there wouldn't be such a demand for it in the fantasy world of videos, films, and magazines.

Even today, there are many people who *fear being seen naked*. Women, especially, are raised in our culture to think their bodies less than sexy if they aren't perfect, in a 'modelly' sort of way. Men too worry about their poor physique, or being too hairy (or not hairy enough). In reality, most lovers don't scrutinize one another's bodies this carefully, but this doesn't stop a lot of us feeling anxious in case we turn our lover off, or disappoint them, by how we look.

Genital fears are still fairly common, even in a world where 'anything goes' and the average seventeen-year-old thinks they're a sex expert! A loose vagina after a baby, unpleasant vaginal odours, a man's fear that his partner's vagina could somehow trap him, that he might not erect, that his penis won't compare favourably with those of his partner's previous lovers, and so on, are all common genitally based fears.

Most of us want to please, so inevitably *a fear of not pleasing our lover* is never far away. This is a greater anxiety than it was when I started my practice thirty years ago. Today's woman is much more critical of her lover's technique, her expectations are higher, and, as a result, many men fear they'll be found wanting. This is especially so early on in a relationship when either partner can fear they won't be 'good enough' for the relationship to continue.

Performance fears are common in both sexes. It used to be just men who were anxious about obtaining and maintaining an erection. Now many are afraid they won't keep it long enough for the woman to have at least one orgasm, and possibly several. Many women, too, thinking their men will like them or fancy them more, fake orgasms and excitement they don't feel. This is really dangerous in a long-term relationship because a man can never know how to behave if he thinks everything he does produces such extreme levels of excitement in his partner. The woman is fooling no one but herself.

Many people say they *fear acting out fantasies*. And so they should. Some say that having once done so, they wish they hadn't. Fantasies are, after all, highly personalized and idealized sexual situations where everything is perfect. In real life this can never be the case and many fantasies, once acted out, are killed off for ever. This can be a real loss to some people. Other individuals fear even revealing their fantasies. Will he think I'm weird? Will he stop loving me if he really knows what turns me on? What will she think if I tell her I fantasise about her best friend? And so on. All this does, in fact, call for careful and sensitive management. We are right to fear our lover's response to such things, though our fears are usually far too great.

Finally, some people are *afraid of masturbation*, either alone or with their lover. Some still see masturbation as somewhat adolescent, and so fear they might appear unsophisticated, or worse, if they suggest it in their love life together. Of course, masturbation is normal at all ages and can be a wonderful bedroom game either alone or together, pleasuring oneself in our lover's company, and/or pleasuring them at the same time.

ASK YOURSELF

▶ How do you think anxiety and fear adversely affect your daily life?

▶ How do you think your partner's anxieties and fears adversely affect you?

▶ What would you most like to change about yourself to be able to cope better in either situation?

▶ Would you say you were anxious as a child? If yes, how do you think you got that way?

▶ Do you think you make your partner more anxious and fearful than they would otherwise be? If yes, how do you do this?

▶ How do you think your partner contributes (however unwittingly) to your feelings of anxiety and fear?

▶ How does your partner deal with you when you are feeling anxious or afraid?

▶ How do you deal with him or her when they are anxious or afraid?

YOUR ACTION PLAN

Overcoming your fears may not be easy but it's possible if you break down the feared situation into small, attainable bites.

For this you'll need to learn how to relax. (See also page 276.) If you are to be successful at desensitizing yourself to your anxiety-producing fears you'll need to be able to monitor exactly how anxious you are at any moment. Anxiety isn't an all-or-nothing phenomenon. You can catch it early and defuse it once you can recognize it.

Here's a useful ten-point scale to help:

0   I am completely relaxed with not an anxious thought around.

1–2 I am slightly anxious. I'm sweating a little but not enough to worry about. I'm wondering if I can carry on.

3–5 I feel moderately anxious with some tension but I can carry on.

6–7 I'm feeling very anxious. My heart is pounding. I'm sweating a lot. My body is shaking and I feel restless. I am really distressed.

8–9 This is horrible now. I want to run away.

10 I am in total panic. This is the worst anxiety I can possibly imagine.

The next step is to think through your anxiety-inducing activity and to break it down into manageable stages.

For example, let's say you're a woman who feels so badly about her body she can't bear the thought of being seen naked by her new partner. Break down the problem into ten steps like this:

1. Lie down on the bed, clothed alongside your lover, perhaps reading a magazine showing a naked woman with a man.
2. Lie in bed naked, under the bedclothes with your partner, with the lights off.
3. Lie in bed naked, with your partner, with the lights on.
4. Lie on the bed naked, with your lover, with no covers and the lights off.
5. Repeat this with the lights on.
6. Undress in front of your partner in very little light.
7. Walk around naked in front of your partner with the lights on.
8. Ask your lover to take photos of you naked.
9. When you can safely do all of this, try the same list of things but now when you're highly aroused.
10. Finally, get your partner to take a Polaroid or digital photo of you caressing yourself, naked.

The starting point for this journey isn't actually to *do* anything at all. Try rehearsing it in fantasy first. Imagine yourself through each step and stop the minute you feel too anxious to continue. Perhaps help yourself by getting aroused. This could help dispel some of the anxiety.

Only when you can happily negotiate the whole list in fantasy will you be ready to try it for real. Whenever you get to a stage that makes you feel at all anxious, stop and go back a step. Never proceed to the next step until you can safely, without any anxiety at all, deal with the one you're on.

There'll always be pressure from one of you to rush at your list too fast. Avoid this at all costs because it'll only dispirit you and make the whole journey longer. Also, be sure to tell your partner what it is he could be doing to help. It's surprising but many of us unwittingly sabotage our partner's efforts at anxiety-reducing exercises such as this, especially if we can't understand what all the fuss is about. This will call for some patience on the part of your lover but it'll be worth it.

Responding when your partner is afraid. The greatest gift you can give your partner when they are afraid is your calm love. The most important thing is not to get infected by their fear. If you do, they'll come to believe that what they fear is even more awful and unmanageable than they already imagine it to be. Listen empathically to what's really going on.

For example, your partner is afraid of going for a job interview because they've had several rejections recently and you know it's reducing their sense of worth within your relationship. Using your insights into their personality and what you've learned from their reaction to previous rejections say something like: 'I can see you're worried about being rejected again. Don't concern yourself about what I'll think about you not getting the job. I'll love you whatever happens. I know you're great. One day these silly sods will recognize it too!' Now it's you two as a team against the world. You can also use this teamwork to build your partner's interview skills by practising how he performs, and looking out for where he might be going wrong. You could even help him write scripts for interviews, find him a good book or something from the internet about the subject and work on it together, go with him to the interview location, and so on.

Responding when your partner is afraid of *you*. This can be hard, especially if you can't be sure what it is about you that makes them afraid. The only way is to ask outright. Reasons might be: you seem too needy; you appear so powerful; you are such a big personality they get swamped when they're around you; you're too sexy for them; you are too demanding; you have too much energy; you're too 'emotional'; you're too unpredictable; you're too outgoing; you're too moody, and so on. Try to talk this through, listening empathically and not taking offence when your partner says something critical. Try to modify your behaviour in ways that help.

Avoiding Risk

Many relationships I see come to grief because one or other partner, or both, is overcome by inertia. Like frightened rabbits in the headlights of an oncoming car, they come to an almost complete stop in their relationship development and growth.

This usually comes about because one, or both, is terrified of taking risks. 'Things might not be that great as they are,' they argue, 'but they could be a hell of a lot worse if we were to stir things up!' Best do nothing.

This is different from, but related to, being too comfortable in a relationship. Here, the couple is accustomed to their lifestyle and their pattern of relating, but knows deep down it isn't what they want, let alone originally dreamed they would have.

But all life is a risk. It's even risky staying in bed all day! It's not possible to be alive and be without risk. It *is* possible to *live* – as in 'exist' – without taking risks but not to be truly 'alive'. Unfortunately, most risk-averse people work on the principle that if they try nothing they'll have nothing to lose. The risk-positive individual works on the principle that unless they try something new they will certainly *not* gain anything.

As with everything in our personal lives, finding a balance can be a real challenge. Some people are forever taking risks and craving change. They can be a real nuisance to their partner if only because life becomes so unpredictable. Yet, paradoxically, such a complaining individual often says it was this exciting, risk-taking behaviour that originally attracted them to their partner. Helping our partner find the right level for them and for the pair of us can be a genuine task that's worth embarking on together. How to help the adventurous one set limits? How to help the cautious one learn that failure doesn't mean 'death'? This can be an exciting journey on which we can both grow. I have even seen things turn around, with the previously cautious one becoming a real risk-taker once he or she gets in the mood! But then, this shouldn't be all that surprising if the cautious one has married the right person in the first place (see page 12).

It's also interesting that in most couples the one who takes the risks does so for both of them. The woman may, for example, project her 'risk needs' on to her guy who then acts them out for her. Perhaps she doesn't have the courage or inner strength to tolerate the failure, loss, or social disapproval that could result, so she gets him to take the risks for her. In this way she enjoys the benefits of the risk-taking when things go well, without having to deal with, or take responsibility for, the downsides when they don't.

This kind of relationship balance works in many other areas of life, of course, not just with risk-taking.

When risk-taking becomes pathological – the individual cannot function unless they are forever pushing the boundaries on almost everything in life – this can be tedious and very hard to live with. Crazy gambles with horseracing, stocks and shares, sex, relationships, workplace issues, sporting activities, and much more can make such an individual a real vexation to live with. But this level of extreme risk-taking is, thankfully, rare.

But even for natural risk-takers, turning their skill on to their own relationship can be hard. Such people fear the loss of their beloved so much that they avoid any form of risky behaviour that could create serious waves. The things with which they are prepared to gamble in the outside world are seen as completely different from their core relationship and its value to them. This, they argue, is not to be risked. On the contrary, some men who are great risk-takers can only do so against what they perceive to be a stable relationship. It can, according to their partners, be so stable it's nearly dead! But for such a man the outside world is where they take their risks, not at home. In truth their hunger for risk-taking is probably satiated outside the home and they then find it hard to create more energy for this type of emotional work at home.

This is, of course, a defence against doing the emotional and relationship business they should be doing but it can be near-impossible to convince such a man that this work needs to be done. He'd rather be out 'killing another bull' than facing the raging beast inside himself.

ASK YOURSELF

▶ What did your upbringing teach you about risk-taking?

▶ How do you avoid taking risks?

▶ What do you think makes you a poor risk-taker?

▶ What sorts of risks are you good at taking?

▶ Do you think you take excessive risks? If so, why do you do it?

▶ How does your partner's risk-taking advantage your relationship?

▶ How does it disadvantage your relationship?

YOUR ACTION PLAN

What do you call a risk? Make a list of things in your life you think are 'risky'. Rate these from 'hardly any risk at all' to 'highly risky'. Talk this list through with your partner. Enlist his or her help with re-framing your thoughts on risk. Try to get to the heart of exactly what it is you are afraid of. For example, your man wants to start a new business but it terrifies you. What is it that scares you so about the risk? Failure in the eyes of your friends? Loss of face? Shame? Losing your home? Feeling powerless about it all? That he's getting his own way again? And so on.

Being 'Right'

We all believe we are 'normal' and so, understandably, imagine that what we believe or think is somehow 'right'. This, by definition, usually suggests that others who disagree with us are somehow 'wrong'. This righteousness (a certainty that we are right from our own point of view) is a real killer to intimate relationships. For such an individual it is often more important to be right than to be loved or to love. I have seen many people, mainly men, who would rather sabotage their whole relationship than admit they might be wrong. They see such 'rightness' as a sign of strength rather than the weakness it actually is. The passionate way they defend such positions, though, betrays their true underlying (unconscious) emotions, which are a fear of being wrong, or not knowing. The internal chaos this creates feels unmanageable so they outwardly protest absolute certainty to themselves and their partner.

The problem with this is that there usually is no right or wrong in most situations. The thought that directly opposing views could both be right (or indeed wrong) comes hard to most of us in the West.

When someone tells me they somehow 'know' something I pull their leg and ask them if they have 'a direct line to God' on the matter! The thing is that when we know something with such certainty it usually means we have little knowledge of ourselves in the matter and yet for all our confidence of being right we remain unloved, unloving, and even unlovable.

When we think we know about *our partner* in this way we are building a barrier to true intimacy. By being so sure we know about our lover – often better than we know about ourselves! – we hide from ourselves that fact that we are so busy becoming an expert on them we spend way too little effort becoming an expert on ourselves.

But the saddest part about 'knowing' and 'being right' is that we spend so little time growing. When we know something in this way we shut out all the other possibilities that could enrich us ... especially those that could be available from our partner. 'Okay,' we argue, 'I'm very experienced at X, so I probably know more than he or she does.' But my view is that most so-called experience is spurious. My contention is that most of us learn rather little from experience. All it does is confirm the way we do things. But this is not growth and change. Having done something in the same, inappropriate, way for years doesn't make us an expert – except perhaps in being wrong!

Real experience comes from being open to change and learning. Because more men are ego-based than are most women, they find it harder to cast aside their over-valued 'experience' in favour of the possibility that their partner might just have a better answer. Such men are often lonely and miserable because they can't connect with their partner yet they still stick to their divine right to be right! Such a man has little fun because to have fun you have to be open enough to play and to accept that you might be wrong. This playfulness eludes many millions of couples because to return to the 'chaotic' uncertainty of childhood in order to play makes them fearful, or worse.

The bottom line here is that how we see matters has little to do with how they actually are – it's simply how we see them through our own, very imperfect, spectacles. The Mayans had a wonderful saying: 'All life is an illusion.' I agree with them. Almost anything viewed from a different angle or at a different time can appear different. The moment we start to believe that our particular angle of vision is the right one we are in serious trouble.

Intimacy can't thrive in such a setting. The job of becoming more intimate (see page 190) involves knowing more about *ourselves*, not becoming more of an 'expert' on our partner. Only a fool would claim to know more about their partner than they know about themselves.

It is only by being truly intimate that we can claim to 'know' anything much in our relationship. This knowledge is rooted in the reality of being in touch with ourselves in their presence. When I do this I am alone in the presence of my partner doing my business, not hers.

It's a shame that living together for many years seduces us into believing that we really *do* know what our partner is thinking, about to say, feeling and so on. In the therapy room I ask the 'sure' individual to write down what they imagine ('know') their partner is about to say. I then ask the other one to say what they were going to say. The results are often totally different from what was predicted, partly, to be fair, because the revealing partner feels able to be truly themselves in the safety of the therapeutic setting. The old saying, 'To assume makes an ass out of u and me' is a good one. Yet every time we make an assumption we are once again trying to prove we are right.

Such 'already knowing' creates havoc in the bedroom too. Once we become certain about our lover's sexuality we are limited by this illusion and, ironically, limit his or her growth too. Many's the time I hear an individual revealing what has happened in an affair. Their listening partner sits there open-mouthed at the revelations. How could their partner, about whom they 'knew everything', have behaved in such a way? It sounds, they say, like a stranger telling their story. This sort of conversation gives us the opportunity of discussing just how boring and repetitive their sex life has become and how their both being 'right' about one another has limited their capacity for creativity and passion. Many people say that 'not knowing' is what makes affairs so delicious. What a cruel paradox!

ASK YOURSELF

▶ In what ways and in what circumstances do you find you need to be 'right'?

▶ How do you think your being 'right' has stopped you growing?

▶ How do you think your need to be 'right' damages your relationship?

▶ How does your partner provoke you into 'having to prove' you are right?

▶ How could you alter your behaviour or thinking to alter this?

▶ Does someone always have to be 'right' in any given situation?

YOUR ACTION PLAN

Being wrong. This is a challenging exercise in which you list all the benefits you can think of to being wrong. Most of us can only think about the benefits of being right, but there are great benefits to being wrong. To start you off, here are a few: not having to be 'perfect'; not having to 'know'; allowing your partner to be right and to learn from it; clearing the ground for fresh ideas and concepts; appearing more humble (and thus more attractive) to others.

Addiction to perfection. Many of those I see who have to be right are addicted to perfection. So insecure are they (though they give out the opposite message) they run their lives on the basis of attainable perfection. Of course, perfection isn't attainable, so they make up for it by being certain about just about everything and right about the rest! Talk this through with your partner and try to see if you could relax into a less-than-perfect model of life. After all, if you are so perfect (or very nearly so) how could you possibly learn anything from your partner? They pick this up and cannot then be truly intimate with you because it is they who (apparently) have all the learning to do in life. Of course, this is nonsense but it's dangerous rather than simply deluding because it shuts out the most valuable source of learning and change you're ever likely to have in your life – your partner.

Relax. You don't have to 'know'. You have no responsibility to the world to be right. And in an increasingly complex and ever-changing world you can't hope to be either, so give yourself a break. All this being right and knowing is intensely self-hating. Let your partner in to love you and to help you learn. You stand absolutely no chance of doing it alone.

Being Too Close

There are few areas of man-woman relationships that are more confusing than love, closeness, and intimacy. Most people mix them up and find that trying for one excludes the other two.

I won't even try to define love but in general terms almost every human relationship can be a form of love. But it is the act of loving that brings rewards, not being loved. Showing love to another should be unconditional, with no concept of being well thought of or receiving sexual favours in return. Loving someone is a privilege, not a chore. All this is very different from being 'in love', as we see on page 202.

If I really love you it allows you to be truly and fully you at that moment. This type of love encompasses both your positive and negative traits. We know we are being loved when we experience being truly ourselves. Although it can sometimes be hard to know when we are being *loving* it is not hard to know when we are being loved. We all need to feel loved to reassure ourselves that the loneliness and separation we fear won't reclaim us. But this experience, however good at a particular moment, doesn't satisfy us for long. We need fairly frequent top-ups of both loving and being loved.

Closeness is a commodity many of my couples rate very highly. They believe that being 'close' will bring them the intimacy they crave. On most occasions, it does not. Paradoxically, closeness, or perhaps more accurately, over-closeness, turns out to be the enemy of intimacy. The problem with closeness is that when we are experiencing it we are more aware of our partner's reality than we are of our own. Such couples focus largely on one another and then when they eventually do focus on themselves they lose sight of their lover.

Healthy closeness, on the other hand, is like a dance in which the two individuals move well together, caring for and complementing one another. They are all too aware of the other's realities and can experience them as unique and special and are prepared to give up areas of personal space to be selflessly loving, interested, and caring. This reciprocal behaviour makes intimacy more likely. None of this is clingy or unhealthy. If we are healthily close we willingly give up parts of ourselves to enable us to expand our awareness of our partner. If our partner becomes dependent on us we 'take care' of them. This is very different from being 'caring'. Taking care of someone isn't part of an intimate relationship; caring certainly is.

Being *close* enables us to really know our beloved, and being *intimate* to know ourselves. When we are close we know our *partner* in our presence; when we are intimate we know *ourselves* in our partner's presence. Most of us know ourselves only in our personal space. When we are intimate we can know ourselves in the presence of another. This enables us to grow, feel free, and to be more alive.

We all have to learn how to separate love, closeness, and intimacy. When we get this right, the rewards are formidable.

ASK YOURSELF

▶ How clinging are you? How does this manifest itself in daily life?

▶ Do you find yourself wishing things were how they used to be? If yes, how would you like to think differently about this?

▶ Can your love cope with change or does it live in the past?

▶ Try to assess how unconditional your love for your partner really is.

▶ Think about the relationships you've had (with whomever, not necessarily lovers) that have taught you most about these matters. What was it about the relationships that did this?

▶ In what ways do you look to your partner to meet your unmet needs in life?

▶ How does possessiveness get in the way of your love?

▶ Do you feel that unless you are totally understood you aren't really loved? If yes, how has this altered the way you run your life?

▶ Do you expect your lover to take care of you? What are your responsibilities in taking care of yourself?

YOUR ACTION PLAN

Family history. Make a list of all your main family members and alongside each make notes about how they individually feel about love, closeness, and intimacy. Now ask yourself where you stand on these matters and what influenced you from your past to create your current position.

Now repeat all this for your partner and try to understand what it is that creates problems for you in your relationship on these issues.

When you feel comfortable enough with all of this, see if your partner could do the same exercise. Exchange notes and talk it all through.

Being of service to your partner. There are many ways of showing our love, closeness, and intimacy and they are discussed throughout the book. A useful exercise that can help you think about the practicalities of this, rather than simply the theory, or 'good intentions' (see page 152), is the matter of service. Highly successful couples not only 'know' in some theoretical way about love, closeness, and intimacy, they act it out in every living moment together. One way of putting this into action is by being of service to one another.

When being of service we: put our partner's needs first; are good at remembering and anticipating their needs; frequently do household and other chores (including emotional chores) that are not usually ours to do; and look for every opportunity to make our partner's life easier and more pleasant.

But being 'of service' has nothing to do with being servile. If we do something from our core, inner strength rather than because we fear our partner won't love us, or might leave us if we didn't do it, we're acting out of power. This is service. My being of service to you shows my love, works not only for your good but mine, and takes nothing away from me even if (highly unlikely) you'll never be of service to me.

One major way we can be of service to our partner is to keep on growing, learning, and teaching ourselves new love skills. If you see your marriage as a safe haven from the troubles of the world, or worse still, a claustrophobic sort of therapy group, then this could be hard for you. If you see marriage as an end-point rather than a beginning, you'll be in trouble with 'service'. True service kills off nagging (see page 228) because both partners are alive to satisfying one another's needs before either gets to this point.

For all of this to be successful we have to be able to let our partner know what our needs are. For more on this, see 'Not Saying What You Mean' (page 238).

Too close, man. Many modern couples expect to be everything to one another. The modern myth that promotes this is based to some extent on the observable fact that many of us have few elders, extended family, or parents available to help. This actually *does* throw many of us together in a way that would have been unthinkable even two generations ago. But whatever the reasons why this has occurred, it is still wrong. We cannot and should not try to be everything to our partner. Having lots of outside contact helps us: keep realistic; put our relationship into some sort of perspective; find seed corn to bring back into the relationship; and so on. The 'desert island couples' I see in my practice are usually in serious trouble. The answer to their fulfilment and happiness isn't only, as they often assert, to be 'better together' but to live in the real world of which their relationship is only a part.

Believing Only Someone Else Can Make Things Better

I look at the victim/rescuer/tyrant triangle on page 290. In this uncon-scious, defensive model we all too easily look to someone else to rescue us. Whether or not we consciously recognize the fact that we are 'needy' or a 'victim', we can quickly find ourselves looking to someone else to make life better for us.

Some people have a family model of this. Problems always get dumped onto someone else in such families and 'they' are expected to sort them out. 'They' could be the medical profession, the social services, public housing services, bank managers, the boss at work, teachers, the local authority, their partner, an able relative, and so on. Some of this is laziness, to be sure, but much of it is not. It is a sense of powerlessness and inef-fectiveness that has been learned from the cradle. Such 'victims' really do believe they can't alter their environment much whatever they try. And to be fair to them, their life experience often bears this out.

But it is no way to run your life, if only because it confirms your victim behaviour, makes others try to rescue (or perhaps even tyrannize) you and because you'll be permanently stuck in a powerless world where everyone else seems to be having a better time of it. Others will also tend to abuse you because you are so 'helpless'. Many such individuals turn to drink, drugs, crime, and violence, for example, unconsciously to prove to themselves that they are indeed 'effective' or 'powerful' — at least somewhere in life, even if it is self-destructive, for instance. A sense of personal helplessness and hopelessness lies at the heart of much socially-disruptive behaviour. Some such individuals consciously feel that, given they're having such a horrible time of things, they don't see why others shouldn't be too. So they go out and create havoc in the world around them.

Many people get married, perfectly unconsciously, of course, to someone they perceive will put the world right for them. Given there are millions of rescuers around – remember these are people who'd rather be focusing on the pains of others and helping them than facing their own pain and helping themselves – finding a suitable partner isn't hard. The 'victim' latches onto a rescuer and they appear 'made for each other'. Many women, especially, say they realize after perhaps many years of being together that they took on their man as a 'big boy' who needed sorting out – a kind of project. In fact, countless women have told me that they see marrying their man as a way of making him into what they want him to be. Sometimes this works but often it doesn't, or the man resents it and eventually turns away from this mother-extension he has married. The sex lives of many such couples are blighted because the man unconsciously knows he can't have 'incestuous' sex with his 'mother', so he backs off and has affairs, or becomes impotent within the marriage.

The reality, of course, is that almost no one can make things better for us, except in small ways and on a temporary basis. The only way we can get a better life is to work for it ourselves, however loving and helpful our partner may be. Certainly our partner can be a facilitator, a resource, an encourager, a supporter, a good example of how we could be, a wise head when we are too deep in our stuff to see the wood for the trees, and so on. But they cannot live our lives for us, and certainly can't make us 'better'. The problem with looking to someone else to make us what we are not is that, if there's to be any kind of justice, we too would have to be doing exactly the same thing for them in return. As soon as I say this to couples they agree it all sounds crazy. Why would I spend my valuable time, energy, life experience, and wisdom trying to live *your* life for you when I should be doing it for myself and you'd get the benefit anyway? Learning to be truly me in your presence is what I should be about, not trying to save you. And even if I am a victim in the world, I can never be truly myself as long as you step in and rescue me. All it will make me is lazier and increasingly ineffective as you 'prove' to me that I can't do it for myself.

ASK YOURSELF

▶ Are you intrinsically a victim? If yes, how do you think you got this way?

▶ Do you feel you unwittingly paired up with your partner so they could rescue you or you could rescue them? If yes, did you have a pattern of doing this before you met your partner?

▶ What was your family's history of problem solving?

▶ How did your upbringing contribute to your belief that you can't help yourself?

▶ What socially disruptive behaviours do you indulge in?

YOUR ACTION PLAN

Family views on personal responsibility. Given that your beliefs and behaviours in this area are coloured not only by your own family's relationship models but also those of your partner, try this exercise:

Make a list of all your close relations down one side of a large piece of paper. Alongside this, write in a word or two about their attitude to personal responsibility. On the right side of the page create an exactly similar list so your partner's 'mother' lines up with your 'mother', and so on. Now fill in what you perceive to be these individuals' views on the subject.

See how everything matches, or does not, then talk all this through with your partner. Best results come from asking him or her to create their own version of this list and then comparing notes.

See also 'Not Saying What You Mean' (page 238).

Believing You Don't Deserve Better

Yes you do! You may not *feel* you do, or perhaps your partner has even told you that you don't, but you do! Getting what you deserve, however, might not be easy. It might even mean *making* something happen!

You've already gone some way towards this by buying this book. It's a great first step because at least it shows you're interested in change. And depending on what you've already read, you'll see that I'm pretty straight-talking about what you can realistically achieve. It's a lot.

I start from the experience – not a noble belief or a wishful thought – that people *can* make their lives better, no matter how crummy their starting point. In fact, many of those who start at the worst point on the scale do the very best. In a sense they have little else to do than improve and they do so. Also, it's a real truth that such an individual making a 5 per cent change to their lives can feel way better as a result than someone near the top of the scale doing the same.

Today's world is a real enemy of one-to-one relationships. From dangerous Hollywood romantic myths, to the daily onslaught at work and play that we all find ourselves involved in, society makes it hard for us to put our relationships first and to grow as a result. We have become almost blasé about the increasing numbers of divorces, dysfunctional families, domestic violence, criminal behaviour, and single-parent families as a way of life rather than treating such phenomena as the exception. This lowers our threshold of expectations and it's easy to see how we can slide downhill not only personally and in our relationships but as a culture.

This isn't meant to be some sort of lecture or sermon – I'm making much of it because it's a very real issue at an intra-personal and inter-personal level in many couples' lives. Much of this arises from millions of people thinking and believing they don't deserve better — and worse still, that they can't make a difference even if they were to deserve better.

Most relationships start off pretty well. You had high hopes; idealized notions of your partner; infinite potential; the failures of other people's partnerships were, you argued, unlikely to be visited on you; your children would be a delight; you'd agree most of the time; sex would be great; your friends would all get on with each other; your careers would harmonize; and you'd end up better people in no time at all.

So, after such a 'wonderful' start, how on earth did you get where you are? What happened? It's a mystery!

The answer, I'm afraid, is that there is no mystery. You set yourself up for this bad scene years ago and have been unwittingly reinforcing it ever since. It's not possible to find yourself in a badly-functioning relationship without having made a real contribution to it. In fact, at the heart of your dysfunctional relationship is a dysfunctional you. This isn't to say that you are to blame in some way. Just to point out that whatever you may think, you are the seedbed of your relationship and the plants that grow and flourish in that seedbed are dictated by its very nature. More to the point, over the years you have been 'feeding' your 'relationship seedbed' with the wrong fertilizer because you've ended up with a plant that's different from what you started with!

This is sobering stuff. But it's real. Your 'fertilizer' from childhood and adolescence has determined how you nourish your seedbed to grow relationships. This said, you can learn how to make better fertilizers that will get you the result you want and need.

When I say you 'deserve better' I don't mean you deserve a better partner. This is part of the 'poor little me' syndrome I so often hear. The only way you'll get a better partner or relationship is by changing yourself. If you were to think you deserved a better car you'd go out and work for the money and then buy it. Yet many people who think they deserve a better relationship somehow expect it to happen in some kind of mystical way, preferably by using the same brand of fertilizer that keeps on producing the wrong plants for them.

This is crazy. But to make any change you'll have to accept that there'll have to be some deep-seated self-questioning and a re-evaluation of many of your long-held beliefs. This will mean starting over in all kinds of ways you thought unlikely, or even impossible. But unless you do this for yourself you'll certainly continue to believe you don't deserve better. And in some sense, you will not!

ASK YOURSELF

▶ What did your upbringing teach you about what people 'deserve'?
▶ How has your relationship tended to promote these views?
▶ In what ways do you run your life as if your partner were to blame for your current state?
▶ How have you systematically let yourself down over the years?

YOUR ACTION PLAN

What do you deserve? Make a list of things in life that you, or others, might possibly deserve. For example: good health; a quiet life; a considerate partner; a loving partner; a great sex life; enough money; nice children; and so on. Now think about how many of these you actually have. Ask yourself what barriers *you* erect, however unwittingly, to obtaining the others. Involve your partner on this if you want to. It can be interesting to see what he or she believes you deserve. Lovingly sharing any differences in these lists can be a real eye-opener and can, if properly handled, help with the self-pitying, 'poor little me' syndrome.

Your relationship seedbed. Make a list of all the things that have influenced your relationship seedbed, and thus your relationships. Get a close friend who has known you for some time, or your partner, to go through it with you and say how they feel your seedbed makes it hard for them to relate to you. Discuss what you could change to improve matters.

See also '"Shoulds" and "Oughts"' (page 266).

Blaming and Scapegoating

Although almost every parent with whom I've discussed the matter assures me they brought up all their children equally, this is obviously nonsense. A first child is always treated differently from subsequent ones if only because when raising our first we have everything to learn and our anxiety levels are high. Subsequent children have an easier time because we function better as parents. Certain personality characteristics of one child are also more appealing than those of another. And some children are more physically attractive than others. Add to this the life changes that shape our behaviour, such as the death of one of our parents; a severe illness in one of us as parents; major, stressful life events; or divorce or separation, and it's easy to see that it is completely impossible to raise all our children the same because we as their parents are not the same from year to year. As we change, the way we parent inevitably changes.

Many people say they really wanted only children of one particular gender. Others tell of their disappointment at having a child of a particular sex first. Others struggle with unwanted babies, even in an age of readily available contraception. It is estimated from genetic studies that just under one in three of all children could not have the father that people believe, so clearly there are major issues here. And so on.

So however well, or fairly, we imagine we are bringing up our children, it's inevitable there'll be inequalities in how we actually behave towards them. Many of these will originate from our unconscious and we'll have no influence over these. With luck, though, these balance out between us as parents so that if one of us finds it hard to like/love/get on with a particular child, our partner will compensate for this. This is one of the many advantages of having two parents.

Having said all this, some children grow up being scapegoated by their siblings, by their parents, or by their family as a whole. They just don't seem to fit in. In such families this child takes all the blame when there is any doubt; is the butt of parental anger, or other unexamined emotions; soon learns that this is their role in life and acts accordingly out of the home and at school; and so on. In a way it's a comfortable role inasmuch as the scapegoated child gets lots of attention. Unfortunately, it's attention of the wrong kind and for the wrong reasons, but the child often doesn't know this at the time.

Imagine, now, such a child growing up and getting married. They will undoubtedly choose someone who will continue this familiar model and their relationship will be in trouble from day one.

Looking now at the other side of the coin, we find the 'blamers'. These people have learned that because they can't take personal responsibility for their actions or lives they need to find someone who could or should. Many come from blaming families where complaining and whining were common and where no one felt sufficiently empowered to do anything much else. Such parents and grandparents (and often their friends) forever blame others, be it the government, 'them' in general, authority figures of all kinds, the system, their neighbours, one another ... in fact, just about anyone that comes to hand. They almost never blame themselves because they see themselves as helpless, powerless, victims of the world who don't deserve blame.

This blaming easily becomes a habit because rather than taking personal responsibility for getting things right in the first place or making things right when they go wrong, blamers look to others to get them off the hook. This is obviously far easier than actually having to change things themselves. After all, if one were to get it wrong you'd find yourself blaming *yourself*! Shock, horror! You have no resources to cope with this appalling situation.

It's easy to see how a blamer and a scapegoat could team up to form a malfunctioning partnership. The passive scapegoat finds a perverse comfort in having a role within such a set-up and the blamer carries on being blissfully unaware of their own inner failings and pains.

Trouble brews when one or other starts to realize how appalling this lifestyle is. This can sometimes occur in the shape of another person (possibly of the opposite sex) who points out how bad things are. This destabilizes the relationship and things have to change if they are to continue living together. Many cannot.

If you think you fit into any part of this model it's a good idea to seek professional help sooner rather than later because, as the years roll by, it can become near-impossible to change. I have seen women in their seventies who are so immersed in their scapegoat role that they can no longer see any benefit in changing the situation. This is very, very sad.

ASK YOURSELF

▶ Would you say you were a scapegoat in your original family? If yes, how did it manifest itself? How did it feel?

▶ Do you find yourself scapegoating others, perhaps even your partner? If yes, how do you do this?

▶ How do you feel when people scapegoat you, if they do?

▶ Are you a blamer? If yes, why do you think you do it?

▶ How do you feel when you are blaming others?

▶ How does it feel when others blame you?

▶ How do you behave when others blame you?

▶ If someone were to claim you deserved to be blamed, what would you say?

YOUR ACTION PLAN

Learn to recognize when you're doing it. Having read the section above, practise realizing when other people are blaming or scapegoating others in your daily life. Get skilled at seeing what's going on, both for the victim and the perpetrator. Watch for the victim's body language. Do they behave in a victim way? Do they get angry? Passive, perhaps? How do they react?

Using this knowledge and insight, start to be more vigilant about how you blame or scapegoat your partner – or even yourself. Many people who are blamers actually beat up on themselves a lot. If you find yourself doing this, try to be gentle on yourself. Enlist your partner's help to stop you doing it. Bad habits, started within yourself, are highly infectious within your relationship.

Looking back at your family. Think about how your family dealt with blaming and scapegoating. Make a list of each family member and alongside each say what role they played in this 'game'. Learn from this how it has affected your behaviour in the here and now.

Looking back at your relationship. Write down a list of when you tend to blame one another. What are your most sensitive situations in this context? Listen empathically (see page 167) to yourself and your partner when talking about this. Try to draw out common themes such as 'I tend to blame when I am scared/lonely/sexually frustrated/angry/feeling undervalued'.

Boredom

This is one of the commonest relationship problems therapists see. As I've said elsewhere, most of us crave novelty and the world around us is geared to providing almost limitless supplies of it. In a way this spoils us and makes it harder to tolerate boredom, or what we now think of as boredom.

A generation or two ago people didn't think of this in the way we do. They tolerated their 'boring' jobs and housework and got on with them. This also meant they coped better with what some today would call 'boring' relationships.

Living with someone for many years would, at first sight, appear to be a recipe for tedium. Indeed, few criticisms hit harder than accusing someone of being boring.

The thing is that we ourselves can become uninteresting – so much so, in fact, that we bore ourselves and then unwittingly project this on to our partner.

If you think you have become dull, try taking up a new hobby, or doing some voluntary work. Anything will serve if it gives you a new outlook on life. This applies to the sexual arena too, of course. Many long-term couples complain of boredom in the bedroom. Letting things slip from how they were at the start of the relationship could be the problem here. Few complain of monotony early on in their sexual life together. Many people have forgotten how to play courtship games (see page 204). Sex is a trade-off between the familiar (so we feel safe and can relax into it) and the novel (to keep our interest up). Getting this mix right can be hard over the years but it's worth aiming for.

No couple can tolerate endless sexual novelty – it's simply too anxiety-inducing. But few of us also want to settle for the same things in or out of bed for fifty years. Sex, like everything else in life, needs some thought and planning if it's to be rewarding. If you fall into the same, familiar routines year after year it would be amazing if you were *not* bored. Anyone would be.

Boredom isn't the fate of all long-term relationships, though, whatever some people say to convince me! As you both grow over the years you may well find you're *more* interested in one another and indeed more interesting as individuals than you were years ago.

ASK YOURSELF

▶ Do you think your life is boring? If yes, what are you doing about it?
▶ In what ways do you think you yourself have become boring?
▶ What bores you about your partner?
▶ How does being boring serve you or your relationship?
▶ How does your boring relationship help you?

YOUR ACTION PLAN

Remember to be yourself. If you don't you'll be shutting the door to pleasures and giving your lover the wrong impression. Reveal your needs in and out of bed and help your partner to be creative. An element of selfishness is a part of every relationship. You need to know what you really want before you can ask your partner to help you get it.

Share fantasies. These could be sexual fantasies or fantasies about holidays, a new hobby, retiring early, starting a new job, or whatever. Rehearse in fantasy things you'd like to do, alone or with your partner, and then share how you could make them happen.

Improve your surroundings. Small changes can make a big difference. I know couples that change the position of their furniture from time to time. Others make love in new settings for a change. Anything that alters your routines even a little can make a big difference to how you feel about them.

Learn to please your partner. Many people who complain to me about how bored they are have become self-obsessed, to the detriment of their lover.

Take the spotlight off yourself for a while and see how you could better serve and love your partner. This alone can start to banish boredom. With luck and a little encouragement you'll find he or she will reciprocate.

Forget about 'being in the mood' (be it for sex or anything else). Start off by banishing routines. When your partner suggests something new, work on the principle that unless it's illegal, you'll agree to do it. When listening to 'bored' couples I'm struck by the limits they put on pleasure. They make love, for example, only when they 'feel sexy', whatever that means. They can't at first understand my concepts of 'angry' sex or 'sad' sex for example. They restrict their pleasurable activities, from sex to going to the cinema, to times when they feel 'right' for it. As a result many such couples do very little because things never seem quite right.

Go to the cinema when you don't feel like it. See a film you'd never normally dream of seeing. Get your partner to surprise you with something they'd really like to do but you would never do if they hadn't suggested it. Try a love-making position you've never wanted to try before ... and probably still don't! And so on. You have nothing to lose but your boredom!

Change

Change is unavoidable if we want to build an intimate life. The problem is that it's always easier to see how others could and even possibly should change than to look into ourselves and see what needs altering there.

Given that even inanimate objects adapt all the time it is clear that change is a part of nature itself. We can't pretend to ourselves that we can get away without it, however threatening we find the idea. Many couples who are too close or too distant can't see how change could make things better. They can envisage only loss.

Life today is all about change. We are daily forced to adapt how we think and behave. But one thing never varies — our fear of change itself. Most of us feel happiest in situations that are familiar. After all, familiarity means not having to re-define life anew every day. We have, in short, to be able to take certain things for granted or life would become intolerable.

Against this stormy sea of never-ending development many people look to their one-to-one relationship as a rock of certainty and 'no change'. How disappointing then to find that the rock we find ourselves clinging to has shifted like everything else in our lives! It is the tension created by the need and desire for change, while at the same time staying exactly where we are, that makes for so much friction in relationships.

Couples often say they know how their partner, or even they themselves, should change. What happens when looking at all this in detail, though, is that the very things they want to alter in their partner are often those that first attracted them. This comes about because we tend to see personality characteristics as being all bad or all good. They are not. Even our partner's meanness, for example, can be turned to our advantage, as they manage our joint financial affairs cautiously. Because we pair with our shadow (see page 12) our very best traits can also be our worst, and vice versa.

But by definition change means starting to think or behave differently. And this can be hard. Not so much the journey as a whole but simply starting with the first step. I usually ask couples to break down an area they want or need to change into several small steps, each one of which can be achieved with ease. (See, for example, 'Anxiety and Fear', page 59.) This makes everyone optimistic. Looked at on any grander scale than this, even I sometimes become dispirited! We all need to make changes in small enough bites that feel comfortable and manageable. Negotiating the setting up of these steps can be a real challenge but is possible with love and application. After all, one individual's 'tiny step' can seem like the Grand Canyon to the other. As we progress through each stage it's vital not to go on unless and until we are happy with where we are. As confidence grows, the steps appear to get easier. Almost all change is about confidence – confidence that we won't fail.

But as with much of the emotional life, paradoxes abound. One of the greatest barriers to intimacy is an inability or unwillingness to change. It might not be anything with the relationship itself that needs transforming. It might be: our job; our hobbies; our lifestyle; our weight; something long ago from our first family; something we need to forgive or to be forgiven for; or something we need to know more about so we can deal with it better. Doing any of this doesn't just occur in a vacuum, though, it is part of our intimate relationship and each tiny step creates change there, whether we like it or not.

The problem is that given that most of us fear change we tend to kill the positive potential of it before we even start. Most of us fear that change will be for the worse but in truth this isn't usually the case. In fact, it often improves life in ways we could never have foreseen. Many people have told me how much better their relationships were at work, with a friend, with their kids, or even their boss since they made a meaningful alteration in something to do with their relationship at home. Of course, changes made outside the home can similarly produce helpful knock-on effects with our partner.

Given that this book is about change, you can see it in several ways. It could be seriously threatening, a task too great to embark on, or even something you'd find it impossible to manage at all – or you could join the journey of discovery, with or without your partner, that will inevitably lead to greater intimacy and love.

ASK YOURSELF

▶ What is it you most fear about change?

▶ How would you like to change your partner, and what does this say about you?

▶ What are your usual responses to change?

▶ How would you like to be better equipped to deal with change?

▶ How could your partner help you cope better with change?

▶ How do you think your expectations of life stop you changing?

YOUR ACTION PLAN

Fake it till you make it. This is a useful little ruse that actually works, if you give it a chance. All change involves doing things we find hard, or wouldn't otherwise do unless pushed. In this 'game' you go ahead and do something that's required of you even though you don't feel like it, can't believe in it, and certainly don't think it will work. You'll be amazed. In the vast majority of cases simply doing it time and again will make it happen! Try using this for everything from: giving your partner a kiss on your/their return home from work, to being happier, more vocal during lovemaking, nicer to the kids, commenting positively on your partner's clothes, avoiding being critical even when you know you are justified in doing so, and touching one another more often. In no time at all you'll discover that doing the little things gets easier and easier and that once you've broken the spell of your 'bad spirit' other good behaviours will quickly follow.

Clarifying. Change can be very threatening. When talking about it, be really sure what your partner actually wants of you. This involves clarifying what they say until we are certain we understand what they mean. Whenever someone says something to another, the message that comes out of their mouth is first somewhat censored and altered by their uncon-scious. The sound then travels across the air and into the ears of the listener. His or her 'internal filters' now alter what was said once more and eventually they respond. At this stage they too may not say exactly what they mean. At every stage there are, therefore, errors and possibilities for misunderstanding.

This makes it vital for intimates to check and crosscheck exactly what they think has been said. 'What did you mean when you said X?' is a good start. 'Did I understand you right when you said that X was Y?' And so on. This is what I call the 'For the avoidance of doubt' strategy. Get into the habit of doing this, especially when talking about difficult areas of your life together.

Try to find positive meaning. When we discuss tricky things such as change we often say things that come out wrong and hurt our relationship. The secret of couples that have great relationships is that they do this rarely and when they do they know how to remedy it. Here's what they do.

Let's say your partner has just said something that really annoys you. You can get furious and start a row or you can say something like: 'When you (say what they did) I felt (your emotion) but I know you didn't mean to hurt me, so what were you really trying to do and how did I misread it so badly?'

Your partner now tells you what it is they were trying to achieve. Perhaps they *were* trying to annoy you. Perhaps to prove a point. Perhaps to stimulate you into doing or saying something – anything! Or perhaps they just mis-expressed themselves.

The next stage is for both of you to work out how best to find a more effective and respectful way of getting that information across without mixed messages or actual ill-intent. How could you better try to prove a point, or stimulate your partner into communicating with you? Thrash this out until you come up with successful alternatives. Ask what would work best for your partner, as the current method obviously isn't effective.

Coping with change. When considering what's worrying you about changing in some way, look at what you're leaving behind and bid farewell to it. Think carefully about what you're moving towards and work out the pros and cons, including your fears and beliefs about it. Remember that all too often it is our fears themselves that are our worst enemies when it comes to change. The old phrase, 'Feel the fear and do it anyway' isn't as ridiculous as it seems.

Remember too that adjusting to change can be, and probably should be, a gradual process. Be gentle with yourself and give yourself time to get used to the new situation. At first it'll be one step forwards and two steps back but even this is change! And you're coping with it. Every so often evaluate your progress and congratulate yourself – or get someone else to.

Children

It might, at first, appear odd to include children in my list of things that destroy relationships – but they do. Or rather, they can. When recently divorced couples are asked what it was that they most disagreed and fought about, money comes very high on the list but children usually come close. Sex is always lower than either of these! Most people have very strong views about their children – their education, their behaviour, for instance – and it is rare for partners to have exactly similar views, even in general, let alone when it comes to any individual child. Clearly the ground is set for conflict. Various studies have found that the more children a couple has, the worse their marital satisfaction. To be fair, these studies were done some years ago when large families meant four or more children. Such families are rare today.

The birth of a first child is the biggest single psychosexually disorienting event in any couple's life. From a cosy club of two (a mistress and her lover) the couple's world is suddenly enlarged by another, unknown, and as yet unknowable, creature. Even couples for whom pregnancy was easy and who like children in general can find themselves amazed by and unprepared for what parenthood brings.

Today's woman, with her full-time job and scant previous experience of real-life babies, often discovers she has feelings she never knew possible, challenges that appear to dwarf those at her work, a man who may behave entirely differently from how she'd imagined (for better or worse), a family that doesn't react the way she thought, a set of feelings for her new child that don't fit in with her fantasy of what mothers 'should' feel, and so on. It is a time of confusion and fast learning. Add to this the fact that few of us have an extended family to hand and so feel somewhat alone and even lonely in our quest to be 'good parents'. And of course, we will even disagree about what that means!

Conflict over relationship matters we had previously taken for granted now becomes frequent, and the rewards and joys of the new little life can be all but lost among the practicalities of night-waking, tiredness, sore nipples, celibacy, work worries, power battles, jealousy, disappointment, and much more.

I have written whole books about this subject, so I won't go into things too deeply here. Suffice it to say that, depending on the personality styles of the individuals involved, this can be a really great time or the worst time in a couple's life. Many men say they feel left out or frankly jealous, as their partner concentrates on the ever-demanding new little life in her hands. The birth of a first baby is, statistically, a very common time for a man to have a first affair.

But there are far more sinister things afoot that need to be confronted. About one in three babies do not have the father that people think they have. Many women tell me they fear what the baby will look like and some even have bad birth experiences, unable to let the baby out because of such fears. Everyone is looking for Uncle Jim's nose, or whatever, but such a mother, guilty about her affair, is searching for characteristics of her lover's appearance that someone might just recognize.

And of course, not all couples are thrilled about having a baby at all. Even in this age of reliable contraception about a third of all babies (some say more) are unplanned. This is not to say they are entirely unwanted; nevertheless the issue is a thorny one and it's easy to see how, for many couples, the 'happy day' is very far from that.

As with everything else to do with our relationship, our fantasies and expectations of babies and parenting go before us. Every unborn child is an idealized object of love but reality often proves different. Becoming a parent can give us the opportunity to be better parents than our parents were, or to provide a better life for our child than they did for us. Some couples see their baby as a sort of glue that will hold an otherwise shaky relationship together. Others are looking to their baby to take the emotional or sexual spotlight off them in the marriage. Some parents look to their child to provide the sort of unconditional love, caring opportunities, intimacy, and so on that they aren't getting from their partner. Some individuals feel they should have a baby to validate their relationship or it won't be seen as 'proper' by their friends and relatives. Some men have a child to prove their virility to themselves or others, or to get back at someone from their past. And so it goes on.

From this tiny skirmish with the subject it's easy to see that having a baby is a hugely complex undertaking and is very rarely the simplistic event it appears. It is for this reason that children are such a problem area for so many couples, though the stage of life at which problems raise their head varies according to the individuals involved. Some individuals are great with little children and babies, others with adolescents or even adult 'children'. Some parents fare badly first time round and settle into later parenting wonderfully and find it a joy. But whatever any individual's reactions and potentials and however well a couple thought they matched as adults, they may have to completely reassess much of this when they become parents. For example, a woman may have previously found her man's boyish charms a delight, but now she needs a 'man' he can be found wanting in her eyes. He too will have ideas about what a 'real mother' should be and finds her lack of housework skills and motherly behaviour annoying or even really worrying. Given that most of us have only our families of origin to go by it's inevitable that we'll compare our partner with our parents in their roles earlier in our lives. This isn't, of course, fair but we do it nevertheless.

I've tended to focus so far on the negatives. After all, this book is about problem areas and how to deal with them. This said, some people, mainly women, say that looking back, raising their family was the single most fulfilling part of their lives. Many women say they grew hugely as a result, and increasingly men tend to say the same. We are having smaller and smaller families today. This in itself brings new problems and opportunities compared with our grandparents' generation. This, and many other changes, has made many older people feel they have little to offer young parents today, as the world appears to be so different. It's true that things have changed beyond recognition in many practical ways, and certainly in the way that society sees women, but young mothers (and indeed fathers) still need support and love from others who've been there before.

Most people tend to focus on the new mother and her feelings, but men have their problems and challenges too. If his partner is taking a long time off from work, many a man worries about becoming the sole breadwinner and a fair number ask me if I think their partner will ever go back to work! This new responsibility can be frightening for the young new dad, especially if he's in his twenties and hasn't yet really grown up himself. His partner may be delighted to have a baby in her late twenties but he may still feel something of a boy himself and thus be unwilling, or fear he is unable, to be a 'real father'. This new-found responsibility means having to alter his lifestyle and definitely restricts his freedoms. Add to this the fear that he might become the sort of father he had (if this was not good) and it's easy to see that many a young man can be very concerned about this change in lifestyle.

Most couples say that once they have a child it seems even more important to try to make their marriage work. Many women also say they need their partner now more than they did. If a woman feels trapped at home with her baby then her man can be her main source of 'news' from the outside world. Some guys find this dependency frightening, especially if they have, however unconsciously, looked to their partner as a sort of mother figure. Suddenly they find themselves having to look after her and this feels strange.

ASK YOURSELF

▶ How have your children damaged your relationship?

▶ How has having a family made you a better person?

▶ How has having a family made you reassess your relationship?

▶ Would you have children again, knowing what you now know?

▶ What are your partner's views on this?

▶ What would you have done with your life had you not had a family?

YOUR ACTION PLAN

Parent, adult, child. Within us all are the characteristics of these three unconscious elements. Get a sheet of paper and put these headings across the top. Under each, list the areas of life which best sum up your way of being in each of them. Now repeat this for your partner. You could find some amazing paradoxes. For example, under 'Child' you may enter 'Family'! In other words, you may identify more with your children as 'co-children' than you do with being their real-life parent. There's a lot to learn from this exercise.

How do you tend mostly to relate a) in the world in general and b) in your relationship? How does your partner tend to function in these spheres?

Many partnerships thrive for a while on a Child pairing with a Parent but the only real, lasting success comes from two Adults relating equally with one another, eye-to-eye and soul-to-soul. This said, remember too that we all shift our position on this triangle throughout life, and even from day to day. A perfectly adult man may, for example, revert to Child behaviour on the birth of his first baby. Some of my patients work a whole lifetime as Parents to one another, and so on.

Being a parent. Take time out to think what being a real-life parent means to you. Explore your feelings, beliefs, hopes, fears, aspirations, and expectations. Talk all this through with your partner.

Make a date. I get lots of flack from my patients when I suggest this. Yet many couples with young families forget that they are lovers and friends first and parents second. Make time in your diaries and busy lives to go out for dates like you did before children. Make these dates a priority and stick to them. Take time to prepare, as you used to. Take a little gift. Make a real effort not to talk about the children, the mortgage, schools, or any of the routine stuff that says you are parents rather than friends and lovers.

After the date tell one another what you liked about it. Make another date at once so you have something nice to look forward to.

Commitment Problems

It's a strange paradox that people are more interested in commitment today than they were say thirty years ago. Perhaps it has something to do with HIV/AIDS and sexual caution; maybe people look around and see the damage done in the sixties and seventies when the 'anything goes' world was booming, with all its disasters. I don't know. But today I see more people prepared to make a commitment, however short-lived, than before. Until fairly recently the word meant a life-long pledge to *marriage*. People today seem more willing to make short-term commitments, but these are no less valuable or worthwhile because of that.

Commitment doesn't just involve things to do with sex, of course. It means promising to dedicate ourselves to our relationship and its future, even if we can't see what the future holds. Most such undertakings involve two processes. The first is a one-off decision to make the partnership special and is the sort we make when we start off together. The other is an on-going commitment to service our relationship and renew it every day. In this we take nothing for granted, watch our step, keep on our toes, and try not to get lazy.

But making a commitment to our lover also involves making a promise to *ourselves*. In a way this is even more important because our lover can't change our life for us. Only we can accept our need for growth and self-development. We can commit ourselves to one another too by agreeing to make the relationship work even when things are going badly.

All of this means putting time, effort, and energy into our relationship but many people fear the work this involves. Whenever I talk about this subject with couples they start to count the cost. Early on in a relationship the costs can seem high and the rewards rather poor. As intimacy grows, though, and commitment starts to pay off, they say that what seemed too great a price at first was in fact the very best investment they'd ever made.

But you can't get very far talking about this topic without coming up against the concept of 'self'. Being committed to a relationship means giving up things we would have otherwise done if we weren't in that relationship. Of course, gains flow from the relationship itself. In fact, in a truly committed relationship one plus one can often make about three! Some people fear a loss of personal 'freedom', but to some extent the surrendering of at least some freedoms is the very basis of a truly committed relationship. The fact that we are able to make such an apparent sacrifice, not for our partner, as is so often claimed, but for the relationship, is the heart of most intimate relationships.

On a day-by-day basis, a commitment means sexual fidelity, making time for one another, behaving in ways that promote rather than harm the relationship, agreeing that the relationship has a future that's worth working towards, and much more. Such a commitment weathers storms well because underneath the daily 'stuff' of life the relationship endures and grows because, rather than in spite of, these problems.

In everyday life, we should strive to balance our other commitments to work, friends, relatives, children, and hobbies in a way that ensures our relationship remains paramount. Nothing should ever come between us as lovers in this respect. There is no more important job. Everything else must take second place or we are not living out our commitment. Many people I see claim that making their career a success has to take first place but they soon discover that however wealthy or successful they are, their soul is empty – or at a more practical level there's no one to share it all with – if they aren't committed to their one-to-one relationship.

The problem is that none of us can swear to give 100 per cent commitment all the time. This can be a real dilemma for those starting a new relationship be it at twenty-two or sixty-two. How can we know with any certainty that we'll be able to remain committed in any given situation?

The answer, of course, is that we can't know. Yet this is the very reason we have to commit ourselves. Such faith in turn shows our love in that we're prepared to risk our love, life, time, energy, sexuality and so on *for the relationship*. We don't do this for our partner. Many people, especially women, find this a hard concept. They say things like 'I'd do anything for him'. This is bad news as it can put their man under pressure. Sometimes this is a relationship breaker in itself. Whilst it can be hard for some individuals to make such commitments *to their partner*, it can be easier and more desirable to make them *to their relationship*. Our partnership, after all, includes ourselves, and we don't therefore need to feel too saintly sacrificing ourselves for someone else. Looked at this way, three set-ups benefit – ourselves, our lover, and the relationship. Commitment now becomes a road to freedom rather than the cage it at first appears to be. It brings joy and liberation to be oneself.

I always advise couples to avoid 'making a commitment' when they are head over heels in love with one another early on. If we are to make a sensible commitment to one another we need to be aware of the other's faults and shadow side – and indeed of our own. Making a commitment before we really know something of worth about ourselves and our lover increases our chances of failure. I always suggest couples get romantic love and lots of sex out of the way before they make a commitment so that when they do so it is made in reality, with some depth of understanding and real chance of permanence. Only then can they make a wise choice that will lovingly bind them together.

ASK YOURSELF

▶ What do you mean by the word 'commitment'?
▶ Do you think commitment automatically follows love?
▶ In what ways do you feel your partner is committed to your relationship?
▶ In what ways do you feel they are not committed?
▶ How do you think you could show more commitment to your relationship?
▶ What's holding you back from doing this?
▶ How do you make the distinction between being committed to your partner and being committed to your relationship?
▶ What areas of your life deserve your greatest commitment?

YOUR ACTION PLAN

Keeping commitment alive. Make an effort every day to actually say something out loud that confirms your commitment. Declare something to your partner. Avoid making promises you can't keep. Try to become aware of patterns in your relationship that disable your ability to feel committed, and talk them through. Ask yourself what it would take to break up your relationship.

Overcoming your fears. Write yourself a list of your past experiences with commitment — be it to a job, a task, a hobby, a relationship, or your family, for example. Make a list of things to which you would definitely say you were committed — and another to which you feel you are not but could/should be. See what trends you perceive. Can you, for example, commit yourself easily to things that need action/money/time/love/emotional intelligence/business skills? See which areas of life you find most hard when it comes to commitment. How does this disadvantage you? How has it disadvantaged you with partners in the past? How is it adversely affecting your relationship today?

Dealing with your partner's fears. There's nothing you can do to make your partner feel better about making a commitment. That's up to them. And no amount of manipulating/sulking/whining/nagging/wishful thinking will make a jot of difference. However, you can help them by avoiding behaviour that increases their fears. A good exercise on this is to sit down together when you are feeling good about one another and each to write a list of what you think are *your* biggest roadblocks to commitment and what are your *partner's*. Finally, make a list of how each of you thinks the other contributes to your feelings about commitment.

Now exchange your lists and read them quietly for a while, trying to see what you can learn. Next, talk things through. You may well have somehow misread certain things about yourself or your lover. Try to be completely honest about your fears. Be gentle with one another as you share these difficult emotions. Next, take one of your partner's fears and look at it in detail. For example, I often see men who fear commitment because their worst fear is that their partner will want to start a family and they feel they're not ready. Quite often the fear is completely unfounded. True, she wants a baby soon, but not at once! True, he doesn't feel ready for fatherhood but in truth she's not that happy about giving up her job at this time and would like to wait anyway.

Suddenly, things take an emphatic turn for the better. Many such fears can be dealt with just by talking and empathic listening (see page 167). Most of us work on false assumptions when it comes to intimacy fears. Loving communication is the answer.

Conflict and Rows

In any human relationship there is one thing of which we can be sure: there will always be conflict, if only from time to time. No matter how much we like or love one another there will be times when we feel so different, and even alien, from our partner that we wonder how on earth we ever got together.

But as with many areas of life, prevention is better than cure, so let's start there. Couples who frequently encourage one another find they experience conflict far less frequently than do most others. It also helps resolve whatever caused the conflict in the first place because there is an underlying well of goodwill into which they can dip their emotional buckets. Setting aside time to share your fears and pleasures in your relationship can also help defuse things before they grow into big issues. Being open about practical, day-to-day matters is also a great help. A lot of conflict occurs over small issues such as who agreed to book the restaurant for that birthday date.

Try to be honest about your expectations because conflict usually arises when there are unrealistic expectations in any particular situation. Try to halt small conflicts before they grow into big ones. Many of my couples say this appears to make things worse because by doing this they seem to multiply their conflicts. But this is just an illusion. Successful couples have a third eye that picks up early conflict and defuses it before it gets anywhere near a pitched battle.

A central part of conflict prevention is to take responsibility for your own emotional business rather than projecting it on to your partner. Most of us create additional conflict, albeit unwittingly, by dumping our own anxiety, fears, frustration, or rage, for instance, on to our lover. Hardly surprisingly, our partner doesn't want this and may get confused as to whether it is their stuff or ours. This confusion adds to the bad feelings of having to deal with our stuff when we ourselves should we handling it, and makes for some of the worst conflict.

These simple preventives may work for you but it won't be easy. Even the most effective of couples that have good preventive skills still experience conflict from time to time. And the more unconsciously attuned they are to their 'shadow' and that of their lover (see page 12) the more ferocious this can be. After all, a lot of conflict we experience with others is simply a reflection of the conflict that rages within us. Finding it hard, or impossible, to cope with this, we project it onto our lover, hoping they will somehow deal with it for us, or show us how to deal with it in ourselves. And this can, of course, occur. Something that upsets us can often in fact be better handled by our partner than by us ourselves, and if we are sharp enough we can learn from observing how they do it. But drawing the line between this helpful way of discovering how to cope with the world and dumping our stuff onto our lover can be hard.

When we first get together, conflict is very common. This is probably inevitable and would occur if we were to start living with a close friend or even a brother or sister. People who have been together for many years say that their worst times were early on when they were trying to get the measure of one another. Thankfully, sex is usually a strong and revitalizing force at this point, so conflicts can be resolved in the bedroom in a way that is less likely later on in life. There is also usually a huge fund of goodwill that the couple can draw on.

When dealing with conflict, one of the biggest problems I find, listening to couples, is their endless ability to confuse fact with opinion. Most of us think that because we perceive something to be right we *are* right. Of course, this is nonsense. Unfortunately, this approach almost inevitably means that if we are 'right' we automatically see others as 'wrong'. (For more on this see page 70.) Let's look at an apparently simple example to do with sex. When I ask a couple how often they have sex the man might say, 'We had sex *only* five times last month', while his partner might reply proudly, 'We made love *five* times last month!' The same 'fact' can mean such different things to any one individual. And to make matters worse, so-called facts that have an emotional element to them (of which there are many) seem to take on a new quality of their own, which can easily lead to conflict.

Once we start down the minefield of opinion we're in serious trouble. To continue with my example: the man might claim that only two of the occasions were what he would call lovemaking at all. She hadn't seemed that interested, hadn't done anything to turn him on, and perhaps, when he thinks about it again, only one of the five would be what he would call 'real sex'. His girlfriend, on the other hand, imagined she had been exactly what he wanted, especially given her recent track record of sex only every few weeks. She thought she had been a virtual sex bomb!

So who is right? The answer is 'both', in these situations. 'Right' from our own perspective. No matter how long we argue or rage we won't convince our partner they are wrong. Listening empathically is the only way out of this dilemma (see page 167).

But however well we listen, and however hard we try to pre-empt conflict, there will always be some. Few couples agree about thorny issues in everyday life such as abortion, affairs, 'perverse' sexual practices, children, women and work, mortgages, in-laws, and so on. There will always be some conflict over such matters and the only mature solution will be to allow our partner to have their views while we retain our individuality with ours. Many couples try to convince me that when they experience conflict over such basic issues it proves they are wrong for one another and that they should break up. I disagree. Given that, on average, we'll be right half the time and wrong half the time, if we stick around one another for long enough it'll give both parties a chance to change, grow, mature, and alter their views. The joy of dealing with couples of many ages is seeing one minute a young couple who imagine such disagreements are the end of the world for them and the next a couple who've been together for forty years who have changed their views and ideas of who's right on such issues many times in their lifetime together.

Most of us like to think we are very similar to our lover. As a result we try to play down differences because they could lead to conflict. Most of us fear being alone, or being abandoned, and so avoid conflict just in case one day our partner will leave us because we are so 'impossible'. But a much bigger disincentive to being up-front about areas of conflict, in my view, is that confronting conflict makes us realize that no other individual can possibly hope to answer all our needs. The cosiness we had hoped for, where our 'significant other' was some kind of soul-mate with whom we almost never disagreed because we were so similar and 'made for each other', can be terribly threatened by conflict. It's easy to see why so many individuals will do almost anything to avoid it, for fear of losing what they value so highly. Finally, looking at our differences with our partner and dealing with such conflict makes us aware of our partner's very real weaknesses – and indeed our own. This can be a harsh alternative to living in the fantasy, lovey-dovey world we think we should inhabit.

The concept of compromise is a vital one in the context of conflict. There are many situations in life where we simply cannot both have what we want. If you paint the living-room wall black, it can't also be white. Some couples try to 'buy' alternate 'gos' in some sort of game. 'I'll get my way this time but next time you can have your own way.' This can work but is terribly arbitrary. And it rarely produces the best result. Who's to say that every alternate time I will be right and on the other occasion you will be? This isn't the equality its practitioners claim – except in the sense that the partners in such a relationship have an equal chance to get it wrong when they could, by compromise or debate, have got it right! The trouble with compromise is that by adopting a middle path, neither will get what they want and neither will be satisfied. I have never found a universally acceptable way round this 'worst-of-both-worlds' situation because on some occasions a middle path can work very well. Almost all successful relationships work on doing 'deals'. Yielding to our lover so they can have their own way can be infinitely more successful for our partnership than trying to find that 'perfect' solution that superficially pleases both yet satisfies neither.

It's largely about ego. If I need, or want, to be right and to get my own way, regardless of the cost, then our relationship suffers. If I am relationship-centred I don't much care whether I get my own way or not; rather that the outcome is best for us as a couple. In achieving this I have indeed 'got my own way', the way to a pleasant and growing life together and within myself.

In Western society the notion still persists that the person we choose as a life mate should be perfect for us. To admit we've chosen someone less than ideal seems to reflect on our character, our intelligence, our instinct, and so on. But when conflict rears its head it questions these very 'certainties'. Perhaps, we tell ourselves, we are bad at making partner choices, perhaps our whole personality is somehow flawed by being so wrong. Our anger at ourselves for having made such a mistake with something so important in life is now all too easily projected, unwittingly, of course, onto our lover who is, after all, the source of our 'problem'.

I'm sure you'll see how crazy this theory is. There is no way we can make a perfect choice. There are no perfect people from whom to choose. And we are infinitely imperfect anyway when making our choice. All we can be sure of is having made *a* choice, which seemed a good idea at the time. The challenge for the mature individual is how to make this imperfect choice work for them long-term. And this challenge would be pretty much the same whomever we chose, and however much conflict they appear to cause us.

Finally, don't forget that conflict isn't something necessarily to be avoided. Growth can only occur when our views and behaviours are challenged. Without conflict we'd get too cosy, complacent, lazy, boring, and predictable. Life is long today and the world around us constantly changing. The mature, emotionally intelligent individual is one that can embrace conflict on a daily basis and use it as a way of growing and extending their personality. Looked at this way, conflict is a blessing rather than a curse.

ASK YOURSELF

▶ In what ways do you feel in conflict with yourself?

▶ Think about the ways in which you create conflict in your relationship. How could you change things?

▶ Think about the ways in which your partner creates conflict in your relationship. What could you change in yourself that would help?

▶ Think about what happens when you have a row. How would you like to be able to manage your emotions and behaviour better?

▶ How do you currently manage compromise? How would you like to be able to manage it better?

YOUR ACTION PLAN

Your stuff, or mine? Much conflict arises because we don't sort out whose 'stuff' is whose. When you're about to get annoyed or irritable about something, stop and ask yourself if the issue is really what it appears to be. For example: if you flare up when your partner asks you to take out the rubbish (a perfectly reasonable request), could it be that it's your problem that you're feeling angry, not hers? After all, she doesn't suddenly become a wicked witch because of this request! Someone has to do it. All you can think of (feel) at the time is that *you* don't want to do it. She already does it four times for every time you do it – you just don't know she does. Is it her fault that you: regress to being a little boy being made to do something you hate by your 'scolding mother' (who was always trying to get you to be clean and tidy); seek to gain some power and control out of the situation (when things are going badly at work and you feel out of control enough already); are using the issue to create a fight to answer your needs for conflict (you haven't had sex for three days and feel under-benefited); are using it as a coded message that you're angry about her weight (you're fantasizing about a slim woman you know when having sex with your partner) – and so on.

With this level of 'stuff' going on in the background it's plain that even the simplest transaction between you and your partner is going to be messy. Unless you sort out who is doing what to whom. This takes time and skill to get good at but it's what successful couples do all the time. They take responsibility for their own stuff and don't let it get in the way of their joint stuff.

Encouragement. Couples that encourage one another all the time have far fewer conflicts and rows. When we encourage our lover we simply express appreciation for what they have done or who they are. Make a list of the sorts of things you appreciate in your partner.

For example:

▶ *I really liked working together today.*

▶ *I appreciate your making dinner last night when I was so tired.*

▶ *I really appreciate the way you deal with Peter, he's not an easy child for me to get through to.*

▶ *I liked the way you listened to me last night. It really helped.*

This is different from praising. When I say, 'That dress you made is really brilliant', I am praising. If I say, 'I really liked that dress, it made me feel great being out with you', that's encouraging. Praise involves a measure of judgement; encouragement is simply a reflection of how you feel as one equal to another.

But encouragement has one further dimension, which is often overlooked. It's vital to notice your partner's *efforts*, not just their results. This helps us feel more appreciative and less irritated by routine stresses. It also keeps us on our toes, noticing the nice things our partner does for us, whatever the outcome. Let's say you call your man at work and ask him to get something from the supermarket on his way home. He goes to the store but they don't have what you want. Rather than getting ratty because he didn't get what you needed, or perhaps you thought he should have gone off to other stores to get it, simply say something like, 'Thanks for trying. It was kind of you to stop off when you're so exhausted at the end of the day.'

Work on the principle that sincere efforts are worth rewarding, whatever their outcome.

Lastly, try not to occupy the moral high ground when trying to encourage. For example, let's say your partner has helped you wax the car but left smears all over their part. It would be easy to say, 'I appreciate your help but I had to go over everything again. There's no point you helping if I have clear up after you!' It's vital to keep your priorities in mind at such a time. It's far better to say something entirely encouraging than to poison any future efforts. Many people say of their boss that he or she never says anything nice when they do things well but jumps in speedily to criticize when they do not. This sort of behaviour isn't fair and is very dispiriting both at work and at home.

The main priority is to get your partner's willingness to contribute rather than proving things have to be done only your way.

Decide to make five encouraging comments a day – and stick to it!

See also 'Failure To Build Your Partner's Self-Esteem' (page 136).

Nice things. Separately, look back over the years you've been together and think about the nicest things you've done for one another. The most important part of this exercise is telling your partner the best things they have ever done for you. Share how this exercise makes you feel.

Detecting conflict early. If you know your partner really well you'll be able to detect very early when things look like getting into trouble. To help with this it can be instructive to draw up a list of things that annoy you about your partner – or even about life in general. Against each topic try to find something that you could do personally to restore your emotional stability. Create a little crib sheet and keep it somewhere, if you have to. You could even enlist your partner's help in this, if you like, so they know what you're up to. This could help them feel they don't have to be responsible (which they are not!) for your emotional stability all day every day.

We all annoy one another from time to time but still need to cooperate and live together. Highly successful couples know what annoys them about their partner and have ways of quickly nipping the problem in the bud before it escalates into a war. Think about two other useful concepts in this context. 'Fake it till you make it' (see page 93) and 'What can't be cured must be endured'. There will always be things about our lives together we won't be able to alter. The wise couple knows how to use their energies to deal with the things they *can* change.

Negotiation. This is something successful couples are really good at. The idea here is to arrive at a win-win situation rather than having one individual feel they have triumphed over the other. If you find yourself competing over who's right (see 'Being "Right"', page 70) or who'll get their own way, you're not negotiating – you're in a contest. The idea when negotiating well is to try to perceive your partner's point of view, and along with this their underlying emotional needs. Far better to give up on our own needs for a while than risk continuing an argument. In this way every 'argument' progresses to a mutually satisfying solution. You'll also need to agree in advance that there are certain lines you won't cross, no matter how heated things become.

This sort of negotiation has been found, by one relationships researcher, to work best if the ratio of positive interactions to negative ones in a couple's life is more than five to one. At this level – the Rule of Five – we have enough goodwill in our 'love bank' to be able to withstand even quite high levels of disagreement, difference, and conflict. Reduce this 5:1 ratio and things falter and fail. Now defensiveness, resentment, bitterness, misunderstanding, and score-keeping (see page 181) kick in and conflict is just around the corner.

See also 'Anger and Rage' (page 51) and 'Jealousy and Envy' (page 176).

Death In the Family

Death is still a taboo in our culture and most of us fear it for ourselves or our loved ones. It's hardly surprising, then, that when someone close to us dies we experience all kinds of emotions, some of which originate from very long ago in our past.

But when we're in a one-to-one relationship these emotions don't just affect us, they affect our partner too. If you have a good relationship, such a loss, especially if there's been time to prepare for it, can build an even stronger bond between you. But if you're already in trouble, a death in the family can highlight all kinds of hidden issues.

Some people find they become braver about rethinking their relationship problems because, compared to the death of a loved one, their other troubles seem trivial. Many people also say that they realize how petty a lot of their relationship issues are and wish they could sort things out in case they or their partner were to die at short notice with matters unresolved. In other words, a death in the family can help put one's own troubles into perspective.

Change usually follows a death and this can empower some individuals to examine other parts of their relationship. At the most obvious level therapists like me often see people soon after a bereavement. Sometimes one partner will say that they want to sort of 'spring clean' their life together, chastened by their loss. Others, realizing that they are now next in line for the Grim Reaper – if it is a parent who has died – accept that life isn't a rehearsal for something, and decide to become pro-active in creating a better life.

Losing a parent can be devastating for many, if only temporarily. Paradoxically, it can offer a potential for growth in others. Many, women especially, feel over-shadowed by their mothers and some have told me how they 'allowed' themselves to feel truly adult only since their mother died. However their mother had in reality behaved to them, they perceived her as being 'motherly' or 'mothering', which prevented them from feeling truly adult. The same can apply to men but it is uncommon because men in our culture are much less influenced by how others see them.

Paradoxes abound too when we lose a parent. In some cases the individual whose parent has died isn't the most affected. Bearing in mind how we choose one another in the first place (see page 12) it's hardly surprising that our partner might have a closer relationship with one of our parents than we do. Their loss can, surprisingly to outsiders, be even greater than ours. Many people soften as they mature and age and we may have seen a more mellow and wise side of our partner's parents than they did as a child. Many's the woman who has said to me, 'If only Jim had known my dad like he used to be when I was a kid, he'd understand why we got on so badly.'

As we lose our parents we can feel abandoned on a desert island where we have no one to look up to, to seek advice from, or even, perhaps, to blame. We now have to face realities we may never have confronted, even if we are in our sixties or beyond. This can be hard for some people.

When working with people who are bereaved I am often struck by how mixed their feelings are. Society in general wants to hear that you are shocked, sad, and sorrowful. But if you are feeling delighted, liberated, released, financially benefited, free to divorce, able to speak your mind to your partner for the first time, empowered in various other ways, and so on, it's far harder to get an audience. It is a rare death that is characterized by grief, sadness, and loss alone.

It is said that it's good to talk about your feelings after a bereavement. I can't go along with this. I think some people find it helpful to talk about certain facets of the experience, but my clinical experience is that many people like to do their thinking and grieving in private. After all, they may not want to air their very personal and complex emotions, perhaps even, or especially, with their partner. I don't see this as a shortcoming ... but then I have never subscribed to the psychobabble tenet that talking is the best medicine. It's far more likely that you'll be useful to your partner by being a good listener at this time. Being available for when they want to talk – if they do – could be the very best service you could offer. For more on this see page 166.

The death of a child is an especially traumatic event for most couples. Even someone who didn't want a child can say they feel a real sense of loss. Some people claim losing a child is the worst sort of loss because a young life is such a bundle of human potential that hasn't had an opportunity to flower. Women who have a miscarriage describe far greater feelings of loss than others can readily understand. In fact, of course, this baby has been a part of their body and soul, and as such is all too real. Being 'unseen' it is perhaps even more real than an extra-uterine baby with whom a mother could have bonded and 'personalized', albeit for a very short time. These mysteries are hard to explain to outsiders but they are all too real.

Many people feel angry when they lose a child. This anger can burst into their one-to-one relationship, especially if their partner could be held, however unrealistically, to blame. Big stuff now hits the fan, as old hurt and anger within the relationship comes out of the woodwork. Now is the time to seek professional help as underlying grief in its many forms can colour our whole approach to even a normal conversation. If we feel suicidal or depressed, communicating meaningfully with our partner can be near impossible. It's a terrible pity that some couples dig themselves into ever deeper holes at times like these. When we are both suffering it can be difficult to support one another as we usually would. Outside help from friends, loved ones, or even a professional can make all the difference.

ASK YOURSELF

▶ What was your family of origin's way of dealing with death?

▶ How does your partner feel about death?

▶ How did you go about drawing up your wills?

▶ What have you learned about yourself from a death in the family?

▶ What have you learned about your partner from this death?

▶ How has your relationship changed as a result of the death?

▶ How would you like to have managed things better from a relationship point of view?

▶ How could you have helped your partner better in the circumstances?

YOUR ACTION PLAN

Grief and mourning. We all obviously mourn the loss of a loved one, but we can also grieve the loss of other things too. After an affair, for instance, many people grieve for their original relationship as it used to be and some the loss of their lover. People can also mourn after any major loss, such as of a much loved home, job, or pet. And it's also possible to grieve after any major life change, especially in a relationship. Okay, your partner may still be physically there but if things are very different in your relationship, for whatever reason, you can easily find yourself grieving the loss of him or her to obesity or addiction, for example. Others might lament the loss of their children to adulthood.

Grieving and mourning are psychological events that have well-recognized stages. Most of us go though each stage after a loss, but how quickly we dwell in any one of them will vary a lot according to our personality, our previous experiences of loss, the amount of support we have, and our current life experiences.

Shock is the first stage. Here, we find it hard to think straight, can hardly believe it's happened, and become somewhat numb. We may also deny anything has happened. Hallucinations are quite common at this stage.

Yearning comes next. You desperately want back what you have lost. Now the anger, disbelief, and sadness set in.

Depression is next, as you go down into yourself and live the inner sadness. You lose your will to enjoy things and feel apathetic and devoid of energy. This is a dangerous time and some people feel like, or actually try, committing suicide.

Finally, *recovery* takes place, as you get used to your loss and start to pick up the pieces. Now you accept life has changed and that you can move on.

This whole cycle commonly take about two years to complete.

Write a letter. Write a letter to your loved one who has died. Open your heart and say things you wished you'd said when they were alive — or even things you did say! Pour out your feelings into this letter then keep it somewhere safe and private. It can be a source of solace and love to take it out from time to time to remind yourself of your loved one. You can even do this for a dead baby or one lost in a miscarriage.

Depression

This isn't a medical book but it's unwise to omit any mention of depression because it plagues the life of millions of couples and damages their relationships.

Most of us feel 'blue' from time to time. Feeling 'down' is a perfectly normal response to adverse events in life and doesn't usually mean we are clinically depressed. When we feel like this our mood alters from day to day and we can function fairly well even though we don't feel full of life. We may be tired all the time and just about coping with everyday existence but this doesn't mean we have the medical condition called depression.

True depression is rather different. Here we feel sad or low, have little or no energy, cry a lot, go off sex and other pleasurable pastimes, have trouble sleeping, and may even feel suicidal. Sometimes anxiety is a part of depression. This collection of symptoms calls for medical help.

When our partner is depressed it affects us very seriously. They may not complain of a poor sex life because they're too low to bother, but it can be horrid to watch one's partner lose their joy in life, become more and more unkempt in their appearance, and lose their enthusiasm for work, family, and even life itself. It can be like living with a ghost of the person we knew and loved. The depressed individual can be so absorbed by their condition that they are sort of 'out of it', but for the well partner things can be very hard indeed. It may fall to the well one to seek medical help for both of them.

Sex also suffers, even early on before obvious depression sets in. Sex and relationship problems can cause depression but the reverse is also true. It's a sad fact that when we feel depressed, the love and comfort our partner offers can feel hollow and even unwelcome as we feel unworthy of their love and can't respond when they show it. This soon gets pretty tedious for the well one too as they realize they are powerless to help.

But some individuals suffer from depression without any of the signs I list above. They can remain cheerful and smiling yet be terribly depressed underneath. They may, for example, go to the doctor repeatedly with migraines, cystitis, or a host of chronic conditions that seem to plague them. Sort out the depression and the rest of their bodily symptoms disappear.

The first sign of a man getting depressed can be impotence. This can also suggest to a therapist that his partner might be the one who's depressed. In this situation he has detected her depression before any clinical signs are apparent. He then shuts off because he sees her reluctance, or whatever, as a criticism of him. Few couples where one is depressed have a good sex life and most find day-to-day relating hard too.

Unfortunately, many of the commonly used drugs for depression cause sex problems in their own right. If this is an issue for you, talk to your doctor, who may be able to find a better alternative medication.

ASK YOURSELF

▶ In what ways do you think depression in yourself or those around you affects your life?

▶ How do you/would you feel if your partner were to say they were depressed?

▶ How would you try to deal with your depressed partner?

▶ How would you like to be dealt with by them if *you* were depressed?

▶ If your partner threatened suicide, what would you do?

▶ If your partner said they felt like dying, what would you say?

▶ How has your personal experience of others being depressed affected your life?

YOUR ACTION PLAN

Getting help. Go through my list of symptoms at the top of this section and ask yourself if you sound as if you might be actually depressed, rather than just feeling low. If you do, talk to a friend or ask your general practitioner for help. Either could help you find a counsellor or therapist. Your GP could be a good start in finding one but there are numerous professional organizations that can be accessed via your local library or the internet. If you're not too depressed, get a book on the subject or join a specialist chat room for support. This can also be very helpful if your partner is having trouble coping with your depression. Give your partner 'permission' to get help if you are depressed. It can be very hard being alongside a depressed individual, especially over many years. Many partners of the depressed feel guilty about seeking help themselves, as it appears they're taking the spotlight off their lover. This is nonsense. You can't support your depressed partner if you too are going down.

Deviations and Perversions

These are difficult subjects that can damage even very loving relationships. There are many different definitions of what the words mean. Unfortunately, many individuals use them very loosely to mean 'something that I personally find distasteful'. For example, one woman might say she finds anal sex 'perverted', yet another will claim it is not only perfectly normal but her favourite sexual pastime.

Technically speaking, a deviation is a practice that 'deviates' the focus of sexual activity and arousal from actual intercourse to other things. In short, the aim is right but it slightly misses the mark.

Deviations usually have their origins in childhood and adolescence where an individual learns that intercourse itself is too anxiety-ridden to be really pleasurable. Only by 'aiming off' slightly can sex be arousing and fulfilling.

A perversion is a situation or practice that habitually by-passes intercourse. So, for example, a man who can get aroused only in the presence of a woman's shoe could be said to be perverted. Sex 'with the shoe' is the only way he can function.

In both perversions and deviations individuals may be frozen at a particular phase of sexual development. For example, the man with his shoe fetish may be stuck at the infantile stage of sexual love where he saw a lot of his mother's feet as he crawled around the floor and became fixed on her feet and shoes as love objects. Perhaps the rest of her was somehow 'unavailable'. Such a man will, at difficult times, regress into this primitive behaviour and his fetish shows itself. At other times he may function perfectly well sexually.

Such individuals often get condemned as weird, or even mentally ill, but they deserve pity rather than punishment. Their sexual lives are seriously flawed and limited to a very small range of activities that most of us wouldn't tolerate.

Such people also have trouble finding suitable sex partners because their needs are so strange to many. Another drawback is that it's easy to become enmeshed in all sorts of sexual sub-cultures. Some 'normal' people see such perverted or deviant individuals as being more liberated or highly sexed but the reverse is usually the case. Such people almost never get their best pleasure from intercourse and this can be a serious social setback for them.

Deviations and perversions are usually thought of as being the preserve of men. But this is changing fast as women become more 'man-like' in their social and sexual behaviour. I have no doubt that many women who had similar feelings about such matters in the past almost never expressed them openly. Today's freer attitude to female sexuality, though, is making it easier for women to express this side of their sexual personalities if only symbolically, perhaps, through fashion.

The characteristics of a true perversion are its fixity and compulsiveness. The individual *has* to do it to become aroused or to function sexually in any way. It can't be overcome by fear, shame, guilt, or punishment.

Common deviations and perversions include sadomasochism, anal sex, dependence on sex aids, exhibitionism, transvestism and transsexualism, incest, paedophilia, and compulsive masturbation, to mention a few. Of course, when I list these things, I don't mean they are all by definition deviant or perverted (except the culturally illegal ones such as paedophilia and incest); simply that a compulsive, fixed indulgence in any of them to the exclusion of any other form of sexual activity is probably not healthy.

ASK YOURSELF

▶ How do you feel about deviations and perversions?
▶ Is there any such thing between a loving couple?
▶ What are your personal experiences of deviations and perversions?
▶ How do you set limits on what is deviant or perverted in your relationship?

▶ Do you think your partner is deviant or perverted?

▶ Would you like your lover to be more 'deviant' or 'perverted'?

YOUR ACTION PLAN

Desensitisation. If you're happy with your 'perversion', all well and good, but if you or your partner find it intrudes and you want to do something about it, this exercise could help.

The aim is to slowly, perhaps over some months, replace your odd thought or practice with something you'd rather have.

Let's say you have repeated fantasies about a fetish object or situation and can't ever have an orgasm unless you think of this object or situation. It is a compulsion.

Next time you're aroused, using the fantasy or practice you want to rid yourself of, wait until you get near to orgasm and then, at the very last moment, change your thoughts or internal pictures to something more acceptable to you. Let's say you're hooked up on fantasies of sex with your husband's best friend and this is bothering you because it might lead to you actually doing something in reality and you think this unwise. As you get close to coming, change the fantasy to sex with your husband (or some other subject) so that at the moment of orgasm this is what you're thinking of. Now, slowly, over some sessions, replace more and more of the fantasy you don't want with the new one and in time you'll find you'll have got rid of the 'harmful' one. This can take many weeks or months but it works well if you stick with it.

If your partner has a perversion. This can be very difficult to deal with but is not impossible. First, how about helping him or her with the exercise detailed above? Second, if you can't bring yourself to get involved, how about helping them find professional support? If they won't go for this, perhaps *you* will need some sort of professional guidance on how to cope. It might be that things are so extreme you'll even think of leaving the relationship. Many partners find they don't need to go this far, preferring rather to stay put and to help their lover deal with the 'problem' themselves, or even to take a limited part in the whole thing. A patient of mine who found her husband dressed in her clothes one night on her early return home found, with therapy, she could tolerate this behaviour (though she couldn't understand it) and eventually actually helped him make up and look nice. She bought clothes for him and encouraged his habit. Within a few months he'd had enough of his 'game' and stopped it altogether. I'm sure her loving acceptance greatly helped.

Emotional 'Armouring'

This is a term with which many readers may not be familiar. By 'emotional armour' I mean the psychic structures we create in the fabric of our body to defend ourselves from emotional pain.

From the very first day of life we are subjected to all kinds of (real or perceived) rejection, loss, alienation, loneliness, helplessness, hopelessness, abandonment, hate, fear, rage, and so on. When it appears that these sensations are too great to handle we start to form a kind of body armour that will protect us in the future from similar onslaughts. It's about personal survival.

This body armour does its job very well but it also has some undesirable side effects, because not only does it keep unwanted stuff out, it also traps other negative emotions inside and can even make it hard for us to externalize *positive* emotions. Many people I deal with in my bodywork are frozen behind their emotional armour and cannot be truly themselves. Their partner knows this but can't say exactly what's going on.

This armour isn't laid down uniformly over the body. For example, someone who feels that their 'burden' of responsibility in life is too great to handle, or who was bullied as a child, will have armour plating mainly over their back area. A woman who was sexually abused as a child, or raped later in life, will experience her armouring in her pelvis and may be subject to sex problems, problems of arousal, repeated cystitis, or other pelvic pathology. A bodywork psychotherapist looks for these signs of armouring and gently removes the armour as the individual comes to terms with what originally caused it. They now need very little, or no, armour and their inner emotions can come out as never before. This may mean they can love, be loved, and enjoy life for the first time.

It can be hard to know how your partner is armoured but the exercises below should help you find out a little. Frankly, such is the depth of these pains it can be a very difficult task even for a skilled therapist to get to the heart of what's going on. If you find you're getting into difficult waters here, seek professional help.

ASK YOURSELF

▶ Which parts of your body do you feel are emotionally armoured?

▶ Which parts of your lover's body appear to be emotionally armoured?

▶ How do you think either of these situations affects your sex life?

▶ How do you think they affect your loving life together?

▶ How do you react to your lover's emotional armouring?

▶ How would you like to be able to behave?

▶ What could you do to reduce the effect of your personal emotional armour?

YOUR ACTION PLAN

If You Are Emotionally Armoured

Confront your fears. Work with a good friend, your partner, or a counsellor, to learn to recognize your fears and then to act on them appropriately. Try not to blame yourself for your armouring. It's not your fault. Also, stop feeling sorry for yourself. It'll do you no good. Confront your fears about being more expressive and intimate. It will tend to deflate them. You'll be surprised how much less of a problem this is than you fear it will be. Be aware of the pains that result as you do all this so you can take a delight as you conquer them over the months in your journey to greater openness.

More physical exercise. Take more exercise. Remember, the armouring is deep inside your body, locked up in muscles and connective tissues there. By physically exercising you'll release these tensions. This could produce some unexpected emotional results, so go gently. As your body yields its pains you'll need your partner to help by being there for you just to love, hold, and understand you. Trust them to do this for you.

If Your Partner Is Emotionally Armoured

Hold them. As he or she embarks on their journey (see above) they'll need holding both physically and metaphorically. People who are armoured have unconsciously come to rely on it to 'keep them together'. They tell me they fear 'falling apart' as they try to heal. Words will not be necessary as you support them. Much of this stuff is pre-verbal. Just listen, hold, and love, and you'll be doing all you can.

Emotional Immaturity

All parents want to see their children grow up to be physically, psychologi-
cally, and emotionally mature. But if physical maturity is difficult to define,
it can be near impossible to define emotional and psychological maturity.
Most of us mature physically but many of us never fully mature emotionally. As a result, at some level we remain child-like in a way that harms our
relationships and ourselves.

A small child is totally dependent on its parents or carers. It takes
rather than gives; consumes rather than produces; is unreasonable and
unreasoning; is governed almost entirely by its instincts; is concerned
largely with its own emotions rather than those of others; and is prone to
outbursts of rage and anxiety.

Ideally, good parenting should take this blueprint and make something
more socially productive and self-realizing for their child. This comes about
by giving our children a feeling that they are unconditionally loved; putting
their needs first; making them feel wanted; protecting them from the
excesses of our own neuroses or relationship shortcomings as parents;
and trying hard not to be over-close, over-demanding, over-indulgent,
seductive, remote, or rejecting.

Parents that refuse to let their child grow up, and treat him or her
perpetually as if they were younger than their years, who oppose inde-
pendence and, in an effort to meet their own needs, encourage the child to
cling to them, run the risk of producing an immature adult who will tend to
remain dependent on their partner. Such individuals regress to childhood
at the first sign of any difficulty in life.

In a sense we never grow up – we just become more elaborate. Our
inner child is present in all our adult dealings with our self and others. A
truly mature adult can let this inner child out to play from time to time without becoming 'childish'. Retaining our child-like capacity to experience
total pleasure, to give total love, to be full of curiosity and excitement, and

to retain a sense of wonder are, paradoxically, signs of the mature adult. Progress towards maturity also, of course, means shedding the remnants of our poor, learned experiences from childhood.

Part of this lifelong journey will involve: ridding ourselves of envy, hate, shame, and guilt; learning not to tell lies (including to ourselves) to avoid trouble; developing the capacity not only to accept failure without disintegration or discouragement but to learn lessons from it and to grow; stopping ourselves from being spiteful over minor wrongs; denigrating others out of fear or jealousy; and being suspicious of the motives of others.

Most importantly of all, in our culture, is the need to control unreasonable, unnecessary, and excessive anxiety. This natural and protective emotion should ideally be used only to mobilize our resources to deal with real, or realistically possible, threats to our comfort or security. Its perpetual misuse leads to inefficiency, inappropriate action or inaction, a reduction in happiness, and, eventually, to psychosomatic illnesses, which can cripple an individual just as surely as any physical illness.

ASK YOURSELF

▶ Are you reasonably independent but not excessively so?

▶ Can you give and receive emotionally? If not, why do you think this is?

▶ Are you largely free of aggression and competitiveness, or can you put such things to constructive use?

▶ Are you cooperative? If not, what are your insights into why?

▶ Are you a productive member of society? If not, how could you become more so?

▶ Are you largely free from childhood feelings of inadequacy, self-centredness, and inferiority? If not, what could you do to make things better?

▶ Are you largely realistic, not governed by self-deception? If not, how would you like to improve things?

▶ Can you control your impulses, perhaps converting their energies into more productive ends? If not, how does this adversely affect your daily life?

▶ How good are you at tolerating frustration? What does this tell you about your personality?

▶ How flexible and adaptable are you? If you are not, how would you like to change?

▶ How good are you at coping with people as individuals rather than stereotypes?

YOUR ACTION PLAN

Your Partner Is Emotionally Immature

Build their confidence. You won't be able quickly to build your partner's emotional maturity however much you'd like to. It will take time and a body of life's opportunities for him or her to mature. What you *can* do is to reward any signs of it with things that he or she enjoys or needs. Lose no opportunity to praise and encourage. Reward good behaviour rather than criticizing bad. Go out of your way to find nice things to say whenever anything goes well. Give them this book to read — or leave it around to be found! Many sections deal with emotional maturity in its various guises.

You Are Emotionally Immature

Use this book. By the time you've read this book and worked on yourself for many months you'll be on the way to considerable emotional maturity. If you need further help, you could seek professional guidance. Your best helper, though, will be your partner. Listen, learn, stay humble, create a working partnership on this, and you'll never look back.

Empty Nest

This is a stage, usually in middle life, when our children leave home and we find ourselves together with our partner, perhaps for the first time in many years. For some couples this is a very difficult time and creates huge stresses in their relationship. It is hardly surprising that this is the second commonest stage of life at which couples divorce.

Unfortunately it comes at a time when many people feel less than wonderful about themselves in middle years. For many men this is when they look both backwards and forwards and confront the realities of what they see. Perhaps they'll never make the grade at work the way they'd hoped; maybe the thought of retirement is too taxing; or it might be they feel liberated by the thought that a period of life (parenting) is coming to an end and that this can open up new horizons for them – but that this very change seems threatening. For some individuals this time of life coincides with the onset of less than good health, or even actual illness. Many women are menopausal, or recently so. Some are mourning the loss of their fertility, others are wondering what to do in the workplace. For many couples, then, this is a time of considerable life change and challenge, whether or not they have children who might be leaving home.

What I'm saying here is that 'losing' our children to the outside world couldn't come at a worse time for many of us. Just as we are coming to terms with our own mortality, the realities of our careers, and thoughts of what we'll do for the rest of our lives, our children appear to abandon us. This can be very hard to take. And few people talk about it or openly acknowledge it, especially men. And then there's the guilt. Could we have done better? Had we done X would they now have a better career/ partner/life? But the job is done and we can't go back. Of course we want our kids to go out into the world and run their lives, this is what we've been raising them for for years. But however we try to fool ourselves, there's still a loss, and for some this is a real period of mourning.

You'll probably have heard the saying, 'It is said that Life Begins at Forty, but it's nonsense. It begins when the dog dies and the kids leave home!' For some this can definitely be true, but I'm not talking about them here.

Having a family is time-consuming; it keeps us occupied; it saps our energy; it is interesting, challenging, and can be fun; it gobbles up a lot of our available money; it brings us into contact with large numbers of others we wouldn't otherwise have met except through our children; it enlarges our view of the world; it helps us learn about ourselves as individuals and partners, and much much more.

It should hardly come as a surprise, then, that when the last child leaves home, things change. Thankfully for most couples, their children leave home slowly over some years, making the situation easier to bear and enabling them to learn how to cope. For the parent whose main joy/validation/sense of worth/sense of self came from parenting; for the individual, or couple, who 'stuck in there for the sake of the children'; for the person who sees their only role as being a parent; and for the couple who have never really communicated other than through their children or in the parent-to-parent role, things can get very tough. For many couples this is a time of test and challenge as they try to live together in a way they did before starting a family but now coming from a totally different place and in a changed world.

As more and more women are employed outside the home there's probably less empty nest angst than there used to be. Few women today centre their lives entirely on their family as they used to even a generation ago. This is healthy, in my view, and greatly helps when the nest is empty – as it will be for perhaps thirty years!

However, empty nest problems aren't just part of a woman's life. Many men miss their children terribly when they're gone. For many it was their only real chance of intimacy, love, and caring in their life. Many a couple's less-than-great marriage is shored up by the emotional support, dealings with and challenges provided by children. When the young ones fly the nest the barrenness of their underlying adult relationship can become all too apparent. Some men say their children provided them with the glue they needed to keep their marriage going.

The nest, once empty, throws us onto one another in a way we haven't experienced perhaps since the heady days of first being in love and living together. But most of us don't feel like this any more. So what's to be done? The challenge now is to create a life together that's not based on the business and busy-ness of raising a family.

ASK YOURSELF

▶ Do you get your main pleasures and rewards in life from being a parent?

▶ What were your partner's experiences of this?

▶ What are your main fears about not having your children at home any more?

▶ Does your partner share these views? If not, how are you helping him or her with their fears?

▶ Do you feel your relationship has been dominated by the presence of your children? How would you advise others to handle things differently in the light of your experience?

YOUR ACTION PLAN

Loss and abandonment. Think back to your family of origin and ask yourself what you learned about loss and abandonment. What have your experiences on these matters been since then? Repeat this exercise with your partner. How do your experiences concur? What can you learn from one another on these issues? If things are really tough, seek professional help.

Failure To Build Your Partner's Self-esteem

Although most people can readily understand how being nice to one another and stopping obviously bad behaviours can build their relationship – as indeed they can – there's more to creating an excellent relationship than simply avoiding the downsides.

One of these is building your partner's self-esteem. When I run groups, some of the most rewarding and moving experiences people have are during the encouragement exercises. I wait until the end of the day, or even of a whole course, and ask people to write something that they enjoy, admire or just like about each individual in the group. They write this on a piece of paper and give it to the individual in a sealed envelope. They, in return, receive comments from all the others in the group.

Everyone then goes away privately and reads the contents of their envelopes. Some cry, some smile, some just look pleased. But everyone loves it. This simple exercise just shows how little we praise one another and how little it takes to make people feel good, valid, and valued.

Yet we almost never do this sort of thing with our beloved. And that's what I want to look at in this section. (See also 'Conflict and Rows', page 106.)

This calls for a whole new way of thinking based on the assumption that you are going to start relating to your partner in ways that build their self-esteem and never destroy it. You will do this on your own with them and in the presence of others.

The trouble is that it can be hard, or near impossible, to increase your partner's self-esteem if your relationship is generally angry, bitter, unfriendly or violent, for instance. So clearly some work may have to be done here first. But it may not. Going out of your way to do what I'm suggesting here can break the cycle of these negative emotions in an almost magical way.

Of course, it's easy to be encouraging when our partner is behaving well. And I'm a huge fan of praising people whenever I can. As a manager in various businesses over the years I have found that people respond best to praise. Even the smallest encouraging comment can yield huge results.

When we most need to build our partner's self-esteem, though, is when they are *not* behaving well! This is the way it works. Whenever you feel the need to criticize or complain about something your lover is doing, actively try to find something good to say that will make him or her feel better about themselves. By doing this you help them, at their very most important time of need, to feel better about themselves and to 'up' their game in a way they wouldn't be able to achieve alone. This is hard to do at first but can quickly become a habit if you let it. The secret is to ignore how your partner is behaving *at that particular moment* (which might not be very edifying!) and to treat him or her as if they were really their best selves. By suggesting that he or she can be better than they are currently behaving, you hold a candle of hope for them. They'll usually oblige you by going for it.

None of this means taking responsibility for your partner's pains, bad behaviour, or whatever. It certainly doesn't mean excusing their bad or abusive stuff. But it does mean helping them to be more of the good selves you know they *can* be, rather than focusing on their bad side. When our partner acts badly towards us it's the easiest thing in the world to counter-attack, defend, or criticize. But by pointing out our partner's ability to behave better in that particular moment or situation we encourage them, gently highlight their inappropriate behaviour for what it is, *but* most important of all, help them change to become a better form of themselves.

For example, my partner starts being rude and critical about a dear friend we have known for years. I could collude and go along with this personality onslaught or character assassination, or I could build her self-esteem by saying something like: 'I can see you're angry about X but it does you no favours being so vindictive about her. You're much more insightful than this usually, you know how I value your wisdom: you're a good judge of character. I'm sure you can find something good to say about her.' My partner is now pulled up short, stops her self-indulgent rant, engages her 'better' parts and in that moment becomes a 'better' person. I too have become a better person as I have facilitated her growth rather than allowing her to fall below her usually high standards. By doing this we both grow.

Lots of you reading this will probably ask, 'What sort of planet does this guy live on?' But it's not that stratospheric, I assure you. Many of us tend, unwittingly, to fail our partner by allowing them to be less than they could be. In a sense we owe it to them to help 'police' their better characteristics, not in a negative, critical way but in an encouraging way that makes it plain we think very highly of them and want to help them keep up to the mark. In return, of course, we rather hope they'll do the same for us!

ASK YOURSELF

▶ What was your parents' model for building one another's self-esteem?

▶ How do you build the self-esteem of others (not your partner)?

▶ How does your partner build your self-esteem?

▶ What could you do to make this easier for them?

▶ How do you build your partner's self-esteem?

▶ How would you like to be able to do this better?

▶ What do you do on a regular basis to encourage your partner?

YOUR ACTION PLAN

You are so special to me because ... But however well we do any, or all, of the above exercises, it's important to remind ourselves and our partner of what it is that makes them so special, not just to the world in general, but uniquely *to us*. In other words, how we value them because of who they are. None of this is conditional. We may even love and cherish our partner for something we don't much *like*. But the fact that it gives us a chance to grow and learn in their presence is beyond price.

Feelings

Almost all men say that women are too involved with their feelings – and almost all women complain that men are too unaware of theirs. Between the two there's a happy balance, if only we can find it.

Most statements we make have at least some sort of emotional content. The trouble is that we often don't recognize what this emotion is, or that we are feeling anything at all. Our senses give us a fairly accurate idea of what's going on in the world around us, but our unconscious is rather bad at letting us know what our hidden emotions are. We haven't got a 'sense' organ for them.

If Susie says to her husband, John, 'I've got so much work to do before the meeting tomorrow,' there are many emotions that could be hiding behind such an apparently simple remark. Is she *desperate* because she doesn't think she'll get it all done? Is she *afraid* that she might not be up to doing it at all? Is she really *asking* John to cook the meal so she can get on? And so on. Many interpretations are possible and even Susie herself may not be aware of some of them.

In this sort of situation empathic listening wins out. If John listens well to her she might just discover what it is that's at the heart of her dilemma, then not only will she quickly feel more stable but their relationship will be ennobled too. It doesn't actually take much to help our partner feel more emotionally stable. Couples who know how to do this greatly prize one another.

Many people get irritated with me when I say how complex emotions are in daily life. They argue, 'If someone's angry, why on earth don't they just say so and get on with it?' The trouble is that as soon as we start to feel strongly about something life stops being simple for us. The emotion involved somehow presses unseen buttons that trigger old memories or behaviours and we start to act in a way that is inappropriate, embarrassing, childish, or child-like, for example. The anger we are feeling in the here and now is now no longer a simple matter but takes us right back to previous times and all the emotions that were associated with anger then.

In the example above, Susie starts (unconsciously) to get in touch with her father's wrath at her leaving her schoolwork until the last minute. She unconsciously remembers his response and fears that John will react in the way her father did. Suddenly the whole transaction alters as John is drawn into her script from the past as she expects him to act like her father did, even if he would not and will not. This now, in turn, triggers emotions from John's past, whether they involve Susie or not. It's easy to see how all this can lead to conflict.

There's only one effective way to short-cut such emotional circuits and that is for the listener to reflect back what he or she has observed the other to be feeling. Now the emoting one can become aware of what they're feeling and each individual can own and take responsibility for what is theirs and what is their partner's. If a couple doesn't do this sort of 'emotion separating', either or both can end up feeling what the other is feeling, even though it has nothing to do with them. Big feelings are infectious and, given that we've all experienced the basic emotional problem areas of life in many settings, it's hardly surprising that our internal computer quickly zaps in to these familiar 'default settings' and we are convinced they are ours rather than a reflection of our partner's. For those who have a 'thin emotional skin' this is a real nightmare. Everything other significant people feel in their presence triggers horrible stuff for them and they almost never feel stable.

Feelings are an inevitable part of life. They are neither bad nor good. They just 'are'. They are usually coped with in one of four ways: being empathically 'heard' (if we're lucky!); ignoring them; denying them; or projecting them onto others. Men tend to deny or ignore their feelings more than do women because of the way males are socialized in our culture. But even if they store them away they still have to be dealt with somehow — usually by drinking, overwork, sex, anti-social behaviour, or substance abuse. Women tend to be more open about expressing their emotions, but can become over-involved with them, often, it has to be said, because the men around them react in the way they do!

Projecting our feelings is one of the most dangerous unconscious games we play. In this we become unwittingly aware of an emotion but immediately sense that it is painful (either in the present or from the past) and so seek to dump it somewhere else, to be rid of it. I often point out to couples how they use one another as cinema screens. The partner is the blank screen and the one with the painful emotion the projectionist. The painful old movie of the projectionist gets played all over the screen of the partner and he or she has to deal with it somehow. If the movie is in full colour and really convincing, the projectionist believes the images *are* their partner – and things can get alarmingly convincing for the partner too. Even being a screen is pretty painful. (See also 'Letting Your Past Rule You', page 209.)

Far better than any sort of projection is to have someone to whom you can entrust your emotions while you sort them out. To change the analogy, think of yourself as a bucket into which your lover can pour his or her emotions when they are too much for them to cope with. Your bucket is heavily coated with Teflon, so none of the contents stick to it. Having dumped all their emotion into your bucket, your partner now feels more stable. At some stage he or she can remove their stuff from the bucket and deal with it – preferably with your help and listening skills. Eventually the bucket will be empty and you will have done the very best for your lover. With this method there is not doubt what is your stuff and what is your partner's because you agree with yourself that you are simply a non-stick container, whatever happens. By refusing to react with your partner's stuff, you force him or her to take responsibility for it.

But we can't go very far in trying to understand emotions before realizing that people have feelings about feelings! These have been called metafeelings. These are different from primary feelings – joy, anger, fear, and rage, for example – and are more 'slippery'. They include guilt, shame, self-consciousness, and hostility, and arise out of social conditioning rather than being intrinsic to our human blueprint like primary emotions.

When dealing with emotions then, we need to be aware of what we are feeling, what our partner is feeling and how we are both feeling about the feelings. Quite a task! It's not hard to see why so many people find feelings impossibly difficult to deal with.

Don't get dispirited, though. Practice makes it possible to get a handle on all this. It takes an initial act of will to embark on the journey, of course, but once you're on it nothing will stop you because the results are so rewarding. Start, as with empathic listening (see page 167), outside your relationship where things are safer emotionally. Because you are uninvolved with the other individual you can stand back and separate out what are your feelings and what are theirs. Once you can do this effectively in neutral situations start practising on friends, and then bring your skills back home.

ASK YOURSELF

▶ What do you feel about 'feelings about feelings'?

▶ What does your partner feel about this?

▶ What did your upbringing teach you about dealing with metafeelings?

▶ How would you like to deal with all this better than you do now?

YOUR ACTION PLAN

Feelings about feelings. Look at the feelings list on page 169 and write them down the left-hand side of a large piece of paper. Alongside each jot what your feelings about it are. You could be astonished as you look at the trends. For example, alongside 'anger' you might write 'fear'. Alongside 'loneliness' you might write 'terror' and so on. This could teach you how afraid you are generally. It could then form the basis of a great session with your partner talking about your fears of many things in life and how this affects your relationship.

Flirting

Flirting is a way we show someone we fancy an interest that makes it clear, but not blatant, something could just happen between us. It's a means of sending fairly direct messages about our sexual intentions without actually committing ourselves. When flirting we spare ourselves the pain of rejection if the other person isn't interested, but leave the door open to take things further if they are. There are two types of flirting. The first is fun flirting. This can make life happier, raise our self-esteem, and strengthen social bonds. It can be indulged in by almost everyone – whether or not they have a partner. 'Flirting with intent' is a different kind of game because here the aim is to get the other person involved with you – hopefully sexually. This should, ideally, be practised only by those who are free to take things further.

Many successful couples continue to flirt with one another even in long-term relationships, but to some extent this is a mis-use of the term because the very essence of flirting is that you are feeling your way and teasing the other person towards a sexual future. If you already have that sexual reality perhaps flirting isn't quite the right word. This said, flirtatious and sexually teasing behaviour can be a huge turn-on for many couples and I encourage couples to go for it if it works for them. Almost all marriage enrichment books advocate it but some individuals find the idea laughable for the above reasons.

Some young men today complain that they find it difficult to flirt in case their intentions are misread. With many women becoming more sexually adventurous, or even predatory, men can be put off flirting because they might be made to look foolish or, in the very worst scenarios, find themselves at the heart of a harassment complaint at work, for example.

Unfortunately, many men aren't that good at reading the flirting 'language' of women. They often misinterpret a woman's flirtatiousness as a prelude to sex. To be fair, in a world where sexual messages are changing all the time, it can be hard for individuals of either sex to know how to inter-pret flirting. The old rules are in the process of being re-written.

Skilled flirters hold that gaze for a second or so longer than is necessary; use positive body language, possibly involving non-sexual touching; employ sexual banter, innuendos or jokes to say 'I'm available'; and generally make it plain that if the circumstances were right, sex could be on the agenda.

All this is very well for the single or the unattached but trouble rears its head when people in committed relationships continue to flirt. I have heard many a woman complain that her husband flirts much of the time, perhaps even in front of her. This is understandably annoying and demeaning to her and for some can mean the relationship should end.

I don't see it quite so clearly. Most people find it hard to accept that others of the opposite sex are off limits for the rest of their lives, and for many flirting is the only way of coping with this. In a relationship where there is a high level of trust the partners see such flirting as a harmless way of letting off sexual steam. In fact, I often point out to women who complain that their man does it in front of them that it is far better that he does it there than behind their backs! How you'll feel about this will depend entirely on how secure you feel in your relationship.

I suggest to couples with a 'flirting problem' that, looked at in an adult way, this could be the best method, apart from their private fantasy world, of coping with the reality of being attracted to others but not taking it any further. After all, as some proficient flirters tell me, they don't actually want to complicate their lives with numerous sex partners – what they most enjoy is the flirting itself. For some it can become almost an art form. The 'potential' that says, 'If things were different, we could take this further', can be more delicious than actually doing so. This, combined with a sexual fantasy involving the 'flirtee', might be the very best safety valve against true adultery and betrayal. Of course, to the purist, flirtation and fantasy *are* true adultery but, I would argue, they rarely result in divorce, unwanted pregnancy, or sexually transmitted disease so, in an imperfect world, I think they're a least-worst option.

Of course, if your partner is flirting in front of you to punish you or humiliate you, there are other questions to be answered. But this isn't usually the case. Early in my career it was always women complaining about their flirting guys. Today it is very much the other way round. Even very liberated men don't like their partner blatantly flirting in their presence, and with good cause. Given that women initiate and control most sexual behaviour, in that without their permission nothing happens, men have every reason to believe that their partner in 'high flirt mode' is in fact likely to act on it. Biologically speaking a flirting woman is more of a threat to her one-to-one relationship than is a flirting man. And most men instinctively know this.

ASK YOURSELF

▶ Are you a flirt? If yes, why do you think you do it?

▶ If you are, how does your partner feel about it?

▶ If you aren't, how would being able to flirt advantage you?

▶ How do you feel when your partner flirts?

▶ How do you use flirting to help your relationship?

▶ How do you use flirting to damage your relationship?

▶ How would you like to flirt more within your relationship?

YOUR ACTION PLAN

Learn how to flirt effectively. Here are my Top Thirteen Rules:

1. **Don't waste your time with someone who's a lot more attractive than you.** Research show that your best chance of success will be with someone of equal attractiveness. Bear in mind that many women under-estimate their attractiveness (especially if they have a thing about their weight) and that most men over-estimate theirs!

2. **Avoid people who are unlikely to be available.** I know this seems obvious but people make this mistake time and time again.

3. **Forget about chat-up lines and showing off.** These are huge turn-offs

and never work. Just be yourself. Body language, the tone of your voice, and how interested you are are far more important.

4. **Make lots of eye contact.** Your eyes are your most important flirting tools. Looking directly into someone's eyes is very powerful. Someone who avoids your gaze is certainly not interested. This said, be sure not to hold that gaze too long. Anything more than one second has been found to be intimidating when flirting. When your target is talking, look at his or her face for about three-quarters of the time. The person talking will usually look at you only for about half the time. In general, then, glance at your target's face more when you are listening and glance away more when you are speaking. Overdoing eye contact will blow things for you.

5. **Personal distance.** When approaching an attractive stranger, keep about four feet between you. This is on the edge of their 'social zone'. Once you are sure of their response it'll be safe to move in to their 'personal zone'. This can be up to eighteen inches from them. Getting too close too early kills things at once.

6. **Read your target's posture.** When we meet someone we fancy we can fairly well control our face. However, it's much harder to control our body posture. There is always a 'non-verbal leak' from our unconscious. Any part of your target's body pointed away from you is a sign that things aren't going well. 'Closed postures' such as folded arms are also a bad sign at this early stage. The thing to do is to 'echo' your target's body language. This mimicking of what he or she does creates immediate intimacy and harmony if your target is at all up for it. People in general like the company of those who echo their body language.

7. **Synchronize your gestures.** Watch two intimate friends (not necessarily lovers) in a bar. See how they tend to lift their drinks together, cross their legs at the same time, stroke their hair synchronously, and so on. When flirting, make a conscious effort to do this.

8. **Touch.** This can be difficult. Touching is powerful and effective but can easily be taken too far too soon – with drastic results. Even a light, brief touch on the arm has been shown to have both immediate and lasting

effects in social encounters between strangers. The rule is: touch but do so carefully. Men should take care not to be too familiar or threatening, and women should be careful not to do too much touching early on as research shows that men easily take this as meaning they are sexually available. A brief arm touch, followed by more eye contact could safely lead to more touching. Touching your target's hand is more intimate, so go carefully here. The next stage is a hand squeeze; then a hand-hold. An arm over the shoulders is the next most safe, followed by a brief knee touch.

9. **How you say things is vastly more important than what you say.** Keep your voice warm and up-beat; avoid quiet talk, monotonous speech, loud speech, and any sort of raucous talk. Don't be negative in what you say. Avoid banality, self-preoccupation, telling jokes, pausing between words or phrases, lack of enthusiasm, passivity, being too serious or earnest, getting over-excited, and don't swear or use too much slang. All these things have been found, in research, to be a killer when flirting.

10. **Listen at least as much as you talk.** If you can listen empathically (see page 167) you'll be streets ahead!

11. **Pay compliments.** These always go down well. Try to make remarks of a somewhat impersonal nature to start with. Comments such as 'That dress is really lovely' go down well.

12. **Personal disclosure.** As you feel things progressing, start to share personal details about yourself in response to anything your target shares. Let's say he or she says they like Italian food, you might reciprocate by saying something positive about a holiday you had in Italy ... Or that your first boyfriend was Italian!!

13. **Clinch the deal.** There's little point putting all this care and effort into a good flirt if you don't capitalize on it. If you want to take things further be sure to give your, or obtain the other person's, telephone number before parting. Don't declare any deep feelings, just ask straight out: 'How about meeting up for a coffee next week sometime?'

Learn how to stop flirting inappropriately. Look through all my thirteen rules above and see which of them you find yourself doing when you shouldn't. For example, do you flirt with your workmates? With your opposite-sex friends? With your boss? With new people you meet – and then regret it? When you've had a few drinks? When you are lonely/nervous/depressed/feeling horny or at certain times of the month? Try to identify your 'flirting weak points' and then try to avoid them.

Coping if your partner's flirting upsets you. This can be very hard. Many people tell me they like to see their partner flirting and being flirted with because it emphasizes their attractiveness to others, yet points up their prior rights over their sexuality. Some women have told me they've instructed their man to do this at parties, for example, because it turns them on. Such a woman likes to see their man getting other women excited before she asserts her sexual position. This is, however, rather rare and can be a game that backfires!

If your partner flirts repeatedly in spite of protestations that it upsets you, it's time to take stock of what's really going on. Is he or she making a statement about their dissatisfaction with your relationship in general? Do they really want to break up and are using the flirting as a way of provoking *you* to leave so they don't have to? Are they using flirting to bolster their poor self-esteem? All of this needs talking through carefully and sensitively. It could be that if your partner really cannot or will not stop flirting you'll have to call it a day. I try to get my patients to rate the severity of the whole thing before they take any such drastic action. For example, if you were to ignore your lover's flirting, what would happen? Do they do it to reassure themselves they're still fanciable even though they're spoken for? Or are they actually on the look-out for promiscuous sex? The former can usually be dealt with, and even built into your joint fantasy life. The latter is unacceptable to all but a tiny minority. This said, the levels of such behaviour people will tolerate if the rest of their relationship is going well astonish me. How you'll respond will depend entirely on what you think and feel about this particular type of 'bad' behaviour.

Giving Up

When we are really young babies and children, if our parents or carers abandon us, ignore us, die, seem not to care, get seriously ill, are depressed, or don't answer our needs, we start to panic and fear the worst. We will surely die. The facts are that human babies are terribly vulnerable compared with the young of most animal species. We can't hope to fend for ourselves early in life. We are highly dependent on the goodwill, love, and caring of others. Unless we get it we can't survive.

This all builds an intrinsic sense of helplessness and hopelessness in to our 'personal computer' that can be triggered later in life when other significant people behave in the same way to us – or even if we perceive that they do. It's as if the clock has been put back many decades and we regress to feeling and even behaving as we did then.

This is what happens when we give up on our relationship and despair that it will ever be good again. It's back to the cradle with all its powerlessness. We now feel unable to change anything. We imagine, as then, that the situation is permanent (whereas our mother may just have been on the phone to a friend and hadn't actually died!), we feel lonely and abandoned, and we feel bad to our very core. We now feel so trapped by our emotions that in reality we find it hard or impossible to learn and change. Anger, murderous rage, bitterness, loneliness, sadness and many other negative emotions cloud our consciousness and we can't move forward.

When we give up and despair, we shut down. To some extent this is self-preservatory. We just can't process any more conflicting information. Our brain gives up. And we give up. Now we can't see there even *could* be a way out, let alone know what it might be. And we can't see even when our partner is trying really hard. It's hell for them and hell for us.

But however true all this appears to be, you can still come back from such apparently impossible situations. All you need is a tiny ray of hope. This could be enough for your partner, this book, a therapist, or a friend to build a small path to your recovery. You don't have to know how this works or why it works, you just have to trust that something *can* work. Soon, what seemed to be an impossible first step up an un-scalable mountain feels like a gentle stroll in the foothills. And this is all you need to get you going.

ASK YOURSELF

▶ What were your childhood experiences of despairing and giving up?

▶ How often do you feel helpless and hopeless about your relationship?

▶ In what circumstances do you feel powerless in your relationship?

▶ Does your partner feel the same way as you do about the hopelessness of the relationship?

▶ Have you a history of giving up on relationships? If you have, what have you learned about yourself from doing so?

▶ Do you find you despair and give up on things generally? If so, would you consider seeking professional help?

YOUR ACTION PLAN

Have you become helpless? Make a list of the signs that you are feeling helpless or hopeless today. This might include: feeling constantly lacking in energy or actually being ill all the time; having accepted almost constant emotional pain as a way of life; feeling there's no point going on; not bothering to put up a fight when I'm attacked or actually abused; feeling lonely or even abandoned; or feeling unable to create a better future for myself however hard I try. If you are experiencing most of these you really should get professional help, as you could be so depressed you'll be unable to improve your relationship or even your own life without it. Getting this kind of care could be the very best thing you can do for your relationship.

What makes you feel powerless in your relationship? Make a list of things such as: I have no control over our finances; I feel a sexual victim; I don't feel heard; I have little say in how the children are brought up; I feel powerless at work; I'd love to change my job but can't; my partner's behaviour is unacceptable to me and I can't change it; and so on.

Now look at each item in turn and ask yourself what you need to do to be able to get more power in that situation. Take an easy one first – one that could be solved by changes in *your* actions and attitudes alone – and then work out, perhaps with a friend or your partner, ways in which you could make something positive happen for yourself. Remember only *you* can regain your sense of power and control. Once you begin to take responsibility for your feelings you'll be surprised how quickly things can move.

Don't at first look to your partner for answers. All you'll need is some support, but even without that you can still get great results.

Good Intentions

It is said that the path to hell is paved with good intentions. As a working therapist I'd strongly agree with this.

Most of us claim to wish our relationship well. Yet it is clear that good intentions aren't enough. Just wanting something to happen or having what I call 'noble thoughts' isn't enough. It can be a start but from thought to purposeful action can be a long journey.

Remember, given the only person you can change is yourself, you must start acting on your troubles right away. By getting started you not only challenge your partner to do the same but you can also 'shame' them into action by your good example. By taking responsibility and telling yourself that, however comfortable you feel, you're determined to make things really great, your partner will be infected by this mood and will soon be taking an active part in the process. Don't wait for your partner to get the ball rolling, or nothing will happen.

All this is linked into comfort levels. Some people are way too passive (see page 244) and too easily settle for where they are. They decide that it's 'okay' where they are – not great but not all that bad either. It's not what they wanted and certainly not what they dreamed of all those years ago but, they argue, it'll do.

The trouble is that even when experiencing this sort of apparent comfort, most of us know we could do better, could really make a difference to our lives, and could help our partner grow while growing ourselves. All this niggles away in the background, creating small but perceivable waves of dissatisfaction – or worse. If we find ourselves in this situation we start to fear change, however small, because rather than seeing it as an opportunity for success we tend to regard it as a possibility we'll lose even that which we have. For many people this is way too dangerous a gamble, so they let sleeping dogs lie.

But risk-takers in life do things losers aren't prepared to try. If you avoid taking risks with the future of your relationship you'll be stuck for ever.

If things really are to change for the better you have to set your sights higher than they currently are. And this is a daily, even hourly, battle. Whenever you do anything that impacts on your life as a couple ask yourself, 'How is this improving my relationship?' 'How is what I just did/intend to do better than what I would have done yesterday?'

What therapists like me see all the time, with depressing frequency in fact, are those individuals who have recently broken up from a long-term relationship. They appear to be new people ... and not, strangely, because they are rid of some terrible 'burden'. Rather, they have turned over a new leaf and thrown old behaviours to the wind. They decided, perhaps with professional help, to clear out their relationship attic, dump a load of rubbish, and make some important and valuable changes. The tragedy is that had such people made this sort of investment in themselves and their previous relationship, they'd still be there, with the one they could have loved so much better. I always tell people about to get out of a relationship that the odds are the one they're in is the best for them. True, maybe not as things are now, but how things could be with some time, energy, and effort.

Unfortunately, a lot of this stems from laziness and familiarity. It often seems easier, or preferable, to invest new effort in new things. Look at the millions of people whose homes are tatty, hardly ever decorated, poorly presented, and less than a joy to live in. Yet when they move home they spend ages decorating, re-equipping, and getting everything just right. As I've already said, we in the West seem to need novelty to make us care for things the way we should. I try to get people to think about how things were when they first met and courted. They were both gracious, loving, caring, interesting, interested, solicitous of their lover's well-being, and so on. In short, at this time we were trying to present ourselves at our very best. How desperately sad, then, that we let things slip and take our partner and even the relationship itself for granted.

Of course, most of us relax and are somewhat relieved not to have to keep up this level of effort and vigilance over many years together. It feels more comfortable, and it's certainly easier. The trouble is that we *should* really keep on trying to impress our partner every day, as we did then, or we'll slowly let things get sloppier and sloppier until the very nature of the relationship changes. Now lack of respect sets in (see page 199), as we let ourselves go (see page 212). Others who treat us like our partner originally did now become attractive and we are soon embarked on a search for that old magic. Trouble beckons.

Some people tell me they don't want to have to go on 'acting' like they used to in the early days. They work on the principle of 'This is how I really am and you'd better get used to it.' But this isn't fair. Why should our partner see us as our 'naked' self like this? You wouldn't go into a shop, or your place of work, and behave like you do in this 'naked' personality state. You'd be very badly thought of if you did. And most people simply wouldn't stand for it. Yet because we feel comfortable and *can* behave sloppily or even badly with our partner we *do*. It's a paradox, isn't it? The very person about whom we should most care gets treated worse than someone we've just met at a social event.

We've all done this, have all been there, so this sad tale is all too familiar. Yet this kind of behaviour slowly destroys our relationship, and it is usually we ourselves who are to blame. Our self-indulgence, our self-pity, our neediness, our pathetic little child, and much more, not only come to the fore but actually start to rule our lives on an hour-by-hour basis.

The trouble is that it is not only our one-to-one relationship that suffers but all our relationships with others, as this kind of thinking and, more importantly, 'being', infects other areas of our lives.

The only way out is to take yourself in hand, to tell yourself that things must change or you yourself will slowly die, not to mention the relationship.

ASK YOURSELF

▶ Are you a wishful thinker when it comes to your relationship? If yes, how does it benefit you both?

▶ In what ways do you feel helpless about being able to improve things in your relationship?

▶ Are you prepared to put up with second best in your relationship? If yes, why do you think you do this?

▶ How often do you ask yourself the question, 'How is this improving my relationship?' If the answer is 'never', why do you think you don't?

YOUR ACTION PLAN

Assessing how inert you are. Most people with noble thoughts and good intentions feel stuck and inert in their daily life. Ask yourself: Are you happiest going for passive activities such as watching TV? Do you find you react negatively when your partner suggests something new? Do you avoid dealing with emotional matters? Do you feel cosy and comfortable yet somehow bogged down? Are you frequently tired out? Do you have very little energy? Do you find you'd rather avoid change?

All this needs to change if you're going to improve your relationship.

Challenge yourself by asking this question: 'If I were starting afresh with my partner (like having an affair) what would I change to make myself more attractive, more energized, more contributory, and more stimulating?' In other words, 'What good intention could I actually act on without too much trouble?' Choose just one thing and make changes. Other, more significant changes will follow.

Guilt and Shame

These negative emotions can dog a relationship and even destroy it. Our experiences of guilt and shame probably originate in early babyhood when we first become aware of our own hostile feelings. These feelings, together with parental injunctions, help decide what sorts of things make us feel guilty or ashamed, both at the time and in later life. Guilt and shame are really forms of aggression turned against one's self.

Defined simply, guilt is a feeling that you shouldn't be doing something, or that having done it, you deserve punishment. You are guilty *of* doing something bad. The expectation is that others will find you wrong or bad and, possibly, that society in general (the law) will seek its revenge.

When we feel ashamed we feel bad inside ourselves, whatever outsiders may think. We now expect our 'inner policeman' to punish us. There's usually some element of pleasure or gratification in the action that produced the guilt or shame. Many people say that these emotions are socially protective in that if they didn't experience them after having done wrong they might well just go on doing it. In short, they are socially-induced regulators that help us behave better than we otherwise would.

The problem is that while we are beating up on ourselves internally (on behalf of the original people who taught us to do it!), we can become self-obsessed, remote from our partner sexually and emotionally, and eventually even truly depressed or suicidal. Depending on our childhood conditioning, our inner policeman will be benign and loving, trying to help us behave better – or tyrannical, violent, and even murderous. We now zap into old unconscious models and act out whatever it was we learned in baby- and childhood. Guilt and shame that is deeply felt can become so destructive that an individual can become impossible to love because he or she feels completely 'unlovable'. This was the way they were made to feel whenever they transgressed as a child. Some people now lose their sense of self-worth and their partner can't get to them.

Fear is at the heart of most guilt and shame. Most of us are afraid that we'll be punished as severely as we were in childhood, be it by society or by our own internal policeman. But this fear is usually unfounded, especially when it comes to shame. Our internalized model of our harsh parent, or whomever, is usually a bigger bogeyman in our imagination than he or she is in reality. Talking all this through with our partner can – provided we aren't so ashamed we can't even talk about it! – help us see that someone who loves us in the here and now isn't that shocked or tyrannical towards us as our original 'policeman' was. Their gentle acceptance of what we have done wrong can help us forgive ourselves and can put the whole thing in perspective. Even if we have done something seriously wrong their love and understanding can help us find a way of dealing with it rather than freezing up, as we would do, if left to ourselves.

ASK YOURSELF

▶ How do guilt and shame affect your life on a day-to-day basis?
▶ What were your childhood experiences of guilt and shame?
▶ How does guilt or shame advantage you?
▶ How does your partner's guilt or shame advantage you?
▶ How does your partner's guilt or shame harm you?
▶ What are your main fears in life?
▶ How do these relate to your main feelings of guilt and shame?

YOUR ACTION PLAN

Areas of guilt and shame. Make a privately kept list of the things about which you feel guilty or ashamed. See what trends you can find. Do you tend to have most problems with things to do with sex, for example? Do you feel guilty about almost anything?

Now make a list of your partner's guilt and shame areas, inasmuch as you are aware of them. What can you learn about your relationship by seeing how these overlap?

The next part is very hard indeed. Try to share with your partner something from your list that's fairly 'light'. By definition you're going to be worried about punishment or worse, or you wouldn't be guilty or ashamed. The reality is that a loving partner will often be far more forgiving of us than we are of ourselves. Let's say you shoplifted something a year ago and the store detectives took you in for questioning but decided not to call the police. You've never told your partner because of your shame. This could be a good starting point for discussion.

Be terribly wary if the subject about which you feel ashamed or guilty has to do with your relationship. For example, I'd rather you didn't come clean about having an affair with his best friend, or your addiction to internet porn, in an effort to get guilt and shame off your chest. Perhaps this will be possible one day but in the meantime stay clear of such things unless you are very sure indeed of your partner's response. I have to say I don't know many people who are!

Inability To Accept Your Partner

This is a very difficult area that causes us all problems, if only from time to time. When I tell people they should largely accept their partner and their behaviours, people often attack me for being unrealistic. But I think it makes sense. I'm not suggesting you should accept what, to you, is unacceptable *behaviour* but that you accept your partner for what they are, who they are, where they are coming from, and for their difference from you. All these topics are covered elsewhere in the book.

When we get together, we make a commitment not just to accept what is easily acceptable but to try our very best to accept that which is not. Annoying personal habits come somewhere near the top of the list when I talk with couples about this subject. Someone will say, for example, 'I just cannot accept the fact that he leaves his toenail clippings in the shower for me to tread on.' Of course, it *is* possible to accept this. With half the world starving, and millions of people having a hell of a life, this hardly rates as a cause of World War Three! Of course, we'd *rather* our lover didn't do such annoying things. Of course, we'd *like* them to be more considerate. And so on. But when they are not we need to try to look deeper at what they're really trying to say by their 'unacceptable' behaviour. We can then, hopefully, do something constructive about it.

The woman here felt aggrieved long-term that her guy never washed the bath or shower, peed all around the lavatory, and so on. The toenail complaint was, according to her, just a part of his generally sloppy and discourteous bathroom habits. To *him* her complaint was yet another way she tried to be a 'bossy mother' to him and thwart his efforts to become an autonomous adult. They even talked about divorce over it! But in reality it was just a silly unconscious game that needed sorting out.

When you come to look at the anger, frustration, or resentment that so often underpins such 'unacceptable' behaviours and your partner starts to own these emotions and do something about them, the unacceptable behaviour disappears. Most such behaviours are the acting out (unconsciously most of the time) of much bigger issues within a relationship.

Far more important than all of this, though, is when we feel our partner him or herself has become unacceptable. Not for their behaviour, now, but for their very 'being'. This is sometimes the result of our unconscious projections onto them – they now carry our rubbish and we criticize them for it when we should be dealing with it ourselves – but often it is not.

The difficulty with such 'unacceptable stuff' is that we all have a bottom line on everything. A few nail clippings in the bath every other month doesn't make our partner 'impossible' or 'unacceptable' – even if it really annoys us. In and of themselves, a few thoughtless remarks, forgetting your birthday, being horrid to a neighbour, or ignoring your best friend doesn't and shouldn't make your partner unacceptable. Taken as a whole, though, and repeated in spite of your protestations, it eventually makes you wonder whether he or she cares at all about you. This now *does* appear to be truly 'unacceptable'. We start to count the cost now, keep score, and begin to de-love our partner. This de-loving can take the form of more frequent rows, less gracious and forgiving behaviour, less sex or no sex, or obviously looking for a new partner, if only in protest.

Of course, your so-called 'unacceptable' partner may simply be engrossed in their own personal pain, doing the best they can to cope with their inner demons, and may still care very much about the relationship. They may see your fear that this says something bad about your relationship as preposterous. But you still have a point and their thoughtless, selfish, ungracious behaviour, or bad spirit needs dealing with. Unfortunately, you cannot do this for them ... and this is when we feel so impotent and helpless. At this stage we feel like looking outside for someone who will want to change for us and be their 'better selves' rather than their 'worst selves'. We know our partner can be far better than this, so why on earth don't they get on and be it, we ask ourselves?

The answers are deep and complex, I'm afraid, and may not be able to be sorted out by you as a couple. Reading this book will definitely help but the deep-seated causes of this bad spirit may not be evident, except in therapy.

Eventually, you may have to draw a line in the sand and say, 'I've put up with X for years and now I've had enough. I just cannot/am not prepared to take it any more.' We all have to find a dignified way of stating our bottom line and then sticking to it. I find in practice it's only fair to give your partner notice that this is what you intend to do. After all, many people don't actually believe their lover's protestations that they'll leave, for instance, and need it spelled out. Give fair notice that you're going to leave if whatever it is doesn't change. I also suggest giving a time scale. It's not fair to ask your partner to stop smoking by next week, or you're off! Agree on a timescale for them to make the changes you need and then stick by it. If you keep on bluffing, your request will be ignored because it'll be treated as a threat – which it should *not* be. You aren't *threatening* to leave. You are saying that something is so unacceptable that you will leave unless things change. This is assertiveness, not aggression or a threat. If, on hearing such a heart-felt plea, your partner still won't change, or get help to do so, then perhaps it really is time to take stock of the whole relationship, if only because things should never have had to come to this drastic stage in the first place.

I hear this sort of story all the time from women whose men are alcoholics or compulsive gamblers. But life isn't a rehearsal. We owe it to ourselves to act with dignity on our strongly held beliefs rather than become a bitter victim of our partner's unchanging behaviour.

ASK YOURSELF

▶ What is there about your partner you find hard to accept?
▶ What does this tell you about yourself?
▶ What do you find hard to accept about yourself?
▶ What of this could you be unwittingly projecting onto your partner?
▶ How do you 'de-love' your partner?

YOUR ACTION PLAN

Signs of de-loving your partner. I mention the Rule of Five on page 114. This states that you need to be doing at least five times as many positive things in your daily life with one other as negative ones. When this ratio falls, goodwill goes out of the window and trouble looms. Now those little spontaneous touches, those tiny eye-catching moments, the 'for no reason' phone calls, the hand holds in the shopping mall, and the cuddles at night, all start to slip and you begin to live alongside one another like lodgers rather than in one another's presence like lovers.

Catch all this as early as possible and actively agree to make efforts to stop things drifting. In this remember the principles of 'Fake it till you make it' (see page 93) and 'What can't be cured must be endured' (see page 113).

Ways in which you've changed. Make a list of the main things of importance in your life together This might include: sex; friends; love; children; home; work; hobbies; dinner parties; money; and so on. Now make two columns alongside these items where you can write against each, 'How you've changed' and 'How I've changed'. Remember: this isn't just about changes of behaviour but of attitude and belief. For example, under Home you might say that it used to be a crash pad for both of you when you were working flat out. Now you have children it's a haven for your children and a workplace for you as you have become a stay-at-home mother. Clearly the significance of your home is now very different. But how have both of you changed to take this into account? Indeed, *have* you both changed? It could be that things like this are hard to accept rather than your partner him or herself for who they are. Perhaps it's their inability to change that's hard to accept.

Inability To Forgive

The French have a saying, 'To understand all is to forgive all.' This is helpful to bear in mind when thinking about this difficult subject, but I keep another, even more profound, saying on my desk: 'He who cannot forgive breaks the bridge over which he himself must pass.'

Most books about relationships don't make much of forgiveness yet it is the very bedrock of most people's intimate life together. It is, unfortunately, blighted by the Western notion of 'Forgive and Forget'. This is preposterous. The most difficult thing is to forgive and remember! When we truly forgive, we wipe the slate clean – not in denial as if nothing had ever happened, but acknowledging that our partner has wronged us and that we forgive them in the certainty that one day we too will need forgiveness.

It is an inevitable part of one-to-one relationships that we wrong each other. We all create, or experience, humiliation, indifference, rejection, hurt, discourtesy, unloving behaviour, and so on. Yet somehow we have to continue without bearing grudges. Of course, it's far easier forgiving someone if they feel sorry, act as if they were sorry and show regret, remorse, or signs of guilt or sadness. But we still have to forgive them, even if they *don't*.

To be honest, in a meaningful, intimate relationship we don't have much choice but to show forgiveness. The burden of carrying our anger and frustration is so great that soon we become the losers and find ourselves killing the very love we are trying to create.

Paradoxically, the individual who cannot forgive often ends up feeling worse as a result. If I feel wounded because someone has wronged me, only I can heal myself. In this sense, if I forgive you I heal myself; and if I forgive myself I help us.

This concept of forgiving oneself is a vital one. It can be relatively easy to forgive our partner if we love them and really want the best for our relationship. But truly to forgive ourself can be extremely hard. Depending on how you were brought up, you'll find it difficult or even perhaps impossible to do this. Just as we can get stuck in a rut of anger and even depression if we don't forgive others, an inability to forgive ourself is also destructive. Many such individuals feel unworthy of self-forgiveness. They argue that if their lover forgives them, that's fine because it's someone else's judgement of their worth, but to do so for themselves takes a far greater sense of self-worth. If you have trouble forgiving yourself it could be helpful to get professional help.

It's easy to love the lovable. It's easy to forgive the forgivable. In an intimate relationship what's really hard is loving the unlovable and forgiving the unforgivable. Of course, nothing and no one is completely unlovable or unforgivable, even if we occupy the moral high ground and kid ourselves that they are. I have seen too many people change their minds over such concepts over even a few years to believe that there's any black and white about the concept. When we are in pain, feel wronged or betrayed, or fear our love-bond is under threat, almost anything can appear to be unlovable or unforgivable. But we are wrong.

Being human and being part of any relationship with others means forgiving and being able to forgive ourselves. To do anything less reduces our value to both ourselves and our relationship.

ASK YOURSELF

▶ How do you feel when you can't forgive your partner?

▶ How does your partner behave when you don't forgive him or her?

▶ Think about how you forgive yourself – or don't. What can you learn from this?

▶ What types of things do you find it hardest to forgive in yourself or others?

▶ How do you feel when someone forgives you?

▶ What is it about certain people that makes it hard for you to forgive them?

YOUR ACTION PLAN

Forgiving and being forgiven. Make a list of the things for which you think you need to be forgiven and those things you need to forgive. These should apply to everything in your life, not just your relationship.

Share your list with your partner, starting with subjects that don't affect your relationship directly. As you become adept at listening empathically (see page 167), it'll feel safe to go on to emotionally laden issues between you.

Inability To Listen

One thing that people, mainly women, complain about is that they don't feel their partner understands them. This usually means they don't feel they are being listened to in an empathic way.

But what is empathy? First, it is not sympathy. When I start practising empathic listening with couples, one or other usually says, 'I know exactly how you feel' to their partner and then recounts something from their lives that illustrates how well placed they are to understand what the other is saying or feeling. This *sympathetic* approach, in which the listener mirrors what the speaker is saying or feeling, *can* be useful later, but until you get good at empathic responses, stay well clear of it.

The trouble with being sympathetic is that, however much you think you're helping your partner, the very fact that you are talking about your own experiences takes the spotlight off them and suddenly you find you're doing your 'stuff' and not theirs. Many people hijack all such conversations with their partner in this way and the speaker never gets heard.

Empathy is different from sympathy in that when I am being empathic with you I put my own business to one side and put myself in your shoes. By doing this I can, if only for a few moments, feel with you what you are feeling. I cannot, of course, feel your feelings *for* you – and I don't want to, they are yours, not mine – but I can get into your skin and identify with you very deeply.

This said, there are no prizes for being a clever clogs, simply to be able to say, 'I really know what Jill is feeling.' You have to act on this information so that it helps Jill. The secret of good empathic listening is to respond to our partner in such a way that they feel their emotions have been identified and to some extent understood.

ASK YOURSELF

▶ Looking at the list above, what are your main roadblocks to listening? How do they affect your partner?

▶ How do you confuse empathy and sympathy when relating to your partner?

▶ How many feelings words could you name unaided?

▶ What are the most easily identified feelings you come across when listening to your partner?

▶ What it is about your partner listening to you that really makes you feel understood and 'heard'?

YOUR ACTION PLAN

Empathic listening. There are three main steps to empathic listening.

First, *put your own business to one side*. Don't jump in with your thoughts and feelings about the topic under discussion, listen solely to what your partner is saying. This can be terribly hard to do in our ego-based culture. We tend to put 'I' first. Men especially find this the hardest step. But with love and practice you'll find you can do this with some skill after only a few weeks.

But saying this and doing it are very different things. Most of us have what I call roadblocks to empathic listening. Here's a list of them. See which apply to you and tell yourself honestly whether you use them occasionally, or pretty much all of the time. To be any good at empathic listening you'll have to become aware of what you're doing that gets in the way. It might take the help of your partner to point out what's most unhelpful to them.

▶ I am preoccupied.

▶ I am working out what to say next.

▶ My feelings are too strong (about what I hear, or about something else).

▶ I don't like the content or feelings of what I hear and so am denying/ rejecting/ignoring it.

▶ What I hear triggers words or feelings that make me feel uncomfortable.

- I try to rescue others by reassuring them.
- I show too much concern.
- My arrogance makes others feel that their thoughts or feelings are insignificant/worthless.
- I compete for attention by talking about my own experiences.
- I silently criticize/find fault/evaluate.
- My insecurity makes me defend myself.
- I interrupt.
- I read too deeply into what's being said.
- I advise/control/interpret.
- I don't notice mixed messages (body language doesn't match with what is being said).
- I question or interrogate.
- I think I know what my partner is about to say because I've heard it all before.
- I race ahead of the speaker in my thinking.
- I jump to premature conclusions.
- I stereotype the speaker and what is said.
- I dismiss what I hear because I don't like the speaker or what he or she has done.
- I fill silences because they make me feel awkward.
- I want to punish or put down the speaker by not listening.
- The speaker hits one of my 'no-go' areas (see page 231).

It's plain to see that if we are engaged, however unwittingly, in any of these roadblocks, we cannot hope to hear what our partner is saying.

The second part of listening empathically is to *identify the main emotion of the person you're listening to.*

Sometimes this is really easy, and sometimes it's very, very hard. If your partner is obviously angry, lonely, afraid, or happy, you might be able to put your finger on things right away. However, if their emotions are 'softer', such as doubt, satisfaction, or confusion, things can be much harder.

I find many couples are unable to name feelings and identify emotions accurately. When I ask groups of people learning about empathic listening to list some common feelings, many individuals get stuck at as few as six! Such individuals can't hope to be very able when it comes to identifying their partner's emotions.

Here is a list of emotions your partner could be expressing:

Sadness	Doubt	Friendliness
Misery	Humiliation	Joy
Loneliness	Inadequacy	Love
Rejection	Shyness	Affection
Unlovability	Embarrassment	Caring
Shock	Tenderness	Determination
Disgust	Comfort	Certainty
Arousal	'Madness'	Importance
Apprehension	Pleasure	Thankfulness
Irritability	Warmth	Surprise
Disappointment	Fury	Relaxation
Hopelessness	Boredom	Relief
Interest	Anger	Betrayal

Take time to ask yourself how many of these you would be able to identify – not just in your partner, in anybody. There are literally scores of possible things your partner could be feeling. The secret is to learn what's most likely to be actually happening and for this we have to be aware of their body language and not just what they are saying but what the underlying feelings are. To get good at this, see page 139 for a discussion of 'Feelings'. As you become more and more proficient at listening empathically you'll be able to identify not only a *main* emotion but several *underlying* ones too. This is extremely helpful to your partner, or indeed anyone else you apply your skills to.

The third and final part of listening empathically is to *feed back to your partner the main emotion you have identified.* This sounds really corny and can indeed appear stilted until you get used to it. The way to do this most effectively is to make your observation as an offering. 'It seems to me you're feeling X' is a good start. If you say, 'You're obviously feeling X', you could get it hopelessly wrong and your partner won't feel understood. By making it an offering you give them the chance to say, 'It's not quite X, it's more Y that I feel.' You now have an opportunity to learn how they express themselves when they are feeling Y. Hopefully this will enable you to identify that emotion again more accurately in the future.

The beauty of this 'open-ended' communication is that the other person cannot simply stop there – they feel bound to say something, once you have made your offering. This almost always moves things on very quickly and effectively. This sort of learning is worth its weight in gold to you as the listener because it can be very hard, or even impossible, for your partner to name what they are feeling, especially when they are distressed about something.

When we are upset, we almost never feel one pure emotion. This results in confusion. If our partner can see through all this and name the main emotion it's a real help for us because we can then focus on that and try to do something about it. Even just naming it can be enough. There may be nothing else to be done at that time.

Here's a typical example of what I hear in the consulting room:

Man comes home from work. He's had a hell of a day.

Man: 'That Patrick will have to go. He's nothing but trouble. If he does that again, I'll have to sack him.'

Wife: 'You think you've got problems? The washing machine leaked, the kids have been hell, and my mother needed me to go round to get her shopping.'

Man: Looks disbelievingly at her. He has not been heard. His emotions haven't been acknowledged. He storms off to the study, sleeps in the spare room and she complains to him in the morning that he never shows her any affection.

Had his wife responded something like: 'I can see you're really frustrated about Patrick. He seems to make your life hell at the moment', whether or not this was accompanied by even the slightest sign of physical affection their lives would have come closer as he felt understood. Such a man now quickly starts to ask her about her day, wants to be helpful about the washing machine and is more likely to want to give her a cuddle. Such a couple don't compete with one another on the emotional stage, they work together to listen to one another in turns so both feel advantaged. It is truly a win-win situation.

This sort of empathic listening is just about the most vital communication skill a couple can have. There are almost no problems that cannot be handled in this way. It builds team spirit, contrasts starkly with what each experiences at work, or other situations in their lives, and teaches their on-looking children how to make life better for everyone.

It is, however, an observable fact that the most difficult person to listen to empathically is our partner. Because of this I always get people to practise this life skill outside the home first. The loss of face, or whatever, when we fail to listen empathically at the grocery store is simple to live with. And listening in this way takes a lot of practice. Be sure not to beat up on yourself when you find you're still struggling with your roadblocks at six months!

Once you feel fairly confident you've practised enough at work and in social situations, start to listen empathically to your partner. Here the road-blocks will be higher and more emotionally laden, so beware because you're bound to fall back a rung or two on your ladder. Remember you have married your shadow and that compared with complaining to the man in the store about your faulty goods, talking and listening to your lover is way harder.

Infertility

I worked with infertile couples for nearly twenty years. It was often harrowing – however rewarding – because many of them became obsessed with their quest for a baby. In a world where we largely get what we want, and where a baby has become a sort of 'designer item', couples expect to 'acquire' a baby as they would a washing machine, or other consumer durable. When this doesn't in fact happen, it can be the first time in their adult lives they experience helplessness and hopelessness.

Taking anything for granted in life is usually a mistake but to take fertility for granted can be worse. Children appear to provide many advantages for us, both as individuals and as a couple, so to be thwarted in this basic 'need', or as some couples try to convince me, 'right', can be very painful, frustrating, depressing, and much more. The pain is all the greater when we try and try, and feel increasingly powerless, especially if we are used to feeling in control in our everyday lives.

Many couples spend most of their sexual lives trying *not* to have babies, so it seems a particularly poignant paradox that some of the worst pains they experience arise from reversing this process. But then it's all about control – and we are used to controlling our environment these days. That we cannot direct this innermost part of our personal environment comes as a real blow to many of us.

Most women think they'll have a baby sometime. 'Being a good wife and mother' is, even today, seen as a goal in itself by millions of women. And I am not knocking this. But it does put pressures and expectations on women that are not there for men. It also means that some women genuinely feel incomplete or even invalid if they are *not* a wife and mother.

Women's lives are more shaped by having a family than are their men's. Once you fear you won't be able to have children your whole life script will need re-writing, even if you imagine you've never written one in the first place. A woman also has her biological clock ticking in a way a man does not. This puts more pressure on her to get things sorted out sooner. This very pressure can be a cause of infertility.

Once you get going on the merry-go-round of tests and investigations, it'll be the woman who has most done. This puts her firmly in the hot seat, with more expectations, more pressure, and more opportunities for failure.

Men too, of course, have their problems with infertility. Not having a baby can be a huge loss for some men. In fact, I am finding this to be the case more and more as time goes by. Some women today are, paradoxically, less bothered about the subject than are their men. Many men think of themselves as only being truly male once they have a child to 'prove it'. They confuse virility with fertility. Others see having a family as a central part of their life and personal growth. To lose out on this, or even the threat of doing so, causes real sadness and even true grieving.

Infertility is usually caused by one partner. This can make the other feel upset because they appear to have chosen a 'dud' and the infertile one guilty or ashamed because they're letting their lover down in this important area of life. Either party can feel angry, aggrieved, sad, lonely, wishing they'd chosen someone else, a source of disappointment to their family and their partner, sexless, sexually disruptive (maybe I *could* have a baby with someone else), and much more. It's an emotional and relationship minefield.

But it's vital to keep talking and loving one another. Try to keep the baby thing in perspective in terms of your overall relationship. This need not spell the end for either, or both, of you as you will fear from time to time. Keep your relationship and its value to you both paramount in your hearts and minds. Remember that you are both unique individuals and that your personal journey through all this won't be the same as your partner's. Try to be there for one another in your individual pains, rather than disappearing, self-absorbed, into your own abyss. Try not to assume that what matters most to you will matter most to your partner. And so on. Remember, you didn't get together just to have a family, so bear this is in mind when the going gets tough. Don't lose sight of your uniqueness and value to one another.

Eventually you'll probably come to terms, however reluctantly, with not having children and can look to other ways of improving your life. You'll have more time for friendships, for business, for perhaps contributing to society in ways that having a family would have precluded on the grounds of time, energy, and cost. You can now enjoy your siblings' children or those of friends and relatives. These 'proxy' children can be a great source of joy to you and you could become a really important person in their lives.

ASK YOURSELF

▶ Could you have become over-focused on your infertility?

▶ How has your infertility altered your relationship for the better?

▶ How has it damaged your relationship?

▶ How has the medicalization of your situation damaged your relationship?

▶ How could you use your current situation to grow your relationship?

▶ What is your biggest fear about not being able to have a baby?

▶ How does your partner relate to this fear?

▶ How do you handle the decision-making on your journey through the tests and investigations?

▶ Assume for a moment you'll never be able to get pregnant. How would this affect your life together?

YOUR ACTION PLAN

If we can't have a baby quite quickly. Although many couples imagine they should get pregnant the minute they stop using contraception, this doesn't usually happen. It can take many months and no medical professional will start to get concerned inside two years, unless you are into your forties. But as time goes by without a result, I think it's sensible to start thinking about alternatives to 'spontaneous conception'. Talk about how far you'd go along the assisted conception route. Would you be able to afford IVF? Would you find it acceptable? What do you think about adoption or fostering? What do you know about it? Have you thought of surrogacy or artificial insemination using a donor? Perhaps get a book on these subjects and start to think things through.

Although many people see this sort of approach as premature until they 'get desperate' I have another view. I think it's better to relax and think all this through *before* desperation sets in. Also, my clinical experience is that couples that are more realistic at this stage and where the woman relaxes into other possible alternatives often get pregnant spontaneously!

Without children we could ... In this exercise – probably done after you've embarked on the merry-go-round of tests without much success – you list all the things you could do if you never had a family by any means. In this way you start to build in fantasy a very real plan for your life together without children. Be gentle with one another because whatever each of you says in discussions like this there'll be a lot of grieving and mourning going on underneath, even if there's still a chink of light coming under the infertility treatment door. There's a whole world out there to be lived without having your own children, though when you're feeling sad, aggrieved, or angry it'll be hard to see this.

Jealousy and Envy

Jealousy is, it appears, an inevitable part of love in Western culture. It's a wholly negative emotion in which the sufferer becomes anxious, suspicious, and angry in response to the real or imagined loss of a love-bond. Some sexual jealousy is normal and probably plays a part in keeping couples – and their families – together. At the very least it makes errant partners less likely to indulge their sexual whims more often than they otherwise might.

We probably first experience jealousy very early in life when we realize our parents have a prior, love-bonded relationship that appears to be more important than the one they have with us. This immediately lays us open to fears of abandonment. Babies and young children also quickly learn to be jealous of their siblings, if only because no parent can possibly be all things to all their children at the same moment.

All of this can extend in some people to go beyond sexual jealousy, to situations where a man, for example, may be irrationally jealous of his wife's girlfriends, her relationship with his own children, and so on.

It is often confused with envy, but jealousy is a triangular situation, whereas envy involves only two people. A boy can be envious of his brother's prowess at playing the piano but he isn't jealous of him.

The trouble is that, given it is such a 'primitive' emotion, people can feel so strongly they can become dangerous. Men in particular, because they are so physically strong and somewhat more aggressive than women, can turn very nasty indeed and even commit murder under the influence of jealousy.

It is a strange emotion because although it appears to be about someone else it is in fact a very intra-personal emotion. It is more about self-love than love. Any situation that makes one partner feel more vulnerable or disadvantaged in a relationship can predispose to jealousy. Impotence, for example, in either partner, can make them fear their lover will seek out someone else. Drunkenness makes people jealous, as do cocaine and amphetamines. Some pregnant women feel unusually jealous but this could be because they feel out of the sex market at this time. Those who have poor self-esteem and are permanently under-confident are exceptionally prone to jealousy, and some such individuals see almost every other person of the opposite sex as a threat. Such individuals almost expect their 'better' partner to go off with someone else and kind of will it to be so. Of course, enough of this sort of behaviour can make such fears become fact.

On the other side of this coin are those who say they have never been jealous. Someone whose self-esteem is this high probably lacks modesty and humility and this can be very unattractive.

It is not uncommon for one member of a partnership to get jealous when there's a lot of change in the air. Their normal stability is thrown off balance and they start to see threats everywhere. Some men, for example, get jealous when their partner goes back to work after having a family. Suddenly all men seem a threat, and not just at her work. Other people find they become jealous when they themselves feel unstable for some reason, perhaps after moving home, being made redundant, or whatever. They unconsciously feel more vulnerable to abandonment and extend this to their one-to-one relationship.

Unfortunately, jealousy can create a terrible vicious circle. By behaving in ways that make us unloving and unlovable we almost tempt our partner into the very behaviour we dread. The jealous one starts to call up their partner 'for no reason' but really to check that he is where he should be; they become almost obsessed with their world of imagined activities. Such people can be driven nearly mad by their endless thoughts by day and night of what their partner could be up to.

The trouble is that so long as we focus on our lover's behaviour rather than our own we are doomed. Controlling our partner cannot and will not work. On the contrary, at extremes such an accused and controlled partner often says, 'Things are so hellish, and I'm not doing anything, perhaps I should just have an affair and be done with it!' Indeed, no amount of good behaviour by the supposed errant partner can hope to make up in fact for the fears in fantasy that the jealous partner has.

The only cure for jealousy is to learn, perhaps with professional help, to be more assertive, to get more confident and to be more self-loving. All this can be hard if your partner has, in fact, ever strayed, and many, of course, have.

ASK YOURSELF

▶ How have you confused envy and jealousy in the past and what effect has it had on your relationship?

▶ Are you easily provoked to jealousy? If yes, what insights do you have into why?

▶ Does your partner's behaviour make you jealous? If so, how?

▶ If you have never felt jealous, what do you think this says about your relationship, or your personality?

▶ In what way are love and jealousy linked in your life together?

YOUR ACTION PLAN

What your partner does to make you jealous. Make a list of what your partner does that makes you feel jealous. Ask yourself whether these sorts of things have occurred in your life before. If so, can you draw any conclusions from these links? Think through how you'd like him or her to behave differently. Ask yourself why they act the way they do and why, knowing what you feel, they haven't done anything about it. The next step is to take all this to your partner. He should let you talk uninterrupted for as long as you need to. He can take notes if he likes. Once you have finished, he can have his say. I want you to feel completely listened to without interruption. Before actually getting into the discussion stage, do this exercise.

Hugging exercise. Before doing anything to explore the sensitive subject of jealousy with your partner, I'd like you to do a simple exercise. You can use it before talking about any difficult topic that you know will cause conflict. Sit or stand and hug one another chest-to-chest. Breathe deeply over one another's shoulder and just melt into each other. Completely relax and really feel your lover's body through your hands and chest. Needless to say, nothing about this is sexual or arousing – it's about connecting physically and at a soul level.

Now break apart enough, or sit very close to one another, so you can look deeply into one another's eyes. Hold this gaze for a long time – several minutes. Keep breathing slowly and deeply and keep relaxed. Don't say anything at all.

Discussing subjects that are riddled with conflict. When you are feeling totally relaxed and loving you're ready to start talking about your difficult topic. You now say your piece for a maximum of three minutes – the time to be kept by your partner who will stop you then. He or she does nothing except listen. At the end of your 'speech' they simply say, 'Thank you for sharing that with me. I'm touched that you have done so and I'll really give it some thought.' You now gently kiss and go about your daily life.

Another day, preferably the following day while things are fresh in both of your minds, get back to the tricky subject and repeat the process with the breathing together followed by your lover having his or her say this time. Do exactly the same thing and enter into no discussions whatsoever. You just listen now and make the rather stilted response at the end. Although it sounds rather silly, it is beautifully neutral and says just what it says.

On the third occasion you'll be ready to actually discuss things. You'll have had time to think about what both of you have said and the emotional temperature will be low, however hot the subject under discussion.

Now:

▶ Listen as much as you speak.
▶ Use all your empathic listening skills (see page 167).
▶ Remember your partner is your best friend.
▶ Avoid all generalizations such as, 'All women are the same'; 'You always do X'.

▶ Summarize your points once both of you have had a say. Actually write things down if necessary.

▶ Make a list of what you *can* agree on rather than leaving the session dissatisfied and believing you can't agree on anything. Believe me, there's always *something* you can agree on.

▶ After the session, write a short letter to your partner saying things you might have not dared to say face to face. In this letter make 'I' statements and keep away from accusations and recriminations.

▶ At no stage in any of this write anything off as 'silly'. Work on the principle that if your partner has a problem, you have it too. This doesn't mean it *is* your problem but that it affects your life and you'll need to find a way of dealing with it.

Keeping Score

Given that life isn't fair, and that in any relationship, not just one between a man and a woman, there'll be times when we feel under-benefited, it's easy to see how we can start to keep score. We live in a competitive world where all forms of competition are rewarded. But this is completely out of place in loving relationships. Our partner isn't our enemy or adversary. As a result, any form of score-keeping does nothing but harm.

The trouble with score-keeping is that it is way too much like playing a game. And our loving life isn't a game. In a game there are winners and losers but in our life together we should both be trying to create win-win situations rather than emphasizing, or even encouraging, competition. A way of creating these win-win situations is to accept that, whilst we might disagree, we could both be right! It simply doesn't matter who is right on the vast majority of occasions. Unless, of course, someone is keeping score!

If our partner gets a great new job, car, or whatever, it takes nothing away from *us*. It adds to the sum of our total 'partnership wealth'. If our partner feels great as a result, this will reverberate on the whole relationship and we too will benefit.

Some score-keeping couples do nice things for one another to earn 'bonus points' so they'll be able to draw on the 'bonus bank' when *they* want something. This is silly and produces bad results. If we love someone and have their best interests at heart, we don't just make them a coffee so that one day they'll make *us* one. We do it on the understanding that it's our pleasure and joy to do so, even if they never, ever make us one! To do anything else is to create a harmful power-and-control game that can only end in tears. Similarly, if I always put down your efforts so mine look better, I am keeping score and diminishing your worth not just in your eyes but in mine. This is dangerous because some day I might just believe my own erroneous publicity about you and convince myself you *are* less than you are. Of course, you are not, but if you have a somewhat weak ego, you might just come to believe you *are*. I have now undermined you – not to mention us – in a way that could be terminal.

Many couples run their entire lives playing such games. They stop being spontaneous or generous to one another, be it in bed, around the home, within the family, or in their personal relationship, because, they worry they'll have to 'pay' for it somehow. Some people say they are even wary of receiving gifts or signs of tenderness because they fear what the payback might be. This is a tragedy. Look at 'Being "Right"' on page 70. Couples who keep score can't ever acknowledge they are wrong because to do so puts them in a weak position vis-a-vis future bonus points. It's a sign of weakness rather than the strength it should be. Being able to admit we are wrong takes some courage in the outside world but should be the very breath of any loving relationship. It costs nothing to admit it – except our pride and possibly losing some crazy bonus points we shouldn't even be keeping – and is a real relationship builder.

ASK YOURSELF

▶ In what circumstances and on what issues do you feel under-benefited in your relationship?

▶ How aware are you of how under-benefited your partner feels?

▶ How do you 'keep score' on a daily basis?

▶ What do you think makes you do this?

▶ How do you run your 'bonus bank'?

▶ How would you like to be able to stop playing 'keeping score' games?

▶ What changes would you make in yourself to achieve this?

YOUR ACTION PLAN

Filling your 'well of love'. If you appear to be under-benefited it's probably because you feel you're forever giving while your partner takes. Assuming for a moment that this is true (which it may not be!) what you'll need is to re-fill your well of love. None of us can forever pull love out of our inner well. Eventually the bucket will come back empty.

Try to think of ways of re-filling your well. Enlist the help and love of friends or relatives, take up a hobby that gives you a new interest, refresh yourself with a break or holiday, pray, enrich your spiritual life, read poetry, take up a physical activity, and so on. You might also benefit from my anti-stress regime (see page 276).

As a result of doing this you may find that because you're more bene-fited you'll be more tolerant in your relationship and will keep score less. You'll also have more to give – if you want to.

Lack of Friendship

In any good relationship our partner is probably our best friend. We may be lovers, parents, business partners, and all kinds of other things, but at the heart of it all is a friendship.

Friends: share their souls; are loyal, value our company and make us feel good to be around them; give rather than take; make sacrifices for us; give us the benefit of the doubt; don't have to be right all the time; defer to our opinions without losing anything; feel understood by us, laugh at the same things, and expect great things of the friendship; respect our feelings and interests; don't count the cost or keep score; and so on. You'll have your own definitions to add to this list. Once we start to think of man-woman relationships as a kind of 'super-friendship', everything and anything is possible.

The thing is that most of our friends are held at a sufficient arm's length most of the time for us to be able to act reasonably with them. Also, it is my professional experience that we choose friends who are like us, and partners with whom we can do painful business (and who are, by definition, *not* like us, see page 12). Therefore we don't tend unconsciously to project our stuff onto our friends as we do with our partner. So, however friendly we are with our partner, the friendship can never, I believe, be truly like other friendships we have. Unlike with true 'friends' where our inner pains and demons are kept somewhat in check — even though we may be very open with them — with our 'partner-friend' everything has a deeper meaning because we have so much invested in one another. Our partner chose us too, remember, to be able to do *their* stuff in our presence. It's a two-way street. And it's a busy street.

The challenge, then, is to try to remember all the things that made you friends — and still do — even when the going gets tough as a result of all the other 'emotional business' you're doing. But no healthy relationship can work on the basis that it deals only with problems and 'issues'. This would be a therapy group of two, not a partnership of friends and lovers! The secret is to think back to what it was that made your partner so attractive to you, what their magical little unique touches of humanity were, how they were so special in an ordinary world. I suggest people look back at old love letters, videos, and photograph albums, and talk to people who knew their partner in the past. Doing these apparently simple things can trigger warm thoughts, help you see that your original, magical person is really still there, if only you can scratch beneath the surface of the 21st-century emotional grime.

ASK YOURSELF

▶ How do you define friendship?

▶ Is there any reason why your partner could not/should not be your friend?

▶ How has your friendship changed over the years?

▶ What would you need to change in yourself so your partner could become your *best* friend?

▶ How would you rate your friendship related to other parts of your relationship?

▶ What, in your view, is the relationship between friendship, love, sex, and intimacy?

YOUR ACTION PLAN

What is a friend? Write a list of the characteristics of a friend, as defined by you. This might include: loyalty; someone who likes me just as I am; someone who accepts me even if I'm being a fool; someone who's just like me; someone with whom I've shared significant life experiences; someone who sort of knows what I'm thinking; and so on. Score each one according to how important each is to you.

Now list your main friends and see how they score, and in what different ways. Lastly, look at your partner and see how they score, and in what ways. Tell yourself how your friendship with your partner differs from your other friendships. How does this affect your life with him or her?

Talk to your partner about all this and listen to what he or she has to say about *their* friendships. Most men have a rather different definition of friendship when applied to their lover. Try to get a definition that enables both of you to understand where you're coming from rather than having unrealistic and unmet expectations of how you could/should be friends to one another.

Your early friendship. Think back to what sort of friendship you had when you first started going out or living together. Make a list of the things that made it a valuable friendship. Tick off what has disappeared today and ask yourself why and how this has happened. Make a side list of new ways in which your lives have grown to create a different sort of friendship. Talk all this through with your lover.

Lack of Humour

Look at almost any Lonely Hearts column anywhere and you'll see that men want slim women and women want men with a 'good sense of humour'! It's rare for men to specify a good sense of humour, so what do women mean by it?

They certainly do not mean a man who tells gags like a stand-up comic, plays practical jokes, or indulges in immature, public tomfoolery. Of course the notion of what is 'humorous' to any one individual and in any particular situation is intensely personal and I can't hope to do anything other than superficially scratch the surface here. There's also a fine line between being funny, witty, or humorous, and being an idiot. It takes a brave individual to tread this line, even socially.

Humour performs many functions. It is said that 'many a true word is spoken in jest'. Indeed, some people like their partner to make perceptive observations humorously as they then appear wise and interesting. Few women feel at ease telling jokes. It is said that this is because to do so one has to be prepared for failure in the eyes of others if the joke falls flat. Few women, until very recent years, have been prepared to face this sort of public 'humiliation'. Also, until recently few women were social 'show-offs', holding the centre of the stage in social groups. Perhaps some women actually like their man to be a bit of a scene stealer, to show off how amusing/talented or whatever he is, in front of other women. This could be a show of his superiority, which she enjoys vicariously and is proud of. *Her* man is funny. This, by inference, makes him a high-testosterone, 'big-dicked', 'real' (brave) man. While lesser men skulk in the shadows, her man is socially dominant and other women wish he were theirs. Perhaps she wishes, albeit unwittingly, that she could be centre stage, the life and soul of the party with witticisms and funny interjections. Unable to do this, she projects her need onto her man who then acts it out for her.

Humour can be used to break the ice in socially demanding or intimidating situations. An individual who can lighten a moment for people in this way is highly prized. Some women say they like it when their man does this as a way of 'rescuing' others from their shyness, embarrassment, or whatever. They see this as 'sensitive and caring', just what they want their guy to be – and to be seen to be.

But I think when most women are asking for 'humour' they're looking more for a lightness of spirit, someone who can laugh at himself, a man who can be 'fun', whatever that means to them, or who can lighten the heaviness they perceive emotional relationships involve. It's about play rather than showing off in front of others. I find that many women see the business of relating as a rather serious – even onerous – one. Women buy the vast majority of books such as this. Women see relationships as 'work', something that can be learned. Men largely do not. Perhaps what women are saying they want, then, is a partner who will see the light side of things, and not get too bogged down in the minutiae of emotional strife. If her partner is 'fun' then she must be 'having fun', she argues. And this is important in front of others. Such a man, her friends assume, must also be 'fun' in bed, creative, light-hearted, invigorating, energizing, child-like, and healing. It is said that laughter is the best medicine and perhaps women pick up on this healing potential better than men do. Letting out our inner child to play can make our partner feel free enough to let their own child out too. Females of all ages past puberty claim to be more 'adult' than their men – at least until about the age of thirty! Could it be that women enjoy a man who can feel free with his inner child when they are feeling somewhat cut off from theirs?

The thing is that when we're being funny, humorous, and relaxed, we are being truly ourselves. Some women say men find it hard to be truly themselves unless they are being funny or fun. And they could be right. When we laugh together we touch souls. And this can be hard for some people to do in any other way.

ASK YOURSELF

▶ How important is humour in your life?

▶ In what ways does your partner fulfil these needs?

▶ If he or she does not, how do you get these needs met?

▶ How do you answer your partner's needs for humour?

▶ In what ways do you and your partner differ in your views about humour?

▶ In what ways do you share your different senses of humour?

YOUR ACTION PLAN

Increasing your fun levels. Draw up separate lists of fun things you'd like to do with your partner. They must be one-to-one pastimes that involve only your partner. They can be mental or physical. Examples could include: tickling; drawing cartoons of one another; using body paints; trying a new and ridiculous sex toy; making silly birthday cards for friends or family; fighting or wrestling; making a sexy video of each other; making love in a special way; throwing him into the swimming pool; having a bath together; cycling; playing a sexy board game; watching an adult video; seeing a comedy show or film together; and so on.

The idea here is do silly things that make you laugh, lighten up, and allow your inner child out to play.

See also exercises for relaxing and reducing stress (page 276).

Lack of Intimacy

The word intimacy means many things to different people. Most claim it is about physical or even sexual contact. I disagree. Modern relationships are redefining dependency, personal freedom, and commitment, and all of this is forcing us to think again about what we mean by intimacy.

Intimacy, as I define it (see also 'Being Too Close', page 74), is about being truly ourselves while our partner is being truly himself or herself and we do all this in the same space. Viewed this way, being intimate is not only one of our most valuable human experiences but also one of the most courageous. Opening oneself up in the presence of another takes courage, but to do so in the presence of *oneself* calls for greater heroism than that required in any other sphere of life. Because it seems so hard many of us never even tackle it. Most people claim that the most important sort of intimacy they seek is with another person yet they have never made such contact with themselves.

Though it's very hard to define what intimacy *is*, it's not that difficult to see how intimates *behave*. First, let's look at what intimacy is.

Being special to somebody is at the heart of it. No matter how many people we surround ourselves with at home, work or play, we crave that one-to-one specialness that only another significant human being can bring.

Having someone with whom we can be truly ourselves, as I've already said, is the next vital ingredient. Knowing ourselves to be imperfect – which most of us do – it takes courage to be open and vulnerable with another. This calls for someone to be alongside us and know us warts and all, and still to love us, not in spite of these things but because of them. Deep down most of us fear being so unacceptable that we'll be abandoned by the one we love. Opening ourselves up to being truly us in the light of this is a tough medicine indeed.

Sharing life with someone with whom we can just 'be' is another facet of true intimacy. We all spend much of our lives 'doing' rather than 'being'.

Many intimate couples say it hardly matters what they are doing together, or if indeed they are doing anything. What matters most is that they are 'being' in the same space. This is enough. Perhaps all this means is that many of us need to reassure ourselves that we aren't condemned to a life of existential loneliness.

A haven, a sanctuary in life's troubled waters, is an important part of any intimate relationship.

Most of us unwittingly pair bond with *someone with whom we can do difficult psychological work on our shadow side* (see page 12). It is very hard for most of us to work out our personal salvation on our own. We need someone to battle against so we can learn from this battling. By pairing with our shadow we give ourselves the best opportunity for growth because our partner is both mirror and shadow.

If, as I assert, the best *sex takes place only between intimates*, then one of the most important parts of our intimate life together will be the exclusive expression of our spirituality through sexual connection.

For those who choose to have children, *the intimate life provides the seedbed in which the next generation can learn to be intimate*. They learn from the love their parents show them and each other. The wise individual grows hugely from their parenting experiences. Indeed, many women say having a family was the single greatest source of growth and wisdom in their entire lives. But parenting doesn't just benefit our children or us as individuals – it's also a wonderful opportunity for us as parents to improve our relationship. Indeed, many couples say they learn a lot from their parenting intimacies that they then apply to their one-to-one relationship with great benefit. Most of us don't get all we could out of this potential for learning but, to be fair, we don't gain as much as we should from many of life's lessons.

Having looked briefly at what intimacy is, how do people who are intimate with one another behave?

Talking: Although most people say intimacy involves talking, I believe the listening end of this two-way process is far more important. We look at good listening skills on page 166. We don't have to be forever talking to be intimate. In fact, many couples I've seen unwittingly use talking to kill intimacy. Being quiet and simply existing alongside our partner can be far harder, and more helpful.

Silence: This is a greatly undervalued commodity in the intimate life. Comfortable intimates use it a lot. To new couples starting out on their journey to intimacy it can seem intimidating and many avoid it. Our culture is partly to blame here because it teaches us that we have to talk to communicate. Of course we don't.

Laughing and crying together: These are greatly undervalued sources of intimacy. Many couples I see hardly ever laugh or cry together. Given that both are good ways of dealing with major issues in our hearts and souls, this is a loss. Most men find it hard to cry in the presence of their partner because they see it as a sign of weakness, rather than an opportunity for more intimacy.

Touching and being touched: Physical touch appears to be the ultimate sign of intimacy in our culture. Many couples, though, hardly ever touch one another except when having sex. For them, experiencing touch outside sex can be very powerful and feel highly intimate. It is interesting that of all my books over more than thirty years, my biggest seller has been that on massage. My second biggest seller is one about non-intercourse sex!

Often the touching of bodies leads to the touching of souls and minds. I was tucking a woman into a blanket one day during a bodywork session when she burst into tears. When I asked her why, she replied it was the nicest thing anyone had done to her for years!

Tenderness: I believe we can't claim to be intimate with our partner unless we are tender with them. The graciousness that goes with tenderness somehow ennobles both giver and receiver. Such love is at the heart of courtly behaviour and enriches our life.

Trust: This is one of the emotions most mentioned when couples talk about intimacy. Millions of people find it hard to trust anybody, not just their partner. For more on trust, see page 205.

Honesty and openness: No intimate relationship can go anywhere much without these commodities. People often ask me whether they should 'come clean' about some indiscretion, for instance, from their past on the basis that 'This is the real me and an intimate lover/partner should know everything about me'. I can't go along with this. Most partners don't want a blow-by-blow account of our past that shaped our current life with them. Getting out our dirty emotional laundry may be helpful but it usually isn't. After all, when we take on our partner we don't do so with some sort of money-back guarantee. We buy into their life, including their past, no matter what it contains. After all, it has made them the unique individual we love.

Forgiveness: This is a major building block of intimate behaviour. We look at it more on page 163.

Discipline: This is a rather unfashionable word today with its connotations of 'being told off'. However, we all need to be *self*-disciplined. A lot of bad behaviour between couples stems from poor discipline and many who are trying to be more intimate are unlikely to achieve it because they behave so badly towards one another. They wouldn't act in the same way to anyone else yet they express surprise when their intimate life is falling apart.

Commitment: None of the list above makes much sense in our journey towards intimacy unless we can be sure our partner is committed to us and our unique relationship. Working at being more intimate can be hard and few of us would feel it worthwhile if we weren't sure our partner would stay around to see the results. In reality, any progress we make towards greater intimacy stands us in good stead for all future relationships as the real work we do is on ourselves.

ASK YOURSELF

▶ Having read what I've just said about intimacy, how intimate do you feel your life is with your partner?

▶ How do you think you manage and benefit from silence between you?

▶ Think about when you last laughed or cried together. How did it make you more intimate?

▶ How do you daily show feelings of tenderness to your partner?

▶ What gets in the way of you being totally honest and open with your partner?

YOUR ACTION PLAN

How intimate are you? Make a list down one side of the page of the major characteristics of intimacy I list above. Score yourself on each. Now add a score that you feel reflects your partner's situation. What do these differences tell you? What do the similarities tell you?

I chose you because ... Look at page 178 where I describe a way to discuss difficult topics and take it in turns to speak uninterruptedly on this subject for three minutes. It can be a very moving and powerful thing to hear. It can also be highly disturbing if what we hear makes us realize how far we have fallen from what we originally had. And this is the idea of this exercise. None of this need be 'critical' in the commonly used sense of the word. Your own internal critic will tell you what's important in what you're hearing from your lover. For example: 'I chose you because I loved the way you kissed me' will mean a lot if you have stopped kissing in your relationship. How much better to go this route than to say, 'I hate that we don't kiss any more.'

My dreams for our relationship are ... Repeat the above exercise but now on this topic. You'll learn a lot about love, closeness, and intimacy by doing this. Remember to keep to 'I' statements and not to be in any way critical.

If you were to die, my losses would be ... This is another winner for getting to the very core of what you most value and cherish about your partner. Remember, these 'speeches' are about celebrating your love, closeness, and intimacy; they aren't an audit of what could, or should have been.

Lack of Joy

Joy is different from happiness and it is of far greater value. Most people who say they want to be happy are somewhat passive and wish it would wash over them in some sort of mystical way to make them feel better. But 'being happy' in a relationship isn't about going out and buying it, it's about seizing every present moment and making it work to your joint joy. In short, joy is a process rather than a product.

There are no 'successful' relationships as such. All relationships are in the process of succeeding or failing at any one time. This means that the journey from one end of the scale to the other can be modified *at any moment* depending on how we behave *now*. Being truly joyful is an effective way of tipping the balance towards success.

Joy is a more active matter than mere pleasure or happiness and reflects a more holistic sense of being. Joy finds delight in the small, everyday details of life. It is non-judgemental, provides its own rewards, asks no questions, and delivers unexpected outcomes. Couples who are able to be truly intimate (see page 190) are in the best place to experience real joy. This is because they feel safe with one another. This safety comes from the implicit or explicit knowledge that their relationship has permanence, so that whatever happens in the short term, they can allow themselves to relax into joyful experiences regardless of the outcome. In other words, couples like this take a long view and build their relationship minute-by-minute in this context.

People who have great relationships 'en-joy' one another's company more than other couples do. But this apparently 'magic fit' is an illusion. Most such couples have made it their business to find out what most pleases their partner and then build competencies and skills in these areas because to do such 'love-work' is a delight and honour rather than the hardship lesser couples see it to be. Linked to this is the observable fact that successful couples take joy in the little things of life that others ignore or treat cynically. Enjoying a view together, sharing a glass of favourite wine, making a positive comment about something the other has done, are just a few examples of what I mean. The trouble is that when I discuss such matters with couples it often sounds corny or trite and some roll their eyes to heaven or pull my leg about it. But it is nevertheless true. We have become blasé and disparaging about these little joyful moments, imagining that successful relationships are based on set-piece activities such as holidays, theatre visits, a new baby, entertaining our friends, or whatever. But, like sex, we can only be doing such things for a small proportion of our time together. The rest is made up of the trivia of life. These trivia – which are in fact what life is really about – are managed in many different ways by different couples. Some treat them as nuisances that have to be got out of the way to make room for the 'real business' of life (events, 'relating', sex, and so on) but successful couples see them as a series of opportunities to celebrate life together and to grow together.

Closely linked to joy is humour. I look at this more on page 187. Suffice it to say here that the best type of humour is whatever supports and nurtures your relationship.

ASK YOURSELF

▶ What would you say gives you real joy in your life today?

▶ How do you think your partner contributes to this?

▶ What personal responsibility are you taking for creating more joy in your life?

▶ Whose responsibility do you think it is that you are not more joyful than you are?

▶ How do you think your lack of intimacy gets in the way of your ability to experience joy?

▶ What do you understand about your past that helps you understand why you are not more joyful?

YOUR ACTION PLAN

Think about the ways you play and express your joy together. Make a list of what these are. Don't just go for big things – take a joy in even quite small ones. Go through the list and see how you and your partner differ on these items. Look back over the last week and see how many of these you have done. What stopped you doing them? What would it take to do them more often?

Make a list of things you know upset your partner if you tease them. Okay, we all like to have fun and be silly together, but there are limits to what our partner can stand. Think about how your teasing goes too far and spoils your, or your partner's, joy.

Sharing your joy. One day when you are both relaxed, sit opposite one another and hold hands, or gently hold one another chest to chest and gaze into each other's eyes. Breathe quietly and slowly for a minute or two. When you are fully relaxed one of you should tell the other what it is about them that gives you joy. Don't take your eyes off your partner the whole time. Start off by saying something like: 'I'd rather be doing X [something you don't like doing] with you than Y [something you do like doing] with anyone else.' Now, while still in this loving position, the other has their chance to tell.

Lack of Respect

Respect is a somewhat difficult concept to define in our lives together, encompassing, as it does, respect for our partner's achievements, abilities, and skills, and for their whole 'self' at a deeper, perhaps spiritual, level.

If we have a loving and intimate relationship, we touch souls in some inexplicable way. We respect our partner's self, their 'otherness', their rights to their own life, and don't define them in the context of us, or indeed our relationship. I personally hate the term 'my other half' for a partner, as if the beloved were half of something rather than whole in themselves. This limits him or her to being thought of only in the context of the relationship. It seems to me to be disrespectful of their humanity and uniqueness.

Many people claim we 'owe' certain others automatic respect. The elderly, our boss, church pastors, doctors, and even the police fall into this category. I personally, and many I deal with, find this a hard concept. I can't see why anyone should respect another just because of their job title, unless, of course, we first and foremost respect them as human beings. None of these groups deserve unquestioning respect, in my view. Such deference and automatic respect is much less common than it was only a generation ago.

In truly intimate partnerships there is no 'job description' like this. We respect our lover in a unique way because they are themselves. This said, we can and should behave in ways that build our partner's respect for us over the years together. To expect that our partner will, or even worse, should, respect us just because we are married to them, for example, seems to me to pave the way for disaster. No one owes us this unquestioning respect. In other words, my experience shows that those who take one another for granted and become lazy over the years fail not only to show their partner the respect they deserve but also don't get any respect for themselves. I think we need to try continuously to gain and retain our partner's respect. By doing this we find ourselves being graceful, gracious, and sensitive to their needs. Anything else is, in a way, positively disrespectful.

Some people tell me that once they've lost respect for their partner it's like a glass that has been shattered – it can't be put back together. I understand how hurt and angry such people feel but, as with forgiveness (see page 163), the one who feels this way is probably the main loser. There are, of course, limits to this. We all have our breaking point.

At some stage in a failing relationship, where one individual loses all respect for their partner either as a human being or as a partner, things can indeed be terminal. The 'failing' partner now becomes so alien to us in their very spirit within the relationship that the only thing we can do is leave. This can occur with alcoholism, drug abuse, domestic violence, incest, persistent work failures, the partner who lets themselves go to seed, one who fails to show moral courage when called for, persistent gambling, repeated affairs, and sexual perversions. Of course, this list is far from complete. Some people are more sensitive to certain such human failings than they are to others. Some women, for example, tolerate years of violence I wouldn't go along with for a week, but stop respecting their man when he loses his job. Clearly our ability to respect others says more about ourselves than the 'disrespectful' behaviour in itself.

To be told that our partner has lost respect for us can be a terrible blow. And understandably, given that a basic respect is seen as central to most people's intimate relationships. You wouldn't want to work for a boss you didn't respect, let alone to be married to someone about whom you felt the same way.

ASK YOURSELF

▶ Who in life generally do you think 'deserves' your respect?

▶ What do you respect about your partner?

▶ Tell yourself how you'd know if your partner disrespected you.

▶ How would you know if your partner respected you?

▶ Think of ways you have lost the respect of your partner and what you are doing about it.

YOUR ACTION PLAN

Rebuilding respect. Think of ways your partner lost your respect in the past and how you mended things. I 'm not aware of any magic formula here. Time is the best healer but works only if there's plenty of goodwill in the system. Forgiveness (see page 163) is also vital. If, on doing a 'respect audit', you find that your partner does lots of things that make you lose respect for him or her, either seek professional help as a couple or think about getting out.

If you don't respect your partner. You may find this is because they don't respect themselves. It can help them if you boost their 'good' behaviours by encouraging them in any way that seems right for you. At the same time spell out the behaviours you don't like. Keep the balance of five (positive inputs) to one (negative) I mention on page 114. Remember to point out that whilst you 'hate the sin', you still 'love the sinner'!

Lack of Romance

The vast majority of books aimed at helping couples say little or nothing about romance. Yet it is a vital part of any lasting relationship. Experience shows that romantic love is seen as a valuable part of most couples' lives.

Although many modern couples see displays of romantic love as rather 'un-cool' they are missing out on a lot. Romantic, loving behaviour has a strong sexual arousal effect on both sexes. It's fascinating to me that getting people to talk about their romantic lives is vastly more difficult than getting them to be open about their sexual ones.

Early on in our loving life with our partner our feelings can be very self-centred. We feel the 'pain' of being so in love and women especially talk of 'suffering' for their love. But as we mature in our love for someone special this self-centredness is replaced by a love that is invested in our beloved for their sake rather than our own.

Learning to love romantically is a skill which, like many others, needs an act of will to achieve. Unless we have learned such love we can't hope to build a future, romantically-based relationship that has substance to it. Those who remain 'in love with love' never get this far and are a nuisance to live with!

Most people in long-term relationships claim that the romantic side of their love life declines as the years go by. For some this leads to affairs, or even possibly divorce. Many men make up for this loss by immersing themselves in work or hobbies and many women turn their attentions to their work or children.

This is such a shame because most couples realize that their love life, their loving life, and their whole enjoyment of one another are linked to their romantic feelings for each other. Even today, when so many women are more up-front about their sexual needs than ever before, most say that they feel sexier and more receptive to sex if their man behaves romantically towards them.

When we make love we re-enact the late-adolescent romantic phase of our learning how to love. Indeed, every time we make love we should try to re-create those courtship magic moments that made our partner so special to us. Many women complain that their relationship lacks 'warmth' and many men ask where the girl who loved them so intensely has gone. But when listening to the sexes discussing the subject, differences become apparent. To men the word 'romance' seems to imply a faithful, dedicated, trouble-free, sexually fulfilling, continuing, exclusive relationship. To women the connotation seems to be based more on occasion, on a particular set of events. Deep romantic feelings and needs seem to cause embarrassment after late adolescence. What a pity!

So how can we get back to where we were all those years ago?

I find the concept of 'making love all day' (see below) is a great start back to the romantic trail that has gone cold. Of course, by this I don't mean 'having sex all day'. Love, like much else in our relationships, has to be 'made'. And the 'making of love' on a daily basis is something many lose sight of.

Intercourse, or indeed any form of 'sex', can be had with just anyone who is willing. But even if we were to have sex every other day for an hour (dream on!) only 2 per cent of our life together would be spent doing it! Of course for most couples it's way below this.

ASK YOURSELF

▶ How would you define romance?
▶ How do you think your notions of romantic love have benefited your relationship?
▶ How do you think they have damaged your relationship?
▶ How do you think you (mis)learned about romantic love?
▶ How do romantic love and true love interrelate, in your view?
▶ What are your partner's views of romantic love?
▶ In what ways could you make your loving life together more romantic?

YOUR ACTION PLAN

Making love all day. We can learn, and keep re-learning, to 'make' love happen whenever we possibly can. Here are some ideas:

▶ Lose no opportunity to touch and kiss one another, 'for no reason'. Many women say that doing this in front of others embarrasses them, whereas some men say it demonstrates to others just how much they love their partner. Find out what you both think and strike a balance that pleases.

▶ Phone or text one another 'for no reason' just to say something loving.

▶ Give one another little presents you know will mean something. They can be really silly yet significant. They certainly don't involve spending much money.

▶ Hide little 'love-you' notes in your partner's briefcase, handbag, or wherever you'll know they'll find them.

▶ Leave a note on their pillow if you're going to be away for the night.

▶ Encourage one another whenever possible.

▶ Find reasons to agree rather than disagree.

▶ Keep quiet about small disagreements and vexations.

▶ Think twice before criticizing.

▶ Never attack one another's personality.

▶ If one of you wants sex and the other doesn't, relieve the needy one.

▶ If things aren't going well for some reason, pretend that they are and change your behaviour. You'll be astonished how quickly good feelings follow improved behaviour.

▶ Listen to what your partner wants you to change about your behaviour and go along with it, even if you don't at first agree.

▶ Keep open conflict to an absolute minimum.

▶ Remember that your partner is your best friend and probably your best chance of having a good life. Don't waste the opportunity.

Lack of Trust

Trust is a commodity that's in short supply today. In society in general, and at a personal level, we tend to trust one another less and less. The pre-nuptial agreement is just one symptom of this 'dis-ease'.

Trust can be hard to define. Perhaps we can learn more about it by looking at its bedfellows: loyalty, fidelity, integrity, and reliability. The problem is that many adults don't much trust themselves and have rather poor role models from their childhood. As a result they are somewhat distrustful of almost everyone they meet. The harsh realities of life in many big cities further reinforce this belief.

When trying to create an intimate life together trust comes high on the agenda. We have to believe that our partner can be trusted to be good to us and to put our needs first. To some extent this calls for a degree of *predictability*, or we'd be constantly wondering what was going to happen next; *dependability*, so we can count on our partner without having to redefine things all the time; and *faith*, that he or she will always be there for us. Human nature being what it is, though, none of these commodities can be totally relied upon. Some people say that until they can be absolutely sure their partner is trustworthy they won't make a commitment, get married, start a family, or whatever. This is probably foolish because none of us can promise *never* to let our partner down.

There are large numbers of everyday situations where we need to be able to trust our partner, from money, children, and emotional support to sex. Early on we have to negotiate each of these in turn as we learn to trust. But as time goes by we gain a sort of 'blanket trust' that covers almost everything without having to be specific. This said, many individuals are highly trustworthy in most areas yet have a personal blind spot. Such a man might, for example, lapse into occasional gambling.

But the area that most of us seem to need reassuring about in this context is sex. In fact, many people think 'trust' within a relationship *means* sexual fidelity. Being committed sexually to someone means not devoting our time, energy, love, and spiritual connections to the search for and dealings with others. Everyone knows that attractive members of the opposite sex don't disappear just because they're in a relationship (see also 'Affairs', page 44) but how this is dealt with is up to each couple to negotiate. All couples have some sort of agreement, even it's unspoken, as to how they'll manage this. Some, at one end of the scale, say that it's okay for their partner to have sex with someone else, provided they aren't told about it and it doesn't threaten their relationship; whilst at the other end of the scale are those individuals who feel terribly threatened even by their lover's fantasies about someone of the opposite sex. To this latter group, even such *thoughts* are 'adulterous' and 'betray' their sexual relationship.

Some people claim that even one, however small, transgression spells the end of a relationship – on the basis that trust is an 'all-or-nothing' phenomenon – while most people say that what they have between them is far greater and cannot, and should not, be jeopardized by a one-night stand, or similar event. Repeated unfaithfulness is obviously a fundamental breach of intimacy and trust and usually spells the end of most relationships. Where any one individual finds their 'point of peace' with this will be unique to them and will certainly alter as time goes by. For example, some women have told me that they were extremely intolerant of their man's dalliances when their children were young but now they are both in middle age and the kids gone, they take a different view.

Even when the rules of engagement are very clear and fully agreed on, once our trust has been betrayed it can take months or even years to get over it. And some people say they never do. I look at this more in 'Inability To Forgive', page 163.

When we do something that brings about a loss of trust we have to take responsibility for it, just as in any other area of our lives. At some level, however unconscious, we decided to violate the trust in our partnership. What made this happen? Why at that particular time? What does it all really mean? All this has to be explored, either alone, with our partner, or perhaps even with a professional. We never do such things 'for no reason'.

There's always a reason, and it makes sense to discover what it is, if we want to stay in the relationship. Of course many people who betray their partner's trust *want* (consciously or unconsciously) to get out and use the issue of trust and betrayal as a way of making it happen. Some emotionally timid individuals do something like this to provoke their partner to call it a day, rather than taking the responsibility for ending things.

ASK YOURSELF

▶ Do you find it hard to trust almost everybody?

▶ In what ways and situations do you not trust your partner?

▶ In what ways and situations do you not trust yourself?

▶ Do you think you deserve to be trusted?

▶ How do you handle loss of trust?

▶ How would you like to be able to handle things better?

YOUR ACTION PLAN

Changing your behaviour. Just because you've always behaved in a certain way when people let you down doesn't mean you can't change. Try to look at your past and see where you learned to behave and feel the way you do. Are you exceptionally sensitive to being let down? Do you easily feel sorry for yourself at the slightest let-down?

The only way I know out of this is to build your own self-esteem. I know this can be hard if you've been betrayed because you'll imagine your partner did what they did because you were useless, or not what they wanted. But this isn't necessarily true. They might well have done what they did even if you had been a saint!

Try to separate yourself from your partner by living life more for yourself. Perhaps you've become too close (see page 74) and have lost your own boundaries. Take up new hobbies or interests; change your job; do some charity work; or do something you've always wanted to do but were inhibited by your partner or relationship. In other words, make your own life and relish it. As you build yourself you'll find that you'll have more inner strength with which to trust others – and more resilience for when they inevitably let you down.

Try to 're-frame' any old tablets of stone, such as 'All men are bastards', that you've been carrying around for a lifetime. Remember that these old 'programmes' can alter your thinking and behaviour in a way that makes people around you act them out! Dump them. They're no good to you.

Letting Your Past Rule You

We are all the product of our yesterdays and our genetic blueprint. There's nothing we can do about this. What's past is apparently gone yet we find ourselves living with its repercussions in the here and now. Many people try to convince me that because of their abused childhood, because they were so poor, because their parents divorced, and so on, they have a hell of a life today and this is why they're so hard to live with, can't sustain relationships, have affairs, gamble, or drink, for example.

Of course, it's a fact that many people have had a terrible past that plagues them all the time. But it's also true that millions of others with pretty much the same sets of experiences didn't end up as criminals, wife-beaters, adulterers, or gamblers. It does, however, take a lot of insight to stop the cycle. In other words, we aren't necessarily and wholly ruled by our pasts. We have a lot of free choice in our current world and don't have to be driven by our old programming.

This said, I'm only too aware that our past scripts do in fact create a mindset, however unconscious, in which we tend to repeat our past behaviours — or even sometimes the behaviour of others in our past. After all, we spend many years in our parental home and it would be naive to believe that we didn't pick up some bad behaviour along with the good. Thankfully, if we choose a suitable partner who will help us confront our inner demons while we are being intimate with them (see page 190), we can re-write many of these old 'programmes' and turn things around dramatically. For example, just because your father used to beat you and lock you in your bedroom doesn't mean you'll end up doing the same to your kids. In fact, quite the contrary will probably be the case. You may fall over backwards to be lenient with your children, never punish them, and so on. This could, paradoxically, produce other problems for them and you.

When we get together with someone to make a new, intimate relationship we bring our sexual and relationship scripts with us. With these histories come a whole load of assumptions and experiences, some of which will serve us well and others that will certainly not. The trouble is that until we get stuck into the real business of relating to that unique individual, we can't know which is going to be which. Expecting things to go as well, or indeed badly, as a previous relationship is natural but probably unwise. After all, although we are still somewhat ourselves (I say 'somewhat' because we all change and in our teens and twenties we're changing month by month) our new partner is definitely not our old one, however similar they may appear to us. They are also not our mother, father, or indeed anyone else with whom we have had a close relationship in the past.

This can be difficult because it's easy to find ourselves using 'transference' – a psychological situation in which we unwittingly relate to someone as if they were someone else. So it can be that our girlfriend does something and we zap into it as our computer tells us this is what our mother used to do/say/think. Within milliseconds we start behaving towards our girlfriend in the here and now as if she really were our mother (in the past) and things start to go wrong. She is so baffled by this response she now might relate to us (in a way known as counter-transference) as if we were someone significant in *her* life – whom we've possibly never even heard of, let alone met – and suddenly we're not really communicating as the both of us at all. It's all pure illusion.

This process goes on all the time throughout our lives but it behoves us to try to understand ourselves so we can learn to distinguish between what's really another person and what is really us. As I mentioned in 'Feelings' (page 139), the mind can take an unattractive feature of our personality and project it, like a movie projector, onto our lover as if they were a screen. The stuff we now see 'on them' isn't really them at all. Again, more illusions. But terribly convincing.

Getting to be aware of how and when we do this sort of thing is a lifetime's work ... but it's worth doing because until we understand how we relate to others we'll always get ourselves into trouble and find intimate relationships difficult or impossible.

ASK YOURSELF

▶ Do you believe you are mainly the product of your past?

▶ If you do, in what way do you think this determines your present and future?

▶ How does your partner's past rule you?

▶ What could you do to make this less likely?

▶ How could you stop yourself running your life on assumptions?

▶ How would you like to be able to take control of your life?

YOUR ACTION PLAN

Talking about your past. Contact a member of your family of origin whom you trust and ask them about various things from your past. This can be illuminating because we all tend to create our own 'fictions', which we then use to run our lives and relationships. Plan and list a series of questions beforehand that could help you understand why it is you let your past rule you in the way you do. Take a tape recorder with you, as there'll be too much material for you to remember easily. Look out old photo albums or family films. You could get some amazing revelations by doing this exercise.

The history of your relationship. Repeat the above exercise but now with your partner. On another occasion switch around and you listen to them. Obviously this 'relationship past' will be a lot shorter than that discussed with your family member but it can still be very useful indeed. Most loving partners can relate to the way we have let our past rule us. This need not necessarily be restricted to your relationship or emotional issues between you. Great lessons can be learned by looking at work, family, hobby, and other issues. Try to learn from your habitual patterns.

Letting Yourself Go

Now we all expect to look good and to stay 'sexy' for the whole of our increasingly long lives – well past the time most of our grandparents would have thought 'proper' – the way we look after ourselves has become an important issue in relationships.

Of course, looks aren't everything, and many individuals don't even see what others do, so delighted are they with their lover's familiar appearance. This familiarity brings a gentle acceptance but it can also allow our partner to become lazy and lose contact with the reality that we don't have to put up with their sloppy dressing or unkempt appearance just because we love them and have agreed to stay with them.

A good relationship can withstand many 'appearance' knocks. When I work with couples where the woman has, for example, lost a breast to cancer, the guy often says he honestly doesn't notice it's gone! And he's not lying. He sees the whole person and loves her for that. Other people claim that their partner's ageing face is more delightful, characterful, lovable, or whatever, than when he or she was young.

But this isn't what I'm talking about here. I'm thinking about the way many people, of either sex, let themselves go and become slob-like, or simply uncaring about their appearance, even if it's only in the eyes of their partner.

Men let their bellies get bigger as they become couch potatoes, their fingers stained with nicotine; and some women take less and less trouble with their hair and make-up, or wear terrible clothes around the home on the basis that 'No one sees them, so why bother?' But our *beloved* sees all this and may dislike it a lot. In such situations people complain that they feel taken for granted.

Some individuals I see about an affair say how lovely it is to deal with a member of the opposite sex who takes the trouble to look nice and to present themselves well. In other words, someone who goes out of their way to make them feel good by their association with them. But few of us go to seed overnight. It usually takes years to let things slip little by little. At the stage the much-fancied partner becomes un-sexy, a notional threshold is crossed. They now seem deeply unappealing, no matter how they themselves feel. Indeed, such individuals often look on open-mouthed when their partner says something like this in the consulting room. They can't see why or how things have suddenly changed. Of course, many other factors can come into play too, a potent one being an involvement, however fleeting, even in fantasy, with someone else. The contrast points up our partner's failings all too plainly and we pass a point of no return.

Problems arise when the aggrieved partner feels taken for granted and ignored, as if they should accept everything their partner does 'in the name of love'. The old line, 'You should love me for how I *am* not how I *look*', is easy to refute by replying, 'I do love you for who you are but I am turned off/upset/disappointed by the way you *look*.' When discussing all this with couples I usually ask the 'errant' one whether they would behave like this if they were embarking on an affair. Of course they say they would not. And this is where the trouble lies. For whatever reason, be it unexpressed anger, frustration, depression, falling out of love, or whatever, the sloppy one is saying something to their partner, and he or she knows it. Getting to the heart of what is actually being said can be hard and may call for professional help.

Of course, we can also let ourselves go in ways other than looks. I tackle these issues in various parts of the book.

ASK YOURSELF

▶ How have you let yourself go?

▶ How do you feel about letting yourself go?

▶ What would you like to be able to change about yourself to remedy things?

▶ What will you actually do to make this happen?

▶ How has your partner let him or herself go?

▶ How do you feel about your lover letting him or herself go?

▶ How could you change your behaviour to help him or her to remedy matters?

YOUR ACTION PLAN

Do an audit. This can be very difficult indeed to do because it can often be hard to see for ourselves how we have let things drift. Still, it's a good start and will teach you a lot for when you get going on your discussions with your partner.

Make a list of the areas where you think you've let yourself go. Remember, we're not just talking about looks here. It may be that your appearance is still great but you've let yourself fall below your usually high standards in your lovemaking; the way you deal with your children; your attitude to work; in sustaining your friendships; and so on. Rate how you think you score out of five on each of the areas that you highlight.

Now, gently ask yourself what you'd like to do to remedy these things and write a short comment alongside each of your listed items.

Next, get your partner involved by asking him or her to make such a list for you (about you). Listen quietly and attentively as they say how they think you've let your high standards fall and see how this matches up with your own list. You could find that you've been too tough on yourself in certain areas and that your loving partner will help you feel better rather than beat up on yourself. However, you may also find that he or she agrees with you and is actually angry about what has happened. Try to discuss things in a mature way, always seeking the insightful route rather than blaming or accepting blame. Look for real answers. Also, be sure to look at how your partner, or the relationship itself, could have contributed to this fall in standards. Your partner may have to bear some of the responsibility in this.

End the session by agreeing how your partner could help you in your quest for the 'better you'. This is a really good example of how a couple can work together. If there are serious underlying problems (such as clinical depression) at the heart of the fall in standards, then it's time for professional help. If it's laziness, taking your partner for granted, arrogance, or a falling out of love, then these can be dealt with between you if you take the time and trouble.

Living Apart or 'Apart'

We have seen elsewhere that intimate relationships thrive best when the partners aren't living in one another's pockets. Some distance and apartness is valuable if we are to have our own lives and then bring seed corn back to share with our partner. It was Kahlil Gibran who wrote in *The Prophet*, 'Let there be spaces in your togetherness ... even as the strings of a lute are alone though they quiver with the same music.' Of course, there's a balance to be struck between togetherness and apartness, but it's also true that many a good relationship can cope with a surprisingly large amount of separation.

Indeed, as all therapists know, Christmas and public and family holidays are times of great relationship strife for some. Many couples today don't actually do all that well when exposed to one another for extended periods of time. And even those that do still enjoy times apart.

When we first start out, every moment seems precious and any time spent apart a loss. As trust grows and we realize that our partner can't be the whole world for us, we start to venture out, believing, in faith, that our partner will be there when we return and will have done something interesting that they can feed back to us.

But some couples, from choice or necessity, opt for a lifestyle in which they are rarely together. Perhaps they fear intimacy. Others really love their partner but find them annoying to live with on a day-to-day basis. Others say they enjoy the times apart because the 'coming together' at the weekend, or whenever, is such fun. Many such people tell me of 'weekly honeymoons', having way more sex than they used to have when they were together every night of the week. The downside to this can be that it can take a day or so to get used to one another again, especially if the woman is angry or tired left alone to cope with the family single-handed, or the guy is exhausted. Some such couples say it can be Sunday afternoon before they feel 'at one' with each other again, and then he or she's off again.

Some people, of course, wish they hadn't got married, either to that particular partner, or indeed to anyone. Perfectly consciously, or perhaps unconsciously, they then seek ways of putting distance between themselves and their spouse. Some men tell me they got on very well and liked being with their partner until children came along. They then realized that marriage had been what they wanted but not parenting. (See also 'Children', page 96.) Such men then take employment far from home so they can avoid this 'chore' of their relationship and yet still feel good about themselves. I think quite a lot of business-driven, 'apart' relationships fall into this category. In other words, it can suit a lot of men, and even couples.

But being apart even for extended periods of time doesn't mean sex has to stop. E-mails, mobile phones, and text messaging have changed everything though, of course, previous generations found their own ways of achieving exactly the same ends. It's now possible to send our lover a sexy picture plus an erotic story, which is fun to create and fun for our at-a-distance lover to receive. Wherever we are geographically today, there's no excuse for being out of touch. Sexy calls, sharing fantasies, cheeky text messages, and so on are all a daily part of the remote lovers' routine. In many ways this can be sexier than actually being there with them because we can masturbate while fantasizing about our lover and make everything perfect. In reality the kids might wake up or the mother-in-law call. In more general terms, too, being apart from our partner can have beneficial effects. The somewhat idealized memory we carry with us can be preferable to the actual realities of daily life with them. Some remote partners find this a real plus to such a lifestyle.

Of course, lots of couples hate being apart like this and find it hard to feel 'connected' and intimate. They miss the cuddling at night, those intimate little moments together, the opportunity to control, bitch, whine, or otherwise abuse their partner, and so on. After all, it isn't just positive or noble things we miss when we're apart. Many women say they feel cheated at becoming effectively single parents when this hadn't been the deal they'd entered into. House-husbands, whilst putting a brave face on it while their higher-earning wife is out in the world, often tell me they would rather be there too, however much they love their kids and feel they're doing a good job. And many a wife of such a man says that he really doesn't do the million jobs around the place that she would have done had she been there full-time.

Living 'apart' is a different sort of thing. In this a couple lives together under the same roof, and may even share a bed, but they share very little else except, perhaps, childcare, and the mortgage!

This sort of 'secret divorce', as I call it, is very common indeed. It's hard to know how common but probably only about three or four in ten couples are really happy together at any one time. Another half will get divorced in some Western countries and a fair number are 'rehearsing for divorce' at any one time. This set-up can, paradoxically, suit many people. They have their partner's social company and continue rearing their children. They can live in a better home than either would be able to afford alone; they can share family events and holidays; and can give the impression to their friends and neighbours that they are a 'happy family'. Some such couples part once the kids leave home but others stay like this for many years after. Although people like me go on a lot about intimacy and sharing a life together, this isn't for everyone. Yet such a couple still wants the social approval and some of the very real practical advantages of neither being single nor divorced. Secret divorce suits them well. Perhaps as single households come to form an even larger proportion of all homes, this balance will change and some who currently opt for a secret divorce will simply live alone and be done with it.

ASK YOURSELF

▶ What was your family model of your parents being apart?

▶ How do you feel when you are apart from your partner?

▶ How does your partner behave when you are apart from him or her?

▶ Would you secretly like to spend more time apart from your lover? If so, what does this say to you?

YOUR ACTION PLAN

Make times apart work for your relationship. Make a list of the good things about being apart a lot. Now make another list of things you could do with this 'freed-up' time that could help you, and your relationship, grow.

Communicating appropriately. Given that you're apart so much, be sure you are communicating in the very best ways. (See page 296). Love letters will work for one type of individual, and tapes or phone calls for others. Those who need lots of touch will be most badly affected by being apart from their lover. Use this section to talk things through between you and to decide who needs what to feel loved and in touch while you're apart.

Do an intimacy inventory. Look at page 191 where I list the characteristics of intimate couples. List these for yourself and see how you'd score your relationship. Now ask yourself how being apart or 'apart' is a result of, or produced by, your findings. Talk about this with your partner.

Losing Touch
With Yourself

If you're in a less than good relationship you'll probably have lost the inner 'knowledge', the sense and essence of who you really are. Not who people – even your partner – think you are, or wish you could be, but who you know yourself to be in the very core of your being. You'll have become disconnected from this inner self to some extent and been sidetracked into ways of being and behaving that don't do you justice, that are neither ennobling nor generous, neither inspiring nor inspirational. In short, the essence – the very 'truth' – of you has temporarily gone astray or been obscured by the trashy clutter of life and an unsatisfactory relationship. The trouble is you may well be blaming all this on your relationship – or even your partner. In reality, whoever, or whatever, is to 'blame', any progress back to emotional prosperity will have to begin with you.

If your relationship is to be mended, you will have to do it. This will mean making friends with your inner self, perhaps for the first time ever, and dignifying yourself as you do so. Most people I see expect to be able to have a great relationship with their partner when they don't have an even halfway good one with themselves. Just think about it. Given you are the only tool you have at your disposal to do the job, how can the job be well done if the tool isn't in good working order? None of this is self*fish*, just because it is initially self-centred. Quite the contrary. We can't hope to be part of a great relationship until we are 'great' to ourselves.

By settling over the years for less than you want and are capable of, you've let things slip and have allowed your partner to behave badly towards you. More important, though, you've cheated on yourself in all this. And you deserve better. Yet you have lost sight of this simple fact. Gone are the days when you were full of hope, goodwill, and optimism. Now you see only the shadows and the beasts that lurk in them.

Your first task, then, is to reconnect with your inner self – that 'essence' of you – and in so doing to take control of the quality of your life and relationship. If you don't you can only expect more of the pain, guilt, shame, fear, anxiety, frustration, confusion, and misery you are currently attributing to your bad relationship. This new-found power won't give you power over your partner to make *them* a better person but it will empower you to be the best *you* can be. And that's the only starting point I ask for. Only by doing a deal with yourself that you're going to commit yourself to a journey of continuing improvement *in and for yourself* will you stand a chance of building a better relationship.

The joy of all this is that it's a win-win scenario. Even if you invest a lot of time and energy in improving yourself, and your relationship still fares no better, you'll still have won out because you're not doing any of this for your partner or the relationship, you're doing it for yourself. Even if, with the worst possible outcome, you or your partner decides to leave, you'll still be better off than you were and will be well placed to make a new and better choice. But if it does work, your one-to-one relationship will provide huge transformative powers that can heal old emotional scars. I never cease to marvel at how a great one-to-one relationship can overcome just about any adversity – from the past or in the present. Its power is awesome. But studies show that great relationships are made not born. Indeed, if great relationships were 'born', how could one explain the fact that about half of all 'exceptional couples' are in second marriages?

ASK YOURSELF

▶ Do you believe you deserve better than you have? Why?

▶ Do you feel your relationship is going nowhere? If yes, how has this occurred?

▶ Do you feel hopeless, pessimistic, and that you've lost your goodwill towards your partner? How has this occurred?

▶ Do you blame all your ills on your 'bad' relationship? If yes, what has made you do this?

▶ Do you feel you're on a journey of improvement in life? If not, why not? Are you worth making an investment in? If not, why not?

▶ Do you secretly fear the change that altering yourself could bring? If yes, what is it you most fear?

YOUR ACTION PLAN

Write your own obituary. I know this sounds macabre but it's a moving and valuable thing to do. Think about how you'd like to be remembered after your death. When you've finished, assess how you're doing thus far.

Write a list of goals or accomplishments you'd like to achieve before you die. Okay, you want to be a 'better' person, in your personal life and with your partner. What would it take to achieve this? Be brave, however stupid things seem when you list them. Work, perhaps with your partner, and together with other parts of the book, to see how you could achieve these things.

Re-assess your personal values. Make a list of values or virtues that are important to you. Go through the list and see how you think you are living these out in your daily life. Some 'virtues' to get you thinking might be: self-control; love; peace; good humour; compassion; open-mindedness; service; generosity; integrity; hope; and so on.

Create a personal motto from this. This could be something like: 'I want to spend my life being of more service to others'; 'I want to devote myself to becoming more wise'; 'I will devote my life to being more loving to everyone I meet'; 'I'll make my spiritual life a real priority'. Now alone, or with your partner, work out how you could achieve this practically. What would it take to make this change? What other resources do you need to make it happen?

Start off with a small step and get going on your journey of self-improvement.

Plot your 'Life Chart'. With time along the bottom of a large piece of paper, re-create your personal life events (written vertically year by year) from birth to the present day. You could be fascinated by the patterns that emerge and how things in your life today click into place from looking at this simple 'graph'.

At the end of the day. Take a few minutes each day to note in your diary, or anywhere private, what you've most learned from that day. Note any 'jewel moments' and take time to cherish them. Make time for yourself to relax, meditate, or otherwise restore yourself.

Money

When divorced couples are asked what their main problem areas were when married, the majority reply, 'Money.' Although most people imagine sex is the biggest source of conflict in failing couples, this is almost never the case. Disagreements over children, and poor communication come much higher on the list. But nothing touches money as a source of relationship conflict.

At first this seems surprising but once you start to think about the issue it's easy to see why. Money has value only because we agree it does. What money does have, though, is many associated emotions lurking on the sidelines, issues that are troublesome to most of us and especially those of us in intimate relationships.

Money is significant to people in different ways. For some it means stability and security; for others freedom to do what they want; some see it only as a problem if there's too little or too much of it; some are altruistic and see money largely as a force for good and doing good for others; some believe money is the 'root of all evil'; and yet others see it as a way of gaining and retaining power or respect.

The symbolism associated with money, or perhaps the symbolic power it confers on its owner, is far more significant than the actual money itself. Rich people actually do get treated differently from poor people and money does indeed buy happiness, even though those who have never been rich strive strenuously to convince themselves that it does not. Of course, not all rich people are happy but far more poor people are unhappy.

The trouble with money in intimate relationships is that the two people involved often have rather different perceptions of what money is for. This leads to confusion and conflict when there is either too little or a lot of it around. Some individuals, for example, like to know exactly how much money they have in their bank account and others don't care so long as there's 'enough'. Some people are aggrieved that they earn less than their partner, even though they do what they perceive to be a more valuable job. People's views on debt vary greatly, with some feeling terribly guilty or ashamed if they have even a small overdraft. Some individuals are meticulous about paying bills on time while others think companies should wait for their money, as they have to in various parts of their life. Then there are savers and spenders.

An interesting game I play with couples is to get each to say what they'd do if they won the Lotto. The result is highly instructive to us all. It shows how each individual balances concepts of play, self-pleasuring, gifts, security, investment for future gain, risk-taking, extravagance, generosity, and much more.

Because most of us have fairly strong views on how we want to spend our money and because it's probably fair to say that most of us have less disposable money than we'd like, it's easy to see how the subject can be a minefield in a relationship. The making, accumulating, and disposing of it are all possible sources of conflict.

The trouble in intimate relationships is that money is very like sex. Of itself sex has no 'value', it is only worth what we say it is. And, like money, it has the power to impoverish or transform relationships. It can be used well, used inappropriately, or even actually abused. It can be bartered and traded for reasons that have little or nothing to do with sex itself. In other words, sex is a highly symbolic commodity, just like money. As a result, we find ourselves dealing with the two most potent areas of our lives together in overlapping ways that are both symbolically laden. Additional problems arise because in our culture it's impossible to be 'too rich' or 'too sexy'. When I complain that my partner spends too much on the children, what am I really saying? Would it be okay if it were *me* spending this money? What would I spend it on if she weren't spending it on them? How much money did anyone spend on me when I was a child? How did I feel about it? How much sex is she 'spending' on me? Why do I feel so under-benefited, and possibly not just about money? And so it goes on. Unfortunately, money is such a minefield for many couples they soon hit 'no-go areas' (see page 231) and retreat. The aggrieved individual sulks, acts out their anger and frustration in other ways (perhaps in the bedroom), and the issues go on hurting both parties.

There is only one way out of all this and that's to talk about it calmly and lovingly, treating our partner as our best friend rather than some sort of financial enemy who's trying to bankrupt, infantilize, or control us. Dealing with difference here can be very hard, though, because having money and being in debt aren't matters of dispute — they are either a fact or they are not. Other relationship 'commodities' such as love, caring, commitment, or whatever, can't be quantified in the way money can. Unlike love and many other things we share, money is embarrassingly finite! Money spent in a bar simply cannot then be spent on a holiday or children's clothing. Money seeks out the realities of relationships because, unlike the 'softer' commodities we daily trade between us, it is either there or it is not. The individual who controls this limited commodity within a relationship has a lot of power to change their partner's life and lifestyle and many people on the receiving end find this hard to cope with.

ASK YOURSELF

▶ What does money mean to you?

▶ What does money mean to your partner?

▶ If you disagree about money, what do you think it's really all about?

▶ If you had lots of money, what would you do with it?

▶ If your partner had lots of money what would they do with it?

▶ How would you like to be able to handle money better?

▶ How could your partner behave to make you happier about money?

▶ What could you change in you to make yourself feel happier about money?

YOUR ACTION PLAN

Bank accounts. There are all kinds of ways of handling bank accounts if you're living together, married or not. The main three are: his, yours, and ours. Make a list of the advantages and disadvantages you can see to each of these. Obviously it's good to have a joint account so you can mutually share the costs of running your home together; there's also a lot to be said for separate accounts so you can give one another presents without the other knowing how much they cost! But there's far more at stake here. What does your thinking on all this tell you about your ideas and feelings on trust; commitment; sharing; power; the need to feel 'free'; and your partner's views on all of these? One day, get your partner to share their list with you and then gently talk it through. Given that money has such powerful symbolic significance, go carefully and try not to offend. You'll be surprised how much you'll learn about one another.

Lotto game. Imagine you've just won the Lotto. List what you'd do with the money – and in what order or priority. Get your partner to do the same and compare notes. What can you learn about one another and your day-to-day attitude to money from this? Take the main lessons learned here and brainstorm a way that you could, today, make a new arrangement about how you handle your money. Don't leave the table until you've shaken hands on a 'new deal' on the subject. Agree that this will be just the start of a more loving attitude to the way you handle money.

Nagging

This is an annoying behaviour in which someone, classically a woman, keeps on and on complaining about something. Of course, men nag too but women do so more frequently because they aren't heard in the first place! Although some people imagine they are behaving positively by stating their needs, this isn't in fact the case because the nagging usually isn't simply a statement of what they want or need; it's almost always accompanied by accusatory generalizations such as 'You always', 'You never', 'Men always', and so on. Such statements are un-answerable, clearly thoughtless and silly, and are guaranteed to turn off most people right from the start. Most 'naggees' feel pathetic and accused by their partner, and many say they reggress to child-like feelings and behave accordingly.

Simply by saying something – the same thing – over and over again is not effective communication. If it needs saying so many times you're obviously not saying the right thing in the right way to get the result you want. When men tell me how much they hate their wife's nagging I ask them what it is they want instead. They say that they could do with less scolding and being treated as a naughty boy and more honest requests of what it is that they exactly are supposed to do. Most people who are nagged don't start to magically 'hear' any better. Quite the contrary. They have selective deafness whenever the tricky subject is raised!

The secret is to discover ways of getting your message heard and acted upon.

ASK YOURSELF

▶ Would you say your relationship was plagued by nagging? If yes, how do you think nagging harms it?
▶ Are there any positive effects to your nagging? Make a short list of them.

- What does your partner think/feel about your nagging?
- What would you rather be doing than nagging?
- What changes could you make in yourself so you didn't have to nag?
- What would you like to say to your nagging partner that could be helpful to your relationship?

YOUR ACTION PLAN

How to stop yourself nagging. I say 'yourself' here because of course you can never stop your partner nagging. At least, not directly (see below). Much nagging occurs because we make one another promises or raise one another's expectations and then can't live up to them. Our partner feels aggrieved and let down and nags. But nagging, criticizing, or pestering your partner into doing something is demeaning and lowers the tone of your whole relationship. Just stop doing it.

Here's how to get a better result. Instead of going on and on the way you are – which clearly isn't working – you'll need to be tough. Let's say you want your man to repair the leaking lavatory outflow that's dripping down the side of the house. You know he doesn't want to do it. Say something like this: 'Would you please try to get that leak done this weekend? It's splashing on my car now. Or would you rather I got the plumber in?'

He'll respond by saying he'll do it. Of course, Monday next he will not have done it. You now get onto a plumber at once and have the thing done. Your partner comes home from work one day and sees it's been repaired. You say something like: 'You said you'd do it over the weekend but you obviously got too busy with other things. I got the plumber by today and it's done.' This hardball strategy actually works because it proves you mean what you say; that you'll find other ways of getting things done rather than sitting around feeling sorry for yourself or nagging; and that your partner actually doesn't have to do everything you want done.

Your partner's response will probably be somewhat hostile at first but if you now assure him that you're not going to let every little domestic nonsense like this become a test of your love for one another, he'll start to soften.

Coping when your partner nags you. There's only one way I know round this – empathic listening (see page 167). By doing this you'll learn how you can change to produce a better result. Let's say your partner goes on and on about your poor dress sense at the weekends. If you were to respond by saying something like: 'It seems to me you feel ashamed of me when I go out dressed like that,' he can either agree or say exactly what it is he does feel. You should now be able to do a deal on what would need to change in your attire that would be the minimum that would make him happy and that would still leave you feeling you were in charge of how you looked. Remember that the idea here isn't for either of you to be right (see page 70). It's for both of you to get rid of a niggling piece of business that gets in the way of your relationship's integrity and demeans you. There is always a win-win solution in such situations, if only we can find it. All you need is goodwill. Listen empathically and you will find a solution, I promise.

'No-go' Areas

Almost all couples – and indeed almost everyone trying to relate to others in any setting – have what I call 'no-go' areas. These subjects are like a minefield, which, from experience, we know is dangerous ground. We tend to avoid them when dealing with our partner.

Subjects as diverse as religion, children's education, affairs, shopping, his hobbies, penis size, her weight are all common 'no-go' areas. They are skirted around but never openly discussed. One partner, or even both, harbours strong views on the matter in hand yet cannot allow them to come to the surface because they know conflict, or worse, will result.

The trouble is that these areas grow and multiply until the couple in real trouble are relating only in the most superficial way for fear of treading on a landmine in the 'no-go' zone. Such couples end up saying little to one another unless it's about safe issues (which they often unconsciously create to busy themselves so as to avoid the real ones), or row a lot because they fear treading on a landmine whatever they say.

Obviously no two people can agree on everything but even a fairly good relationship can withstand a considerable amount of disagreement. Many 'no-go' areas aren't that serious anyway: they are often the pretext of the current battle. The war is really waging deep down in the couple's lives. End the war and the mini-battles cease.

The trouble with 'no-go' areas is that they can be hard to sort out on your own. It makes sense to involve a third party who can put things into perspective and manage the apparently 'impossible' minefield. A good friend can be a great help. Professional help may be needed if this fails.

Sex is one of the most common 'no-go' areas. When working with couples who profess to have sex problems I always treat their claims with some scepticism because experience shows that sex is usually the innocent bystander that gets crushed by the marital bus running out of control on the sidewalk. Sex problems and their related 'no-go' areas reduce tender feelings and it's usually the woman who first goes off sex as a result. Many men see this as a sort of punishment – and indeed some women do use sex to punish their husbands for not being empathic/sensitive/caring, or whatever. Many men can withstand a woman who rows with them, even though most men know that women have the upper hand in such arguments, but they can't stand a partner who refuses to have sex. This really is the last straw. The guy now sees himself as no longer loved – on the basis that he sees his partner having sex with him largely because she loves him – and he withdraws into himself, his work, his hobbies or other outside interests to avoid having to deal with an 'unloving woman' with whom he has no intention of dealing on his 'no-go' areas. This downward spiral all too often leads to the divorce courts if not caught early and dealt with.

But such 'no-go' zones don't just harm the couple themselves; they deter the individuals from talking about such matters with their children. This can lead to disharmony in a whole family and, at worst, a new generation of young people who are crippled just like their parents. This makes it vital to learn how to deal with 'no-go' areas successfully.

ASK YOURSELF

▶ How do you think 'no-go' areas affect your daily life?

▶ How do you feel about this?

▶ In what kinds of situations do you feel you are most affected by your 'no-go' areas?

▶ How do your 'no-go' areas advantage you?

▶ Why do you think you'd like to be rid of your 'no-go' areas?

▶ Could you easily list your partner's 'no-go' areas? If not, why not?

YOUR ACTION PLAN

Make a list of your 'no-go' areas. Rate them from 1 to 5, where 1 gives you little trouble and 5 the most problems. Now extend this list to include what you perceive your partner's 'no-go' areas to be and rate them too.

What patterns can you see emerging? Are there subjects you both avoid? Which of your list could you possibly talk about, just to get the ball rolling? If you want to involve your partner, have them create an exactly similar list and compare notes. Listen empathically to one another (see page 167) as you talk this through. Remember that many 'no-go' areas are, by definition, hidden and that you might not be aware of what some of yours really are. Listening to your partner's views on this could be helpful.

Work on a no-go area. Remember that the reason the mines in your mine-field are there is because you are afraid to defuse them. Identify a fairly unthreatening mine – one that you are consciously aware of (obviously), yet something you wouldn't normally be able to raise with your partner. This will take courage. Let's take oral sex as an example. I know you may think I'm crazy asserting that this subject could be non-threatening but, believe me, there are far more dangerous subjects you could be tackling from your list.

You know he wants you to fellate him but you've long given up trying because you are dispirited and feel the whole issue has got out of proportion. Neither of you has raised the subject for years but it simmers away nevertheless.

Write down a private list of the things that most upset/concern you about performing oral sex on him. Here are some ideas that might help:

▶ I feel such a whore when I do it.
▶ He knows I hate it so why does he persist in demanding it? I feel so controlled.
▶ It's as though he's putting my love for him to the test and I hate this.
▶ My previous experience with other men is that I hated the taste and smell of semen.
▶ I had a bad experience once when I nearly choked on a guy – it scared me.
▶ I feel he gets his own way sexually enough of the time without this thing I don't like.
▶ I couldn't bear it if my mother knew I did this sort of thing.

Now look at each of these points from your partner's point of view and ask yourself how you could meet him on even one issue. What is your absolute minimum starting point?

Next, talk the subject through with your partner, armed with your prepared thoughts. How about something like this?

'I know you want me to perform oral sex on you but there are lots of issues for me about it. [You now go through your list, while he listens silently.] I know many of these things will seem crazy to you but they're real to me. I'm not crazy because I can't or won't do what you want but perhaps we can come to some sort of compromise on things. You never know, in time I might change my mind if I see you're prepared to give a little too. I've been giving the matter some thought and I'm prepared to get things moving because I can't stand us being divided over this.'

He can now listen empathically to you and within no time at all you'll be finding ways of addressing the 'no-go' area positively, even if neither of you immediately (or indeed ever) gets the *total* result you want.

Now it's time to do a deal. Ask him what his lowest acceptable point of entry would be to the subject other than just talking about it. If he says, 'occasionally kissing my penis', for example, you might feel you could accommodate this. Remember that most of our 'no-go' areas have magnified over time and come to occupy much more psychic space than they need. A woman in this situation, for example, may fear that her man will, given the least encouragement on the matter, forever want *only* oral sex, *only* to ejaculate into her mouth, or whatever the most extreme position she can think of happens to be. None of this may be true. Yet at the moment he's getting nothing of what he wants and her inability to approach the matter means that all kind of imagined threats will remain just that – imagined.

Now repeat the process by asking him to name a 'no-go 'area of his that you could helpfully address.

No Sex

Many people say they can't imagine 'a relationship' with someone without sex. In fact, some try to convince me this is a contradiction in terms. 'Having a partner' to them means having a sex partner. But 'no sex' can mean many different things to different people. It can be a temporary situation, as after the birth of a baby, or after an operation or serious illness; or it can become a lifestyle. How each is dealt with will vary greatly. Temporary celibacy can be coped with by the couple finding alternatives to actual intercourse (if that's what's off the agenda). This is what successful couples do. They can happily and lovingly sustain this behaviour for months or even years.

Millions of couples never, or almost never, have sex and claim to tolerate or even enjoy the situation. It's very hard to know how common sexless marriages are but figures of one in eight seem about right to me. Of course, given that definitions of sex vary so greatly it can be hard to know what such couples mean. To some people oral, anal, or other forms of intercourse that don't involve vaginal penetration aren't counted as 'sex'. So it is that I can see a man who complains he 'hasn't had sex for months', only to find that his lover masturbates him regularly, and even performs oral sex on him even though she doesn't want true intercourse. Are such a couple 'having sex' by any usual meaning of the term? I think they are.

Now let's look at much less obvious types of 'sex'. Let's say a couple claiming to have no sex cuddle and kiss, and have a loving relationship in all kinds of other ways. Can they be said to be having sex? I think they can. A sexual relationship isn't just about penetration. If such a couple are exclusively involved with physical, emotional, and spiritual intimacies, I think most people would consider it to be 'sex'. I can tell you that any partner of someone who is doing this in an affair certainly calls it sex – albeit not intercourse!

A life without intercourse is, of course, perfectly possible and even enjoyable. Millions of people who have no partner live like this all the time and don't crack up. Even if they'd rather be having sex, and many would not, they transform their sexual energies into other productive things in life. After all, intercourse isn't the only way of expressing love, creativity, intimacy, fun, delight, or whatever. That it *can* be a source of all these things in a one-to-one relationship doesn't make it *necessary* in such a relationship. Of course, the difference is that the single, the widowed, or divorced, and so on haven't chosen their lifestyle in the expectation that it will have a sexual element to it. They may be tolerating a sexless life but wouldn't necessarily have chosen it. Those of us in relationships expect to have sex because this was part of the 'contract' from the start. Understandably, we feel aggrieved, betrayed or cheated when this vital part of the contract is declared null and void.

Some 'no-sex' couples are adult enough to renegotiate their sex contract. A few, realizing that they themselves no longer want sex but want their partner to be happy, allow extra-marital activities, provided they don't threaten the relationship. (See also 'Lack of Trust', page 205; and 'Affairs', page 44.) This is almost impossible to guarantee, of course, and most such deals founder in time. Other couples come to arrangements in which inter-course is banned but the 'under-benefited' partner is pleasured in other ways, irrespective of their partner's feelings about the actual ways them-selves. In other words it is possible for such a partner to answer their lover's needs but to be cut off from the actions themselves. If this symbolic form of 'sex' takes the pressure off the relationship, I think it's an intelligent solution to a difficult problem.

ASK YOURSELF

▶ How do you handle times when you're not having sex?

▶ How does your partner handle them?

▶ How would you and your partner handle your sexual needs if he or she could never have sex again?

▶ How do you think you mis-use sex in your relationship?

▶ In what ways do you feel controlled by your partner not having sex with you?

YOUR ACTION PLAN

You don't want any sex but your partner does. Make a list of all the things that you'd consider just as nice as sex in your relationship. Get your partner to make a similar list on his or her own and exchange views on them.

Discuss which of these you'd be prepared to do together instead of having sex or to trade for the minimum sexual activity your partner wants or needs. For this you'll need a list of mutually agreed 'sexual' pastimes, even if they don't involve intercourse. These could include: cuddling; massage; sexy talk; watching one another masturbate; and so on. If you are completely 'off sex', obviously none of these will appeal, even to keep your partner happy.

If this is the case and you can't even bring yourself to play this game, perhaps you'd benefit from professional help. This will only be necessary if your partner finds the situation too hard to bear.

Your partner doesn't want any sex but you do. Build up your fantasy life; create new masturbation games; use porn more; enlist the help of your partner, if possible, in any of this. As a very last resort, talk to your partner about how they'd feel about you seeking sex outside your relationship. You could be surprised. I've seen people who are delighted to have the 'burden of sex' taken off their shoulders by this suggestion. That this solution could lead to the end of your relationship must be kept in mind but this needn't be the outcome unless you fall in love elsewhere. This is always a danger.

Not Saying
What You Mean

This is one of the most important barriers to communication for many couples and one that can subtly kill even quite good relationships. It is a technique many of us unwittingly use to sabotage our relationship and was learned early on in childhood. At its heart is the fact that what's real never gets said and what *does* get said is never all that real.

Perhaps in your childhood you discovered that your parents, or other significant adults, didn't listen to or couldn't cope with what you said, so you gave up on saying anything, or got into the habit of saying things you didn't really mean.

When we behave like this we unconsciously give our partner unhelpful signs and directions to distract them from knowing what's really going on for us.

This usually takes the form of side-tracking them with 'safer' topics that have nothing to do with the matter in hand. For example, it's all too easy to focus on some trivial behaviour – such as never locking the garage door – rather than on the deeper issues of feeling unheard or ignored over much more important things in life.

Of course, it's easier to sort out your partner's behaviour over garage doors than it is to get to the heart of your feelings of being ignored or unworthy of considerate action in the eyes of your partner, or even the world in general, but the real problem lurks in the background un-dealt with. Even if one such simple issue is resolved – as it might be with effort or consideration by your partner – another will certainly rear its head. Now your lover gets irritable because however hard they try you'll always come up with more 'misdirections' to throw them off the scent of what's really wrong. Deep down you want your partner to hear, as if by magic, some hidden, yet probably well-disguised, inner voice. But they do not. This, in turn, makes you feel worse because, you tell yourself, if they really loved you they should know what's going on for you. It's your childhood history repeating itself in the most painful way.

All this makes you feel more emotional, more out of control, and more hopeless that you'll ever be truly heard. Your relationship suffers. Worse still, one day you may explode in some way, acting out years of frustrated 'not saying'.

Unfortunately, this is dangerous behaviour for your partner too because by throwing all the decoys in their path you force them to use huge amounts of emotional and loving energy trying to sort out problems that aren't real. Or you unwittingly walk the dog, have sex, make a meal, or deal with the children – anything rather than deal with what really matters at that time. None of these is genuine, and as a result, doesn't provide you with the emotional or spiritual 'return' you need.

ASK YOURSELF

▶ Do you get defensive when your partner asks what's wrong? If yes, how do you think this advantages you? How could you behave in some other way?

▶ Do you postpone talking about things you know are bothering you? If yes, why do you think you do this?

▶ Do you focus on trivial complaints a lot? If yes, how have you found this helps you?

▶ Do you vehemently discuss other people's problems, hoping your partner will detect it's your relationship you're on about? If yes, how does this advantage you?

YOUR ACTION PLAN

It takes huge courage to say what you mean, especially if you've been together as a couple for some time and haven't ever done it. As we've seen throughout the book, you'll make progress only by actively managing your behaviour and taking personal responsibility for the outcomes. This is risky stuff and you'll feel terribly vulnerable at first when you do it. Take time to congratulate yourself every time you pass a new milestone on this journey. This might sound childish but it isn't. I hope that in time your partner will start to congratulate and encourage you as you get better at saying what you mean, but in the meantime you'll have to give yourself this encouragement.

Reward yourself in some way that matters to you, so as to reinforce your new behaviour.

Make no mistake – being this brave is what improving your relationship is all about. You have choices on this. You can stay where you are or you can make things better.

First, let me help you acknowledge that you might not be aware of what the real underlying issues are. *This doesn't matter*. I'm not asking you to be your own therapist. All I am asking you to do, from today, is to start doing things differently.

Practise saying what you mean in public. Next time you're in a shop or other public place and feel something strongly, make an effort to deal with it there and then.

Do this firmly but without aggression, trying to leave the individual on the receiving end with some sort of pleasant feeling about having dealt with you. For example: 'I'd like you to replace these shoes that have broken after only one week. I'm sure you'll agree it's not reasonable and that a shop as good as yours wouldn't want to sell such badly made things.'

Keep practising this sort of assertive, non-whining expression of your feelings about things that are outside your relationship with your partner. Doing it for real with them should be tried only once you are confident that you can express yourself without blowing up or getting defensive outside your relationship. My work with couples and groups shows me that all these tasks are better practised in the outside world first. You'll need to get confident and feel free to make mistakes without the emotional baggage of your relationship getting in the way. After all, what does it matter what the woman in the shoe shop thinks? All that matters is that you've tried and have moved yourself on – not a mile, just a step.

Say what you're feeling at that moment. Next time your partner asks, 'What's wrong?' focus on what you are *feeling* at that moment rather than trying to psychoanalyse, ignore, or dismiss the issue. For example: 'I'm really upset you're later home than you said. I'd gone to a lot of trouble to make a nice meal and now I feel under-valued in spite of my efforts.'

By making this response you'll have done some important things:

▶ Used three 'I' statements – and no 'You' ones.
▶ Won't have accused him of being late at the office with the woman you're afraid he's seeing too much of (whether it's true or not).
▶ Given him an opportunity to apologize rather than get defensive/ aggressive because you've nagged him.

In other words, you have given yourself the very best chance of being heard, without creating bad feelings in your partner. Any other response will be guaranteed to generate the very sort of reaction you so fear from your partner – and you'll have 'proved' yet again why it is you don't say anything.

Warning: Don't concern yourself at this stage with how your partner responds to your statement. That's their problem and you'll have absolutely no control over it. All you are trying to do is alter *your* behaviour. How your partner eventually alters their behaviour in response to the different you is their responsibility and is outside your control.

Congratulate yourself that you have said quietly and with dignity what you felt and leave it at that, unless, of course, your partner goes on to make some sort of positive, constructive remark, in which case you should openly and warmly acknowledge it.

Ignore opportunities to react badly. Next time your partner does something trivial but annoying, actively remind yourself you have the freedom not to let it get to you and you can choose to ignore it.

There is no law that says because you can get angry, you have to.

By letting go of getting annoyed with your partner over small things you'll clear the ground for airing your feelings about real issues and will be better able to say what you mean when it matters. Getting mad at small events is self-indulgent and easily becomes a self-righteous bad habit. Just stop doing it.

Try to stick to the subject in hand. Ask your partner to let you know lovingly next time you are talking together and they find you change the subject. Try to think through to yourself what it is about the issue that makes you uncomfortable and perhaps later, on your own, jot down some notes to yourself. Making the matter 'concrete' by actually committing it to paper will help you make it real. If you feel comfortable, try to discuss with your partner what it is that made you change the subject. Here are some ideas to work on:

▶ Did you feel threatened?
▶ What emotion *did* you feel at the time?
▶ Did it feel familiar, perhaps from your life as a child or from another adult relationship? Give yourself time to think through what's going on.

Stop focusing on other people's problems. Next time you find yourself going on and on about other people's problems ask yourself what this could be saying about your own life. Ask your partner what he or she thinks is going on.

List your worst fears about expressing yourself. One day when you have some time and are feeling okay, sit down and make a list of the worst things you fear about expressing your real feelings. Here are some ideas to trigger your thinking:

▶ I'm afraid/have actually experienced that by doing so I'll be unacceptable or unlovable.

▶ Whatever I say, I won't be heard.

▶ I get scared of my own feelings when I talk about them.

▶ I fear I might go mad if I really let them up to the surface.

▶ My mother/father was: like this/neurotic/mentally ill, and I fear I'm
getting like them.

▶ I don't want my partner to be burdened with my crap – he/she might
stop communicating with me altogether.

▶ I don't want to sound childish and silly. I'm an adult and should be able
to sort myself out.

▶ It doesn't matter what I say, my partner won't understand.

There are many more, of course.

Warning: Whatever reasons you come up with, none of them need, in reality, stop you saying what you mean. Your fear is your worst enemy. I have
seen people with many or even all of the things I've listed eventually learn
to say what they mean perfectly well. To use any of these excuses to stop
yourself saying what you mean is a cop-out, and completely within your
control. Don't allow yourself to be self-indulgent.

Passiveness

People who are passive often appear to be 'nice' and most outsiders can't understand why their partner has such a hard time with them. They aren't openly aggressive or hostile, like their partner might be, and seem so reasonable, smiley, and generally 'good sorts'.

Underneath, though, such individuals are very dangerous indeed – largely because none of their hard work at damaging the relationship is apparent.

Such individuals are known by psychologists as passive-aggressives. They work away covertly – albeit often unconsciously, to be fair – to wreck things in a way that leaves them looking good to the outside world. They always have an excuse or a convincing tale to tell yet you can't pin down exactly what it is they've done to ruin your life. Such individuals undermine their partner's confidence and achievements, and end up doing exactly the reverse of what they claim to be doing. They sort of go along with what their partner wants but subsequently thwart it in some mysterious way. The partner of such an individual finds all this infuriating because they never quite know what they're dealing with. All they *do* know is that they feel terribly controlled and manipulated, and they can't put their finger on quite how it happens time and again.

Let's say as a couple you are deciding whether to buy a new car. Your partner tells you what they want to get and you disagree. If you're a passive-aggressive you don't come out with your thoughts there and then but go along with their decision, perhaps even quite pleasantly. But as soon as things get real you start to show your previously un-expressed views as veiled aggression. Now, you argue, the main agent is way too far away; the car isn't available in a colour you'd be prepared to live with; the financial terms are unappealing; perhaps you should do something for the home or the family rather than buying a car at all, and so it goes on. Anything to get your own way (not to buy the car at all) except saying at the very beginning, 'I don't think we can afford/need/should buy a car right now', and face the consequences.

The roots of such passive-aggressive behaviour go way back into child-hood. In some households any form of disagreement is seen as threatening, dangerous, or socially unacceptable; others teach their children that settling for a quiet life is the best thing to aim for; some families believe that *any* disagreement is by its very nature aggressive or an expression of anger; others mix up being assertive with being angry; in some households there is so much anger and aggression about that the children learn to avoid being tainted by it by becoming 'passive'; some people are too shy to express their views, or fear ridicule if they do; some learn that, whatever they say, others overrule them or ignore them, so why bother? And so on. It is here, in child-hood, that much unexpressed aggression starts and grows. But because 'nice' people shouldn't show their feelings in an aggressive way, such indi-viduals unconsciously argue, they must find another way of getting what they want. And they do. Unfortunately, it can cost their relationship dear.

ASK YOURSELF

▶ In what ways and in what situations do you feel passive in everyday life?

▶ In what ways do you feel passive in your relationship?

▶ How do you express your passive-aggressive tendencies?

▶ How did your family of origin express conflict, anger and discord?

▶ In what way would you say you were a 'nice' person?

YOUR ACTION PLAN

Assessing how passive-aggressive you are. Do you: Tend to find excuses for not doing things? Start sentences with 'Yes but ...'? Find you have mysterious ailments that get in the way of something you've agreed to do? Suddenly 'find' you're hopeless at doing something you've agreed to do? Agree with things your partner wants only then to sabotage them later?

Change things like this. Next time your partner suggests something that you're not keen on, come right out and say so at once. However scary this feels, or however at odds with your usual behaviour, simply say no. See what happens. In fact, nothing you fear will happen. Try saying something like this: 'I realize what a pain I've been by saying one thing and then sabotaging it for you later. From now on I'm going to say right out if I don't agree and then we'll both know where we are. If you don't like it, we can discuss it and we may even fight over it but I can't go on being passive like this. It also doesn't suit you because I just end up being a nuisance to you at a later stage. This has got to stop.'

Power and Control

Issues that relate to power and control are high on the list of topics that couples bring to therapists. We all want to feel we have a degree of both within our relationship, and for some individuals this need is very great. Perhaps they felt un-empowered – or even dis-empowered – in previous relationships and are determined to make this one different; perhaps their childhood was characterized by permanent feelings of powerlessness; or they may just be reflecting modern society's changing views on the matter.

Over the millennia of recorded history there is little doubt that it was men who had the overt power in both families and society in general. I say 'overt' because this power was somewhat illusory at the family and inter-personal level. The old truism 'the hand that rocks the cradle rules the world' was valid then, and still is today. Women have always had consider-able power in relationships, largely conferred upon them by the fact that they have control of a commodity that men value highly – sex. Females are also much more verbally adept, with most women able to out-argue most men. Women are also provably better at multi-tasking. Many of these female and feminine skills make men feel inferior today just as they must have done in ancient times.

Add to this the obvious 'inferiority' of men when it comes to the contin-uation of the human race – sperm is cheap but eggs are expensive – and it's easy to understand why men have been seeking to exert power and control over women in whatever way they could since time began. On this note, with continuing advances in reproductive science, it won't be long before men are completely removed from the reproductive cycle. This will produce even more problems, which will show themselves as issues of power and control within relationships.

As a result of changes in society over the last thirty years women are now in an increasingly ascendant position on the 'power' ladder as they obtain power in the workplace as well as in the home. Women now increasingly rule public and private domains and many men are finding it hard to know where they stand. Male skills involving greater physical strength and certain other innate brain abilities are becoming less valued in a culture where mechanical diggers and computers can be used equally effectively by women. Even the way big business functions is dominated by more feminine concepts than used to be the case. In this increasingly 'feminized' world many men feel unskilled, undervalued, square pegs in round holes, and somewhat by-passed by history. They have lost their historic roles as hunters and fighters and are struggling to find new ones.

All this makes for altered relationships at home between men and women. No man can 'un-know' this social picture when dealing with his personal relationship because everything in his private life reflects it.

The notion of 'power' in a loving, one-to-one relationship confuses many couples. That power shifts are occurring is without doubt. The way I have found to make sense of all this is to constantly shift the centre of power and control within the well-balanced couple. In certain settings, then, one partner takes what could be called 'control' and in others, the other partner does. In this way each has their own 'speciality' areas (though these, too, will shift over time) and together they constitute a formidable team. In this model it's also vital to bear in mind that just because the woman has a 'powerful' role at work, she may not want to continue this behaviour at home. Many's the high-flying woman who has told me how she likes to turn off being a 'bossy boots' at home and have her man take 'control' over much of their life together.

And this last point is an important one. For the tired, multi-tasking woman who also wants sex, it's a delight to have a forceful man who takes 'control' in this area and makes things happen for her. Unfortunately, an increasing number of men are so unsure of themselves, they have lost their bedroom skills and confidence so, for fear of getting things wrong, with the associated criticism, back off altogether.

The beauty of sex to many people is the 'loss of control' associated with it. At a more serious level, some individuals find their sexuality controls them or their partner and this can call for professional help. In certain relationships one seeks to control the sexuality of the other. Again, help can be valuable, especially as this often points up the paradox that the one seeking to control is usually feeling out of control or lacking in power in other areas of their life. Deal with these and the sex problem sorts itself out.

Couples with power and control issues at the heart of their relationship sometimes find a useful haven in sadomasochistic sex games. I encourage these because they are ways of harmlessly acting out deeper needs, with the added bonus of great sex. Some of the most powerful businesswomen I have dealt with in the consulting room say how much they like to be taken over during sex. 'At last,' they sigh with relief, 'somewhere I don't have to make everything happen!' None of these women are what anyone would call 'passive' yet they happily hand over sexual control to their lover.

It's a sad fact that the words 'power' and 'control' have become synonymous for many couples. In the sort of relationships I try to foster, both individuals have their own sources of power and control within themselves. Having power isn't at all the same as being 'powerful' in the negative sense; just as having personal control isn't about 'controlling' our partner.

The only control worth having is that which we exert over ourselves. The only power worth having is that which empowers our relationship. Any other definition and we're in trouble.

I like the saying, 'Don't walk in front of me, I may not follow; Don't walk behind me, I may not lead; Just walk beside me and be my friend.' This is the model for the sort of power we all need as couples. It empowers both of us to be truly ourselves; enables us to grow year on year; creates a bond that no human power can assault; and in a world of fragile relationships ensures our durability as friends and lovers. Looked at this way the notion of who has power or control over whom seems outdated and tedious.

This model leads to what I call an Alliance of Equals. I see every successful man-woman relationship as a sort of exclusive club – with just two members. The teamwork is not only ennobling to the individuals involved but is also arguably the best way to cope with a complex and hostile world. Such a couple draw on one another's strengths, rather than focusing on their weaknesses. This alliance enables both people to grow, is a formidable role model for their children, a source of strength for their friends and family, and is the backbone of a successful society. There is no substitute for it.

ASK YOURSELF

▶ What could you do to make yourself feel more powerful in life generally?

▶ What could you do to make yourself feel more powerful in your relationship?

▶ How does your partner dis-empower you?

▶ How do you dis-empower yourself?

▶ In what ways do you think you try to control your partner?

▶ In what ways do you feel controlled by him or her?

▶ How do issues of power and control affect your sex life?

YOUR ACTION PLAN

Who's in control? List all the important areas of your life. Alongside this write who is most 'in control' in these circumstances. If it's joint, say so. Now score each one to let yourself know how satisfied you are with the current set-up. Get your partner to make a similar list. Compare lists. Ask your partner to give his or her view on your scoring. Lovingly discuss the issues that arise. If one of you tends to be over-controlling, try to discover why this is. Is this just a bad habit? Could it be that they feel out of control in the rest of their life? Have you become lazy, thus almost forcing your partner to take control in situations they'd rather not? Where could you start to take joint control where you are not? See what comes up. Try, wherever possible, to get to a situation where you have joint control over most things, even if you actually *do* the things separately.

Now extend your discussion to include issues of power. Do power and control mean the same to you both? Talk about power without responsibility.

Previous Bad Relationships

It's probably fair to say that we all carry the scars of previous relationships with us wherever we go. These may have come about from bad relationships with our parents, teachers, siblings, relatives, religious influencers, strangers, and many more. Any human relationship in which we felt used, abused, bullied, tyrannized, damaged, put down, ignored, rejected, unloved, abandoned, lost, or depressed can leave us with a memory of what this feels like. It seems to be a part of being human that we are constantly expecting others to repeat this pattern, if only because our internal 'emotional computer' is set to recognize it.

Even when we have unfortunate dealings with someone whose behaviour comes even close to any of our previous 'default settings' for pain we unconsciously expect them to repeat exactly what we think, from experience, we need, deserve, or fear.

It's easy to see, then, how bad relationships with members of the opposite sex can plague and haunt us for years after the individuals themselves are out of our lives. And given that we tend, unless we have considerable insight, to choose the same kinds of partners time and again, it's hardly surprising that our 'emotional computer' not only expects disaster with people who are similar to those who have given us grief in the past, but actually inserts little programmes to be sure that the picture is complete.

The problem, as I see it, is that few people actually sit down, with or without a professional, and ask themselves why any given relationship has gone wrong. They whine about it, complain to their friends, feel sorry for themselves, court sympathy from anyone who'll listen, lament their bad luck, offload their emotional rubbish on those who are too insecure of themselves to prevent it, damn half the human race ('bloody wo/men!'), and much more besides. What they almost never do is to ask themselves in their heart of hearts, with bleeding-knuckles honesty, what it is that *they* contributed to the failure of the relationship.

I always tell people that their previous bad relationships are a heaven-sent gift. How else can we hope to learn how to make good ones? Or how to avoid making the same mistakes time and again?

ASK YOURSELF

▶ What do you think you have learned from previous bad relationships?

▶ If you have learned little or nothing, why is this?

▶ What is the pattern to your bad relationships?

▶ In what way have you contributed to bad relationships?

▶ How do you behave when you are in a bad relationship? How does this behaviour serve you?

▶ How would you most like to be able to behave when you're in a bad relationship?

YOUR ACTION PLAN

Starting over after a bad relationship. When I see people, especially women, who are recovering from a recent bad relationship the biggest single problem is that they think they are somehow flawed in having chosen such an individual. Of course, this could be the case but it usually isn't. It is also not the end of the world. I always tell such people that new relationships are rather like buses – there's always another one coming round the corner!

Whilst it's vital to sit yourself down and think very carefully through how and why things went wrong, it's also important not to get too heavy. Look for repeating patterns in your failed or unsuitable relationships. Do you always choose control freaks? Do you choose people who can't commit? Why do 'bastards' appeal so much? How much 'danger' can you stand? Are you incapable of true intimacy and so choose (unwittingly of course) people who will ensure you don't get it? And so on. Get professional help if necessary to explore these patterns. Every failed relationship is a godsend because we can learn so much from it.

Until you are happy that you *have* learned, stay out of the market for a while. Feeling 'hurt' (usually anger), or any other major emotion, clouds our ability to choose well. Being without a partner is better than being with an unsuitable one. Take your time and wise up about yourself in the meantime.

Relatives

When we settle down with someone we don't just take them on as individuals, we 'buy into' their past, their whole family. Given that we are all the product of our pasts, those most important in creating this past will almost certainly be our family. Of course, religious pastors, teachers, youth work leaders, family friends, and many others will have importantly contributed to our personality development but it's our close family that plays the biggest part.

But not all families are the same. The roles that parents play, notions on gender, views on everything and anything in the outside world, handling crises, birthdays, work, play ... in fact anything you can think of will have been differently handled by your partner's family of origin than it was by yours. This will have programmed their emotional computer to work in a very particular way. And it will be different from the way yours works.

But it's not just social attitudes and beliefs that will be so different. Your partner may be very close to their father and hate their mother, or the other way around. They may have siblings of one gender only and be inexperienced in how to behave towards the opposite sex. And so on. Some people's expectations are of keeping in very close touch with their family after they are married, and others see it as their chance to break away and become 'more adult'. Some individuals see themselves as permanent 'children' in the eyes of their parents and may even act like this in their marriage. Others are brought up to be highly independent individuals with parents that are almost equals.

It's easy to see that when you start looking at your relatives, the potential for difference and misunderstanding between you is great. All this is greatly enhanced if your partner's family, or your own family of origin's situation, is other than the 'norm'. In practice, the norm today for most families is not 2.4 children living together with their married parents who will stay married for a lifetime, with the man as the main breadwinner.

Today's families are very diverse, with racial mixes, parental age differ-ences, religious divides, educational chasms, gender issues (gay-parent families, for example), parents who may or may not work, man-woman work role-reversals, and much more. All this makes for complicated emotions between you as you try to make sense of it all in the context of your relationship, especially in the early years.

Whatever you feel or think about your family, though, you won't much like it when your partner criticizes them to you. It'll take time with you two working together as a couple to come to sensible, balanced views about your families that will separate you from them in a healthy way. Early on after your marriage you'll probably still feel part of your family. As time goes by, though, you'll become more a part of your relationship and its own dynamic, and eventually you may have your own family about which you'll then feel most strongly of all.

Ideally, when we get married it's best to treat our new family as a massive source of new inputs and resources. After all, the person we love so much we want to spend the rest of our days with must have had something good going for them at home or they wouldn't be the unique individual they are. Some people find they get on better with an in-law than they do with their own parents. This is hardly surprising, given that our partner may be very much like their mum or dad.

Whole new alliances can be formed when two families get together, with all the growth this can bring.

But however good things are between you you'll inevitably end up making comparisons. Even if you don't say it you'll find yourself thinking, 'This isn't how we used to do it in my home.' Of course it isn't, but then you didn't marry your clone, remember? Part of the joy of merging with another family is that they can give new insights into life and open new doors for us, just as our family does for our partner. Of course, this is challenging, and even very stressful, especially early on, but if you stick in there you'll eventually reap huge rewards. Even when you can't agree to adopt a particular family pattern or practice, dealing with these differences can be used to grow and strengthen the bond between you as a couple. In good relationships, both partners are mature enough to look for what's good and bad about their respective families and then to draw on the best to make their life together better still. It's crazy to re-invent the wheel. If one set of relatives has worked something out well within their family, it would be mad not to learn from it.

ASK YOURSELF

▶ How has dealing with your in-laws helped you understand your own parents?

▶ How has dealing with your in-laws helped you understand yourself better?

▶ What have you learned about your partner by observing his or her relatives?

▶ How could you put this knowledge to good use in your relationship?

▶ How have you in fact done this?

▶ How do your relatives damage your relationship?

▶ What could/should you do to prevent this happening?

▶ How do your partner's relatives damage your relationship?

▶ What could he or she do to prevent this happening?

YOUR ACTION PLAN

Your parents' marriages. List, on your own to start with, the features of your parents' marriage. Now ask yourself: What's the main positive thing you've taken away from it? What's the main negative thing? How is your relationship better than theirs? How is your relationship not as good as theirs?

Now ask your partner to do the same, then compare notes. Use this exercise to see what you can learn about how you two relate.

Sex Problems

Having written whole books about sex problems, I find it difficult to summarize the topic in a small space. Great sex doesn't make for a great relationship. And the reverse is also true. In fact, some couples claim to have a wonderful relationship and to have no sex at all (see page 235). This said, for most, sex is important if only because it is the only commodity that the partners agree to source entirely from within their relationship. We are all happy if our partner finds love, interest, fun, creativity, and other human relationships elsewhere, but we feel especially protective of our faithful sexual bond. To many their sex life is the main, or only, thing that distinguishes their relationship with their partner from relationships they have with others.

When sex is going well it makes up a very small percentage of the average relationship. We take it for granted. But when it's going badly it makes up a very large one, which, like a runaway bus, kills a lot of innocent bystanders as it careers down the street.

Sex can, of course, be healing, fun, relaxing, make us feel accepted and loved, a unique opportunity for extreme intimacy, a relationship glue when life gets tough, and much more, but it can also be bad for us. Many men especially can't understand when I talk about 'bad' sex. To them, every sort of sex is, by its very nature, 'good'. But all of us mis-use sex, if only from time to time, to control our partner; for our own personal, selfish ends; to act out previous abusive experiences; as a way of healing ourselves or advantaging ourselves even at our partner's expense; and so on.

Given that we all put a different emphasis on how important sex is within our life together, it's clear that the way we define 'sex problems' will vary hugely. In general, I work on the principle that, in a loving, committed relationship, if I have a sex problem, then my partner has it too. After all, even if it has nothing at all ostensibly to do with her, if I am her monopoly supplier we both have a problem that needs sorting out. In fact, whoever's 'fault' it is, we share the problem and we should try to find a way round it.

It is now that problems with mismatching rear their head because almost no couple has exactly the same sexual appetites, needs or agendas. One may see something as a problem yet the other be perfectly happy. This mismatching can occur on a practical level or at a psychological one. For example, a woman may feel that if she isn't a rewarding partner in bed she isn't being loving or desirable to her man; and her partner may feel he lets her down by not being sufficiently potent, powerful, or masterful in bed – or indeed out of it. Only frank discussion will uncover what each really wants, rather than what they *imagine* the other wants. Many so-called sex problems can be dealt with very quickly like this. Simply redefining the terms can help a lot.

The trouble with sex in a monopoly supplier situation is that when things do go wrong, the under-benefited one can feel angry, rejected, abandoned, unloved and unlovable, disappointed, bitter and much more. Depending on their personality type they can now get punitive, vengeful, or hateful and the whole relationship starts to suffer. The other partner then, obviously, doesn't feel very sexy and the whole situation spirals downhill rapidly.

This state of affairs happens to all couples at some stage, perhaps repeatedly over many years. For most it is temporary and they find ways of healing things and returning to a sexual life that pleases, if only on a 'good enough' basis. When matters get more serious, one or other starts to make sweeping statements or harsh judgements about the other and wonders whether they should find a more suitable partner.

This can be hard because, given that sex isn't an all-or-nothing phenomenon, and that sexual pleasure can be so hard to define, it's easy to make perfection the enemy of the good. Yet defining what we mean by a 'good enough' sex life can be hard and few couples readily agree – even if they agree to agree for the sake of peace!

After all my years in this business I don't know the answer to this one. It is inevitably stressful – and some think it preposterous – to expect one individual to answer all our needs over many years in an area that can be as important as sex. Of course the overwhelming majority of people look outside their relationship, in fantasy, to answer their unmet needs, but to do anything more than this is to put severe strains, or even terminal pressures, on the situation. When this occurs within a loving relationship where every-thing else is working well, the dilemma is a huge one. Many people remain in deeply unsatisfactory and unsatisfying sexual relationships that are in all other respects highly enjoyable. How long any one individual can toler-ate such tensions will depend on many factors. Some older couples tell me that they are just waiting for their diminishing sex drives to take over in such situations, trying in the meantime to focus on the more positive sides of their life together. Younger couples understandably find this harder to do.

Because sex is the main way that we are 'allowed' to regress with one another as a couple (during lovemaking we re-live babyhood, child-hood, and adolescent love scenarios), when this is unavailable we can find ourselves regressing in other ways. These can be unhelpful, or even destructive, at work, at home, or within the family, let alone within our one-to-one relationship.

I know it's a truism, but sex doesn't just 'happen' within a relationship. The making of love (see page 204) takes time, effort, creativity, and care. These exercises could help get you back on to an even keel. If they don't, you might want to get professional help, or discuss with your partner what ongoing sex 'problems' mean for you. Perhaps you'll be able to find a solu-tion even where a professional cannot.

ASK YOURSELF

▶ How do you feel about sex problems in your relationship?
▶ How does your partner feel about them?
▶ Who do you think is responsible for any sex problems you have?
▶ How do you handle sex problems that occur?
▶ How would you like to be able to handle them better?

YOUR ACTION PLAN

Go back to courtship. Most everyday sex problems sort themselves out with time. And some cease to be 'problems', even if they don't change at all.

The best way to handle things is to stop even trying to have sex and to get back to romantic, courtship behaviour (see page 202). This takes the pressure off sex completely and opens the doors to other pleasurable and sensual experiences. Learn how to do sensual massage.

Sensual holidays. A sensual holiday is an evening, a day, a weekend, or longer, in which you throw out all your old routines and roles and start over again, teaching one another to be physically intimate. I advise couples to take it in turns to plan the holiday. If they like, the organizer can send the other little notes, e-mails or text messages teasing him or her about what's to come. He might buy her a set of beautiful lingerie, and she him a small gift too.

Send one another love tokens ahead of time. These will be redeemable on the sensual holiday at any time your lover chooses. Ideas for these could include: champagne in bed; making love in a semi-public place; going out with no underwear; playing customer and call-girl games in your hotel room; and so on.

Stay off sex for the first day, if it's a weekend together. Build up the tension in other ways and tease until you can't bear it any longer. Get back to your old courting days when you longed for one another and the novelty of your relationship. Do something wild you wouldn't normally do. Break out of familiar bounds.

Once back home, talk through what worked well, use it in your fantasy life together, and plan your next 'holiday' at once so you have something great to look forward to.

Sexual audit. Make a list of every sexual activity you can think of. Now rank them in order of what you most like, or would most like, if you're not currently doing a particular thing. Now rank each one on a frequency rating of how often you actually do it.

Get your lover to create a similar list. Compare lists and see what you can learn. Many so-called sex problems arise from one or other partner being bored, not getting the sort of sex they want or need, or some sort of anger or bitterness because things have become so jaded and familiar. Challenging one another with a list like this can do the trick and dispel even quite 'serious' sex problems. But for this to work, you'll need to be totally honest and to listen attentively and empathically to what your partner says. If this exercise results simply in more rejection and prohibitions, it'll be a waste of time and could even do more damage. Find ways of compromising; do deals; be more adventurous than you think you could ever be; 'Fake it till you make it' (see page 93); and remember that 'What can't be cured must be endured' (see page 113).

Sexual Orientation Confusion

Although most of us are sure whether we are heterosexual or gay, some people are confused because they sometimes fantasize about, or feel actually attracted to, someone of the same sex. Although this isn't a 'sex book' I think the subject is worth airing a little here because it can cause relationship problems.

Clinical experience shows that most people are neither wholly heterosexual nor homosexual. We all fit somewhere along a continuum. To confuse matters further, individuals who strenuously deny they have, or even could have, any attraction to others of the same sex are usually in some sort of denial of their attraction to the subject. I find this is especially true of men.

Some men worry about whether they might be gay if, for example, they find nipple play exciting. They see this as something women like and then (erroneously) fear they might be gay for wanting the same thing. Some men who discover the eroticism of their anal area also worry this might mean they could be gay. Of course, this isn't the case because anal sensitivity and eroticism are universal human pleasures – they have nothing to do with being gay. In certain Arab countries men openly walk hand-in-hand down the street with their heterosexual friends. This would definitely be considered gay behaviour in Western culture.

Similarly with women. Just because you think you'd like to kiss or cuddle a girlfriend doesn't make you a lesbian. Quite a few women fantasize about 'making love' with another woman, and some even act it out in a playful way in what has become known as 'lipstick lesbianism'. Such women don't sacrifice their sexual life with men – at least not permanently – they simply add on the pleasures of same-sex activities as a form of play. These games usually last for only a few weeks or months and the women I see who do this certainly don't label themselves as 'lesbian' in any meaningful way.

What characterizes true gay behaviour and practice, in my view, is when someone seeks out love and social connections with same-sex individuals. Almost no 'lipstick lesbians' claim to have a 'love affair' with their partner. And even fewer would dream of becoming part of the 'gay scene' except perhaps in a fun way to make a statement. And it is the same with men. Gay men are in love with other men, indeed they say they can only have a meaningful, love-bonded relationship with another man. No heterosexual guy who simply enjoys anal pleasures or fancies another man fleetingly ever says this or wants to become a part of the gay subculture.

There will always be a fascination for same-sex activities in some people, even if it's only in a stylized form in fantasy. If you think you'd like to act on such pleasures I suggest starting off with controlled game-playing in the safety of your heterosexual, one-to-one relationship rather than actually seeking out someone of the same sex, or diving headlong into the 'scene'.

In this way a woman could, for example, indulge her man's interest in anal play and even penetration by using a hand-held dildo, a strap-on dildo or a G-spot vibrator. And he can ask her what her same-sex fantasies involve and act on these, if she wants to. After all, some such individuals, of either sex, are aroused, intrigued or fascinated by particular erotic techniques and behaviours they associate only with same-sex relationships. Of course, they don't need to be restricted in this way.

If, after reading this, you still think you could be actually gay, you'll probably want to discuss your feelings with someone who really knows what they're talking about. I don't advise going to gay people to find answers because, like all social minorities, gays feel somewhat under siege and many have a need to evangelize and gather members into 'the club'. Some unsure individuals can soon find themselves drawn into the true world of gay life even though they don't really fit there. Some perfectly good heterosexual relationships have foundered unnecessarily because of this.

A few people who are married, or otherwise pair-bonded, say they'd like to experiment with the gay life. I think this is unwise unless they are very sure they're prepared for the consequences. Few individuals are prepared to stay married to someone who has an alternative 'gay life' as a hobby, and with HIV/AIDS being the problem it is, this is very wise. Whatever many gays may think, I feel it's advisable to contain one's 'gay' desires and 'needs' within a heterosexual relationship – mainly in fantasy – perhaps even aided by one's lover. Taking this interest, or even potential interest, outside the relationship is a step too far for most partners.

Hopefully, if one of you decides you really are gay, your partner will be able lovingly to accept it and let you go to start afresh. Many partners, though, find this almost impossible to deal with and feel cheated for all the 'wasted' years they spent with someone who really didn't want them heterosexually. It often helps explain their poor sex life over many years, and some find this helpful and reassuring.

ASK YOURSELF

▶ How would you feel if you were to think you were gay?

▶ What would you say to your partner about it?

▶ How would you feel if your partner declared they were gay?

▶ What is your experience of gay and bisexual people?

▶ How has your personal sexual history informed your views about all this?

▶ Would you really like to be bisexual, or even gay? How do you think this would advantage you, or your relationship?

▶ Do you feel in any way trapped in your heterosexual relationship? If so, how?

YOUR ACTION PLAN

Talk it through. Get your partner to go through the questions you've just answered and share your findings. This might be the first time in their lives they've had to confront such issues, whereas for you it could be a subject that's occupied your thinking or fantasy life for years. Take things very gently. Most partners feel terribly confused, betrayed, and baffled. Most heterosexual people simply can't understand the attraction of same-sex others, especially if it's an attraction that means they're out of a job! Anger may soon follow, so be aware of how rejecting your comments will appear from your lover's perspective.

'Shoulds' and 'Oughts'

Although related to 'Being "Right"' (see page 70), this is a different kind of relationship minefield.

However well we were raised, we end up as adults with a collection of 'shoulds' and 'oughts'. These, often perfectly conscious, scripts guide our daily behaviour with our partner, and others, and are underscored by many other unconscious ones. Together this raft of 'ways of being and behaving' guide our life minute by minute.

Many such precepts are, of course, useful and socially necessary. We 'should' drive on the correct side of the road or we'll get killed. We 'ought' to behave decently to others, if only because experience shows us that they then tend to do the same for us. Many 'shoulds' and 'oughts' make the world a better place and are valuable in our one-to-one relationships.

This said, once our 'shoulds' and 'oughts' start to rule us, once we see ourselves unquestioningly acting them out from unconsciously written historical scripts that no longer apply, we're in trouble. Problems come about because rather than believing that these long-held concepts are flexible, practical lessons handed down, unfiltered, from our parents, teachers and so on in early life, they appear to be moral tablets of stone that are immovable. We are now very close to being 'right' on such matters, which soon means our partner is wrong if they don't agree.

And this is never more acute than when we discover that – shock, horror! – our lover has a different collection of 'shoulds' and 'oughts'. Confusion reigns. Our life 'givens' are suddenly challenged and by someone we thought we knew well and want to 'be like'. The very truths by which we ran our life can seem threatened and we wonder if we've made the right choice in someone who clearly isn't working off the same script. This can be very upsetting, or worse.

Of course, the truth is we could *both* be right in our assumptions – after all, 'shoulds' and 'oughts' are assumptions, however apparently useful – or we could both be wrong! 'You should always be respectful to the elderly' is a typical 'should', but it is clear that not all elderly people deserve automatic respect unless you have it set as a tablet of stone that they 'should'. The trouble with 'shoulds' and 'oughts' is that they seem entirely self-evident to the owner but faintly ridiculous or improbable to outsiders.

'A woman who doesn't feel like sex should go along with her man's needs and, who knows, she might start enjoying it' is another sort of 'should'. 'I've just given birth and should feel loving and maternal towards my baby' is yet another. There are thousands of them.

I find it can be helpful to look at where such notions arise from in our past. Something that made perfect sense when you were a child could be total nonsense today. But doing this can be painful because it appears to create differences between you as a couple that could be hard to reconcile. Suddenly the peace you thought you shared is shattered by several, or even a mass of concepts that the other finds alien, and even alienating.

What's to be done? As with all notions of difference (see page 12) there are ways of tackling the issues without surrendering either your entire personality structure or your beliefs. And this is important to bear in mind because we aren't simply a collection of our beliefs. True, they have accumulated around us as a result of our experiences but some of these experiences are clearly flawed and so, as a result, are their associated 'shoulds' and 'oughts'. Therapists like me see individuals who were, for example, beaten as a child in the name of love. Their chastizing parent told them they were doing it only because they loved them. Such an individual then grows up believing that someone who really loves them will punish them 'for their own good'. It's easy to see that such a woman, for example, could unwittingly marry a sadistic man so her 'shoulds' on this level can be fulfilled. Likewise, someone who was punished for sex, say as an errant teenager, can come to enjoy it as an adult only if they are punished before or after, even if the punishment is only symbolic in the form of a sado-masochistic sex game. And so on. 'I should be punished for my sexual behaviour/needs/pleasures' is the 'should' here; and the 'ought' further reinforces the belief because 'If this is how I feel/behave, I not only "should" be punished, I *deserve* ("ought") to be punished'.

On a less sinister level millions of 'shoulds' and 'oughts' rule our lives with our partner. One patient of mine, even after many years of being with her man, still got thoroughly annoyed when he walked on the inside of the pavement when they were out together. Her 'ought' was that a respectful, caring man 'ought' to take the outside and act in a chivalrous way towards her. Every time he didn't do so she took it as a sign of his uncaring, unthinking behaviour and it blackened her view of him, if only for a moment.

ASK YOURSELF

▶ What was your family of origin's attitude to 'shoulds' and 'oughts'?

▶ In what way do you think you have brought these into your relationship?

▶ What are your views on punishment? How do these relate to your 'shoulds' and 'oughts'?

▶ What would you like to change about yourself to be able to deal better with this?

YOUR ACTION PLAN

How do your 'shoulds' and 'oughts' affect your life? Make a list of your 'shoulds' and 'oughts' and alongside this, one for your partner's. What does this tell you about yourself and why you chose your partner? How do these lists match and differ in significant areas of your life together?

One day when you're feeling loving, get your partner to create similar lists and discuss the similarities and differences. This can be a challenge! When I do this with couples I often find they strongly disagree about the other's 'shoulds' and 'oughts'!

Spiritual Alienation

Defining the word 'spiritual' can be difficult. But if this is hard, trying to say what our 'soul' means to us can be near impossible.

First, most of us have a rather personal definition of what we mean by the term 'spiritual'. To some it is linked inextricably to their religious beliefs and practices, and to others it has more to do with their inner connections with a 'higher being' and their part in the cosmos. Some individuals look at me as if I'm mad when I raise the subject, yet the majority of people in Western cultures today, according to surveys, claim to have some sort of spiritual beliefs, even if they aren't at all 'religious' in the traditional sense of the word.

For those who have a clearly defined and valued religion, choosing a partner who shares their beliefs and enthusiasm isn't just desirable but vital. They may see their earthly life together as part of a journey that doesn't necessarily end with death and, whatever their faith, want and need their partner to be a part of its daily practice and implementation. Such individuals put great importance on their faith and beliefs, and tend to run not only their personal lives by these precepts but also their significant relationships and their families. Troubles arise in such partnerships when one member can no longer subscribe to the same truths, or loses their faith entirely and 'goes off' all forms of religion. This can put huge strains on the relationship because not only is the remaining one terribly upset for their partner's loss (and the loss of their partner) but it can also mean their practical life changes as one, for example, refuses to go to formal worship any more. The couple that were until this moment part of, say, a Christian or Jewish community, now function rather differently and this reflects on their everyday life. Certain Christian denominations claim, 'The couple that prays together stays together.'

Problems also arise when one partner feels that because they experience spiritual matters in a certain way, their partner should too, or they aren't suited or compatible. It's possible to debate this long into the night, but it's usually pretty fruitless. I'm always encouraged when someone says they have deep spiritual beliefs, whether or not they are shared by their partner. The important thing is to be tolerant. Even if we do share a spiritual life together, who's to say we experience it in the same way? And should we? I don't think so. We are very different individuals – or we wouldn't have chosen one another in the first place – so why should we share the same experiences in exactly the same way? On the contrary, I have found in my personal and professional life that growth can occur when couples do *not* share things as if they were 'one'. We don't marry our clone, and this goes for our spiritual life, as elsewhere.

When it comes to larger, more loose, definitions of spirituality, difference can be tolerated more easily. Most people tell me they are attracted to someone who shares their general beliefs in this area, but aren't that bothered if the details of what they believe are different from theirs. It can be hard when a couple are out for a walk on a beautiful evening and one is profoundly moved by the sunset and the other simply sees it as a collection of pretty light patterns. The 'soul connection' the sunset-loving partner experiences cannot be shared with his or her partner and they can feel somewhat alienated. When people say they are 'soul mates' they mean, among other things, that this sort of experience touches them at their innermost core and that in doing so they feel more at one with each other. Such couples don't need to talk, they share such experiences at a profound level even, perhaps, when they are physically remote from one another. Of course, one doesn't need to be partnered with someone to experience this with another human being.

Most people are confused by what they mean by their 'soul'. When I ask people where they think their soul or 'spirit' resides in their body almost everyone holds their hand over their chest somewhere, be it heart or lungs. The English word for breathing in – inspiration – is a shortened form of 'in-spirit-ation'. It also has special significance in its other meaning: as in 'inspiring someone or something'. In this latter meaning we 'give life' to the situation. The ancients knew this and held that the essence of a person's soul had to do with breathing. The 'breath of life' is a well-known phrase and certainly at a biological level we cannot stop bringing this 'inspiritation' into our bodies or we physically die.

Most people I have asked feel, or believe, that their heart is the seat of their most important 'love' emotions and that their lungs are 'at the heart of' their 'soul business'. Synchronized breathing is a particularly soulful experience, as we will see in one of the exercises below.

There can be little doubt that couples that share 'soul stuff' do extremely well in the rest of their relationship. Whether this comes about through some sort of mystical connection, a common thread of the universe that runs through both of them, or because their shared religious beliefs unite them in a similar way, hardly matters. The outcome is the same. Such individuals feel bound by a much bigger bond than their mere behaviour towards one another, and experience a love that transcends the earthly trivia of daily life.

ASK YOURSELF

▶ How many of your partner's views on issues of 'soul and spirituality' do you share? What are they?

▶ What gets in the way of meeting one another on these issues?

▶ How would you like to alter things so as to have a more rewarding spiritual life – alone or together?

▶ What is it about *you* that gets in the way of achieving this?

YOUR ACTION PLAN

Synchronized breathing. Many of us are so 'uptight' in our relationships because our bodies are closed off to our partner – and indeed to ourselves. An exercise I find helpful, to release both emotions and body tensions, is synchronized breathing. This is rather like the breathing described on page 178 but goes further. In a sexually active couple, truly rewarding sex occurs only if they are attuned to one another in body and soul. This exercise helps achieve this.

In a warm, safe, uninterruptible setting, and when you are both feeling good about one another, get undressed and sit opposite one another on your haunches. Place your foreheads so they are touching and your hands on one another's shoulders. Shut your eyes and start breathing deeply. Each breath needs to come from your belly and go right to the top of your lungs. Breathe together in rhythm, accommodating your breath depth to match the size of your partner's chest. Continue this for as long as you want while you sense the unique connection with your lover. Many people tell me this is the only time they feel as if their souls are touching – outside having sex.

Talking of sex, next time you're making love, try this. Sit on, or astride, your man's erect penis, so it's very deep inside you. Don't move at all but both close your eyes and breathe very deeply as I've just described. This is especially effective if your chests are touching. Feel your sexual arousal moving up from your pelvis to your head. This can be helped by contracting your pelvic muscles. Now direct this energy down to your heart area. Keep on breathing as you 're-circulate' it to your vagina again. Many men complain that their lover withholds her sexual energies. This exercise helps dispel this. It also produces a sense of oneness and soul business that is unique.

Stress

This is an over-used word that means very different things to different people. Lots of people claim their one-to-one relationship is plagued by stress. They are, they say, too stressed to be nice to one another, to further their own and their partner's development, and perhaps even for sex.

So what is stress? Drawing a line between 'pressure' and 'stress' can be hard. Many people, probably most, function best when they are under some sort of pressure. Their expectations of themselves are high, they try harder, and they often get their best results when under a certain degree of it. This feels normal for many people and can indeed be so. It is almost certainly healthy.

At some point, though, this pressure can escalate into something less positive and even rather dangerous. The body and mind now start to suffer because of the 'pressures' placed upon them and we feel truly 'stressed'. Of course, the level at which one individual feels actual stress and another just helpful, creative 'pressure' varies hugely. Some people are amazed at the high levels of what they would call stress others can tolerate, or even thrive on. At the other end of the scale are those who are so used to stress they see it as normal – which it is not.

When we get truly stressed we start to malfunction. The body's normal response to stress of any kind is to produce more hormones such as cortisol and adrenaline. These increase our heart rate, raise our blood pressure, increase our metabolic rate, and get us ready for 'fight or flight'. When all this is working well, and at moderate levels, we continue to function well enough. But at a certain level our body and mind start to fail us. And if we are continually exposed to high levels of these hormones we can become anxious or depressed as a way of life.

Causes of stress in a couple's life include money, children, work or lack of it, the relationship itself, problems with in-laws, affairs, divorce, deaths in the family, and so on. The response of any one individual is unique to them.

Some people appear to thrive in such stressful situations, they become more energized and pro-active, their best personality characteristics come to the fore and they manage crises well. Others fall apart and become helpless and hopeless. Most of us lie somewhere between these two extremes.

The trouble with stress within a relationship is that whatever caused the stress in the first place affects us both at the same time. For example, if our child is diagnosed with leukaemia, or our family business goes bust, we both have to face up to the stresses and challenges. This can be harder than when one of us has a stressful situation that doesn't directly affect the other. In the latter one of us can help, support, nurture, and love, while our partner becomes more stable, and weathers the emotional storm.

Problems are greatest for couples when the stresses they experience find the cracks in their relationship — cracks that were, of course, already there but had been papered over. It's now that such a couple experiences real strife, starts blaming one another, hits out emotionally or even physically, and generally regresses to less than constructive behaviours that are bound to damage their relationship.

But this is exactly what most of us tend to do. When the going gets really tough we tend to resort to our worst coping strategies because they are so deeply ingrained and primitive within us. Our partner is handily there to act as a punchbag (see page 286) and we take our stresses out on them.

So it is that under stress some people start to get depressed, others to act out their pains from the past in socially disruptive ways (perhaps by having an affair, or taking to drinking, drug taking or gambling), others to be continually anxious (not sleeping, feeling edgy, being unable to relax, having always to be on the go), and yet others to feel physically ill all the time, and so on. People usually think of stress as a disorder of the mind, but the body suffers greatly too. Part of this scenario is that sex starts to become less frequent, less enjoyable, and eventually perhaps even impossible. Many impotent men claim stress is at the heart of their problem and many a stressed woman says she never feels like sex. If sex were the glue that was holding things together in our relationship, its loss at a time when we need glue more than ever is not only sad but destructive.

But so-called stress can, in fact, be many other things. Many people who are angry, full of rage, guilty or ashamed, frustrated, depressed, anxious, lonely, grieving, bankrupt, physically ill, suffering from a chronic medical condition, and many other things, all say they are stressed but often don't realize what's at the seat of their stress. For some who have very poor housing or very little money, perhaps combined with poor social and coping skills, just existing is stressful. It is hardly surprising that such couples find it hard to maintain their one-to-one relationships.

This said, I find that many middle-class couples who see them-selves as being a million miles away from this helpless/homeless stereotype can be just as stressed – or even more so – than their under-benefited brothers and sisters. Goals that are set too high, unrealistic expectations of themselves and others, 'keeping up with the Joneses', and the inexorable desire and expectation that life will get better and better, are just a few things I see time and again with middle-class and professional couples. When they fall even a little short in any area of life, things get stressful, largely because they are walking a business, financial, emotional, relationship, and family tightrope. The dividing line between this apparently 'enchanted lifestyle' and disaster may be only a heartbeat away.

Modern life, then, is bound to be stressful. The only things we can do are to stress-proof ourselves as best we can and to learn how to cope with stress once it hits us. The exercises below should help a little.

Look up the various topics in this book that apply to you, when stressed, and see if you can change things.

ASK YOURSELF

▶ Are you aware of how stress affects your life?
▶ How do you make the distinction, for yourself, between pressure and true stress?
▶ How does your partner's stress affect their life?
▶ How does your partner's stress affect your life?

▶ How do you contribute to your partner's stress?

▶ How does he or she contribute to yours?

▶ Are you more or less stressed in this relationship than in others?

▶ What do you think your stress is really all about?

▶ How would you feel if someone said they were magically able to remove all your stresses from you tomorrow?

▶ How would this affect your life?

YOUR ACTION PLAN

There are many ways of de-stressing yourself but in a book such as this I can give only a few pointers. If your problem is that your *partner* is very stressed, then help them by going through this list and finding ways you could do things together that would help.

Find new ways to relax. There are many ways of relaxing and you may find that your idea of what's relaxing will differ greatly from that of your partner. Try to do something that's really relaxing every day. Here are some ideas: going to a movie; watching TV; receiving a massage; giving a massage; listening to, or making, music; gardening; sex; reading; cooking and eating; phoning a friend; having a cuddle; having a bath; having your hair done. It's worth thinking about how you could relax more or in different ways. Most of us are rather limited in what we do to unwind. Talk to your partner about things you could do together.

Practise deep breathing. When you feel under pressure, put your hand on your stomach and take a slow deep breath in. This will make your hand rise a little. Exhale slowly, letting your hand subside. Take around six of these deep breaths, making sure that you fill right up to the very top of your lungs each time. Repeat the cycle if necessary.

You'll be surprised just how effective this can be in a moment of feeling even very stressed.

Progressive muscular relaxation. For this you need to find a quiet, warm place and preferably to sit or lie down. Start by breathing deeply 'into your stomach'. Check by placing your hand on your stomach and then seeing it go up and down. Repeat this for a while until you feel relaxed.

Now firmly clench your foot muscles for three or four seconds, holding your breath as you do so. Now relax your feet, letting go of your breath at the same time.

Repeat this cycle but now with your calf muscles.

Work up the whole of your body, area by area, slowly contracting and relaxing all your muscles in a systematic sequence.

At the end, sit quietly for a few minutes, or even sleep for a while.

Stress management strategies. It's not just a matter of learning how to relax. There are many other factors that need addressing if you want to stress-proof your life.

Try working on these alone and/or with your partner. Every one of them has proven effects: eat healthily; eat regularly; reduce your caffeine intake; take daily exercise; get enough sleep; make time to play; find a hobby; go on vacation; spoil yourself; be free with laughing and crying; spend time in meditation or prayer; make your surroundings more attractive; have realistic expectations (page 282); boost your self-esteem; challenge 'shoulds' and 'oughts' (page 266); see stress as a challenging opportunity to learn; learn to say no; dwell on positives rather than negatives; tolerate situations you can't change; separate thoughts from feelings; don't jump to conclusions or make assumptions; accept yourself; be assertive rather than passive (see page 244); improve your decision-making skills; set realistic deadlines; delegate; nurture your one-to-one and other intimate relationships; nurture your friendships; enlist the help of friends; get professional help if you need it.

Unplanned Pregnancy

It's impossible to know what percentage of babies is born unplanned but about one-third is a commonly accepted figure. It is probably much more. Many of these pregnancies are subsequently accepted. Abortion is the way the rest are dealt with.

Increasing numbers of children throughout the Western world are born out of wedlock and this is becoming more socially acceptable. Many women have extra-marital affairs and, as I have already mentioned, genetic testing shows that just under one-third of all children cannot possibly have the father they appear to have. (See 'Children', page 96.) Clearly there's a lot of reproduction going on that isn't what it seems! This is largely because women are more biologically promiscuous than are men. This has been known since time began and is why men throughout history have tried to control the sexuality of women.

Whenever I talk about unwanted pregnancies, people throw their hands up in horror and harangue me about the scandal of teen brides and gymslip pregnancies. In reality these are very few compared with the numbers of unwanted babies born to married women.

So why, in an age of apparently successful and readily available contraception, do women still have so many unwanted or unplanned pregnancies?

Bad luck. Some women claim to have repeated bad luck with their contraceptive methods. Scant psychological work with such women shows this is nonsense. Most such women in fact get pregnant to show their love for their man, to add satisfaction to their relationship, or to secure a failing one. Sometimes it is to replace a lost child, or even a lost boyfriend. Women who have repeated 'bad luck' usually turn out to really want a baby at some level, however unconscious. Some never really settle down with any contraceptive method – and claim they are all 'useless'. An underlying cause can almost always be found to explain these so-called 'bad luck' or method failure women.

Depression. This can lead to carelessness over contraception. Other depressed women hope a baby will 'cure' them.

Uncertainty over sexual identity. A few women seek to prove they are really female by having a baby.

To punish their parents or their partner. If a girl has very repressive parents she can get pregnant to spite them. Some women in later life get pregnant 'by accident' to get back at their husband or partner for some wrongdoing, misdemeanour, or shortcoming.

Wanting fun before settling down or later in life. Some young women take contraceptive chances before getting married and some middle-aged women do the same in a reproductive 'panic' when they see the menopause beckoning.

Personality problems. Some women who have repeated unwanted pregnancies have problems seeing themselves as the source of their plight. They can always convince themselves it's someone else's fault, or that they have persistent, inexplicable method failures.

Partner reasons. Although most unwanted pregnancies are the result of issues within the woman herself, some are created by their partner. Some men, consciously or unconsciously, want to test or prove their own fertility; to demonstrate their virility, to themselves or others; to save or secure their relationship; to add to their personal status; to give their partner something to worry about or to get her off their back; to punish her for some reason; to exert power and control over her; to replace a dead child or one 'lost' through divorce or separation; because they don't like her chosen method of contraception; because they are emotionally immature; or because they fear that her using a reliable method such as the Pill would encourage her to be sexually active with other men.

Psychosexual issues. There are many possible conscious and unconscious factors in women who get pregnant when they know they shouldn't. The biological imperative to reproduce is deep-seated in almost all women, whatever their brain tells them. In addition to this, some women, even today, feel that sex is really about babies and so cannot justify, or perhaps even truly enjoy, sex that isn't linked to the possibility of getting pregnant. A few women believe that deep down, sex is bad or sinful, and that getting unwantedly pregnant is a punishment for their 'wicked appetites' and pleasures. Some women see sex as something that men 'do to them' and so don't bother with contraception because to do so would be a contradiction. Some women who have problems accepting their sexuality get drunk, or use social drugs to relieve themselves of the responsibility for their actions. A teenage girl who has recently started having sex can misuse it to win or keep a boyfriend; to keep up with her peer group; to prove to herself or others that she is a 'real woman' rather than a 'silly girl'; to punish her parents; to provide an interest in an otherwise dull and unrewarding life; to get her out of the education system; to create someone who will love her more than she feels she is currently loved; as a route to a home through public housing; to live out her mother's desire for a baby for herself; or even, perhaps, to prove she is a 'virgin' (by not using contraception she kids herself she isn't really having sex). I have seen many 'part-time' virgins. Such young women believe they are virgins even though they have sex from time to time. Obviously as one is a virgin one doesn't need contraception, they argue.

ASK YOURSELF

▶ How have you contributed to your unplanned pregnancy?
▶ How has your partner contributed to it?
▶ What has the unplanned pregnancy taught you about your relationship?

▶ What has the pregnancy taught you about yourself?

▶ How do you intend to ensure it doesn't happen again?

▶ How could your partner help with this?

YOUR ACTION PLAN

Coping with an abortion. How you do this will depend on many things, including your personality type. Some people, of either sex, go about their daily life as if almost nothing has happened and others grieve for many months, or longer. Try to give one another all the support you can. This can be hard because with other bereavements you can usually enlist the support and love of other family members and friends. Many couples grieve their aborted child alone, and this can put strains on the relationship. Remember it may not (just, or even) be the woman who's feeling down. Many women I've dealt with fare a lot better than their men in these circumstances. It's his loss too, don't forget. Listen empathically to one another to see what's really going on. There'll be many lessons to be learned about your relationship, if only you're open to hearing them. Seek professional help if things get too deep for you to manage.

Unreasonable Expectations

Unreasonable expectations abound in intimate relationships. We live, as we have seen, in a culture that makes young people believe that the sort of love they feel early on will continue 'for ever and ever', just like in the movies and romantic fiction.

To be fair, though, it's not just society that's responsible for this. We do it to ourselves too as we invest our love, hopes, and future in someone special. We tend to idealize both them and the relationship in general and this soon leads to expectations that can't be realized. To some extent this is healthy and desirable. We need to believe that our relationship has almost infinite potential if we are to persuade ourselves it's worthwhile investing everything in it to make it succeed. Unless we thought, or at least hoped, all this was going to be worthwhile, we wouldn't bother. And in a culture that puts great stress on making a partner choice and sticking with it, perhaps we have to fool ourselves, or just have faith, that everything will turn out not just well but really well, in order to make such a commitment at all.

All this makes it hard to differentiate between unrealistic expectations and perfectly reasonable hopes and aspirations.

There are many areas where our expectations can fall short. Here is just a tiny selection.

I EXPECT MY PARTNER TO:

▶ **Make me happy.** If we marry someone on the basis that their 'job' is to make us happy, we're in for a bad surprise. No one should take this burden on their shoulders. The only person who can make us happy is ourself.

▶ **Be completely reliable.** No one can be 100 per cent reliable. We ourselves can't promise to be so for our partner, so why should we demand or expect it of them?

▶ **Put out the rubbish.** Don't bank on it.

▶ **Be really intimate.** Intimacy doesn't just happen. It has to be grown and worked at over many years together. Many couples never experience it over a whole lifetime. If we 'expect' it to just 'happen', we're in for a serious disappointment.

▶ **Give me a great sex life.** This, like intimacy, takes time and effort. We might get lucky and happen upon a 'good enough' sex life but anything more will mean making an investment.

▶ **Be a soul mate.** This will only follow high levels of intimacy and trust. Some couples find that building their spiritual life together helps here.

▶ **Be someone I can trust absolutely.** No one can be trusted absolutely. Human beings will always let us down somehow, some time, however rarely.

▶ **Be totally faithful.** Almost everyone is unfaithful in some way, even if it's only in the mind.

▶ **Be honest and decent.** No matter how decent anyone is, they'll be open to temptations in life and may succumb to behaviours that aren't typical of them.

▶ **Be a good parent to our children.** Who knows? Whatever our partner says at the start, he or she might not even *want* to have children when it comes to it. And none of us can know what sort of parents we'll make when we eventually have children.

▶ **Want what I want.** Let's hope they don't *only* want what we want or life will be very boring. Hopefully there'll be enough difference to keep things fun and growing.

▶ **Know me better than I know myself.** Not likely. However insightful our partner is it's unlikely they'll be able to do this for us. And we definitely can't rely on them being able to do so.

▶ **Rescue me from life's pains.** We are the only one who can deal with our pain. We cannot and should not expect our lover to do this for us, even if they might help.

▶ **Take over where my parents left off.** Although it's tempting to think a loving wife could make up for imperfect mothering and a husband for less-than-ideal fathering, this isn't a healthy model on which to run an adult relationship.

▶ **Rescue me.** Hopefully not. Only we can rescue ourselves.

▶ **Help me grow.** Maybe, but don't bank on it. Unless you have a truly intimate relationship you'll find you are living, however pleasantly, alongside one another, growing at your own respective rates. If you *are* being truly intimate with your partner you might grow as a result of this, but not because he or she is being intimate with you. Growth occurs only by you being intimate and truly yourself in your partner's presence. They don't do it *to* you!

▶ **Change my life.** This expectation will definitely come true, however you define change. Most people who say this to me, though, mean, 'make wonderful changes to my life that I couldn't do for myself'. This is a false hope and smells of rescuing.

▶ **Create a better marriage for me than my parents had.** Unlikely, I'm afraid. Perhaps you'll be able to create this as a team but your partner alone won't be able to do it.

So where does all this leave us? It's impossible to enter into any new situation without *any* expectations, be it working for a new boss, buying a new car, moving home, making a new friendship, or agreeing to spend the rest of your life with someone! But in my opinion, it's better to err on the side of starting with a clean slate than slowly ticking off, however unconsciously, the failed expectations as the years go by. In a way it's an arrogance to 'expect' anything from our lover. After all, we can only hope and try to do our best for them. Why should we expect more of them than we can possibly deliver ourselves? This is neither honest nor honourable.

How much better to say, 'This is me being wholly me. I'm starting off with you being wholly you. Where it will take us, I have no idea, but wherever it is I want to be there with you.'

ASK YOURSELF

▶ In what ways do you think your life together is dogged by unreasonable expectations?

▶ Which of you is the more 'guilty' of this?

▶ What do you think is at the heart of these unrealistic expectations?

▶ What would you like to be able to do to run your life on a more realistic basis?

▶ What's stopping you doing this?

YOUR ACTION PLAN

Assessing unrealistic expectations. Look above at my list of expectations. Copy them on to a piece of paper, plus any others of importance to you that come to mind, and then rate them from 1 to 5 according to how strong such an expectation is in your life.

Now look at the highest-scoring items and see what patterns jump out at you. For example, do most of your unrealistic expectations have to do with yourself or your partner? Or the relationship? Do most of them arise from childhood things? How does your current relationship stand up to scrutiny on these issues compared with others you've experienced? Is this making you count the cost? And so on.

Using Your Partner As An Emotional Punchbag

It is easy to create and perpetuate bad behaviours in our relationship, behaviours that we wouldn't dream of exhibiting elsewhere. Using our partner as an emotional punchbag is one such.

In this we, usually unconsciously, to be fair, lay into our lover as if they were some sort of devil, or our very worst enemy rather than our best friend. Once we get into the 'feel' of this behaviour it can be hard to stop, especially if our partner doesn't draw a line that makes us stop.

Such attacks are usually out of all proportion to the issue being dealt with and we resort to all kinds of underhand tactics, including character assassination and undermining our partner's self-worth, to make our point. What started off as an argument at best, or even frank aggression at worst, now becomes a full-scale war. An issue that could have been settled with an air pistol brings out the Exocet missiles.

The thing is that we all know deep down exactly what to say, or do, to our partner to cause them the most pain. Sometimes this can be achieved without even appearing hostile. It might take the form of being silent, cutting off sex, being passive-aggressive (see page 244), avoiding them, and so on. But the message is the same – I loathe, condemn, and am disgusted by you.

Once communicated, these sorts of feelings are hard, or impossible, to undo. Some people say they can't ever forgive their partner for having said such things. They remember them for a lifetime, and it alters their whole relationship. Other victims of such behaviour are able to withstand the character assassination, or whatever form the abuse takes, but withdraw into themselves and build up more emotional armour (see page 127). A part of the relationship has died.

The trouble is that when we're feeling and behaving like this, it isn't really our partner we're being horrid to. It's almost always someone significant from our past about whom we feel, say, murderously angry. In this 'as if' relationship we vent our deep, unconscious pains from the past, spewing them over our partner for reasons they can't understand. All they know is they don't deserve it, didn't ask for it, and don't want it. They can't be expected to be a psychoanalyst at that moment – they just feel attacked and hurt.

To be fair, we too later feel terribly hurt, ashamed, guilty and much more when we act like this. We can't explain to ourselves, let alone anyone else, why it is we felt so awful, hateful, vengeful, loathing, murderous, or whatever. We also feel helpless and hopeless at the time as our emotions take us over in a way that's scary and out of control. What, we fear, might we do? Could we actually kill our partner, or hurt them physically? Could we damage ourselves by lashing out at a table, a wall, or whatever? Might we give ourselves a heart attack, or burst a blood vessel? All we know at that moment is we being absolutely foul to our dearest person.

Look at page 12 and see what I say about pairing with your shadow. If, as I assert, we unconsciously choose someone who'll help us work on our inner demons, it's not surprising that we unwittingly project our worst possible characteristics onto someone else and then take it out on them. Of course, while we're doing this, it's impossible to be aware of this unconscious mechanism.

Perhaps there is no way of short-cutting such outbursts on these hellish occasions. Perhaps the only way our partner can deal with us is to bear in mind at the outbreak of such hostilities that it is not *they* who are the real target. This can be hard but it's vital if you're on the receiving end of such behaviour to separate yourself emotionally and even physically from the source. If, as is usually the case, your partner is acting out an 'as if' relationship from the past, you don't have to stay and be the blank screen onto which they project all their hell. When the warfare ceases you can calm them, love them, and help them return to a stable state. In the heat of the battle you cannot hope to do this – and I advise you don't ever even try. I have had patients in this state nearly kill me, and I'm six foot six!

ASK YOURSELF

▶ How do you use your lover as an emotional punchbag?

▶ How do they use you as one?

▶ Have you ever felt you might actually harm your partner physically? How did you handle this?

▶ What help do you think you'd need to be sure this would never happen?

▶ In what ways have you let your relationship become emotionally lazy and self-indulgent?

YOUR ACTION PLAN

Knowing which of your partner's buttons to push. Make a list of the areas of your partner's life about which you know they are especially sensitive. You'll be able to identify these because you'll have unwittingly hurled them at your partner on many occasions in the heat of the moment. It might be their: religion (as in, 'You Jewish bastard'); weight ('You fat cow'); sex drive ('You impotent bastard'); height ('You little man'); looks ('You ugly bitch'); money ('You mean cow'); parenting ('Call yourself a father?'); and so on. If you ever hear yourself saying anything like this in a sneering tone, or catch yourself being sarcastic, cynical or condescending, you'll know you're on to something important.

Now you're aware of what you're doing you can take steps to avoid it. Much of this sort of thing is pure self-indulgence and you can stop it if you want to. Ask yourself just what good such insults are doing either of you. Does any such behaviour get you a better result? I doubt it. So, apart from the fact that it's familiar behaviour, why continue with it? It's vital to find other ways of expressing your anger, frustration, and pain. How about taking yourself away from your partner when you feel like this? Try doing something else, such as going for a walk, or even hitting a pillow in another room.

Stop yourself being used as an emotional punchbag. I know it's hard but try to bear in mind that when your lover is 'punching out' at you, they aren't being strong, they're being weak. At that moment they may not know any other way to behave. And right then you can't hope to teach them. The only thing you can do is to get out (see page 55). Some people can shut off so they hear nothing and thus have a sort of 'internal' time-out whilst remaining in the room. Others need actually to remove themselves from their partner's presence until they have calmed down and started to behave reasonably. Do whatever works for you. But don't under any circumstances stay there to be emotionally punched further. By removing yourself from your irrational partner you disable them from their self-indulgent behaviour and rob them of their power.

Needless to say, if any of this results in actual physical damage to you, it's time to consider getting out altogether. People who abuse their partner in this way rarely stop unless given a tough ultimatum. You will never change such a person, however contrite they appear afterwards.

Victims, Rescuers and Tyrants

This subject is a potential minefield of which every loving couple should be aware.

Within every one of us are fragments of various different personality types. None of us is all one thing or another. Of course, there are hundreds of different personality characteristics that are present in human beings, but there are three main ones that get in the way of an intimate lifestyle. Most of us exhibit at least one of these traits and some of us have all of them operating at full tilt the whole time.

A *rescuer*, in this model, is someone who focuses on the needs and ills of others. More rescuers are female than male. They quickly home in on those who need fixing and take them over. They can't avoid others with pain and they move in to help. They find difficulty sharing, or even recognizing, their own woundedness and, as a result, appear to others to be 'together', or even 'saintly' people.

Such an 'over-functioning' individual often pairs up (quite unconsciously, of course) with someone who needs their services. This is the *victim*. To the entire world the rescuer appears to function better and be stronger than the victim but this isn't in fact so. Rescuers spend much of their life turning their psychic spotlight outwards on others for fear of turning it in on themselves and seeing the trouble there. Rescuing is an unconscious defence mechanism that protects us from knowing our inner pains.

Victims feel negative about themselves a lot of the time, believe others think badly of them, turn their pains inwards and become angry or depressed, feel unworthy of improvements in their lives, unconsciously seek out rescuers to do their emotional work for them, and generally hide their woundedness in inertia. They are a magnetic attraction for rescuers!

A *tyrant* is someone who seeks, unconsciously, to punish others or themselves.

Now imagine a triangle with each of these types at a corner. Most of us function in one major mode but can, with some alacrity, speed off into one or other of the other two. Scratch the surface of a rescuer and you'll find a victim. Provoke a victim and out comes the tyrant. And so on.

Deprive someone of their role in one corner of their triangle and he or she will soon occupy another and start to act out their pain in that particular way.

Now let's complicate matters further and bring the real world into play. Imagine another triangle super-imposed on the original one. This second triangle has the same labels at each corner but doesn't line up with the first one. Let's assume your triangle was the first one, the second one is your partner's. Now it's easy to see that while you are being mainly a rescuer, for example, he might be obliging you by being a victim, or he may be in tyrant mode. The way these two triangles overlap in any one minute, hour or day varies all the time, producing rather different results.

A woman may, for example, have started off her married life with an unconscious need to be punished in some way for something. This suits her man well because he wheels out his tyrant and duly 'punishes' her. But as she matures in her thirties and her original need wanes, she finds it tiresome and unnecessary. Now he can't play his tyrant card any more and their relationship has to change. Perhaps he now starts acting like the victim he really is deep down. She now zaps into rescuer mode and they play another game for a few months, or years.

Such couples often say how close they are. But they are never truly intimate (see page 190). This is because their 'closeness' is based on unconscious game-playing that arises out of both of their old hurts. As we have seen, intimacy results only from two people being truly themselves in each other's presence. When our triangles overlap so our victimness is being dealt with by our partner's rescuer, for example, things can feel comfortable and familiar. But they are not healthy.

The bottom line here is to sort out how you both function in these models and then to start on the royal road to discovering the origins of your victimness so you can go some way to healing the original pains that made this entire, elaborate triangle necessary in the first place.

As each of you acknowledges your pain you can now stop rescuing and be truly helpful; stop punishing and start learning how to encourage one another; and stop being a helpless victim as you both teach one another how to survive and grow in more positive ways. This is a huge task and can take many years. But it's worth it, even if it needs professional help. This said, many couples can produce excellent results on their own. Working with the rest of this book will definitely assist you on your journey.

ASK YOURSELF

▶ Which do you think you are most of the time: rescuer, victim, or tyrant?

▶ Which is your partner, most of the time?

▶ When you are acting at your worst, which are you?

▶ When you partner is at his or her worst, what is s/he?

▶ How do you think this way of behaving has damaged your personal relationships in general – not just with your partner?

▶ How do you think it specifically affects your relationship with your partner?

▶ How do you think it affects your sex life together?

▶ What would you most like to change about yourself in all this?

YOUR ACTION PLAN

Recognize which role you're in. This can take time to get good at. Try to look down on yourself from the outside, as if you were in a helicopter, and become aware of which role you are in at any one moment. By getting good at recognizing when you are acting as victim, rescuer, or tyrant, you'll be able to curb your behavioural and emotional excesses and will help your partner and the relationship by stopping dangerous games getting out of hand.

Recognize which role your partner is in. Repeat the above exercise but now trying to identify your partner's role in that moment. Try really hard not to mirror this role, or indeed to snap into an 'opposite' role. For example, you may well be able to pick up that your partner is being a 'victim' in that moment. This is good but it's only really helpful to your relationship if you then ensure that you don't try to rescue or tyrannize them.

Recognize historical roles. One day when you're feeling calm, sit down with a piece of paper and write down a list of occasions in your relationship when you thought things were going badly. Now alongside this list, try to identify which of you was in which role at the time. Look at this and use it to think about which types of situations in life generally you react to in which mode (victim/rescuer/tyrant). Try to gain some real insights into how you and your partner interact in this way. Share these findings if you want to.

When Love Dies

Most of us think we are in love when we settle down to start a relationship. And we are probably right. It appears that our love will last for ever. It is unique, indestructible, and will outlast anything anyone else has, whatever the setbacks. This kind of love can often be a sort of 'sickness' and not real love at all.

And this is the problem I find with individuals who say their love for one another has died. It usually means that their Hollywood romantic model has died and they have nothing to put in its place. They now have to live in the real world with a real individual, the rose-tinted spectacles are off and they don't like what they see.

Of course, someone in this situation may be right. It could be that once truly back in the world they realize that they have chosen the wrong person. If I had my way such risks would be greatly reduced because I would forbid people to commit themselves in the early, heady days of romantic love. It is simply all too overwhelming and dampens or destroys our critical faculties. We deserve better and so does our partner.

Unfortunately, some people, women especially, are in love with love. Unless they are 'suffering' for their love in the Hollywood sense they aren't, by their definition, really in love. Yet, they complain to me, such love always dies and the story repeats itself time and again with man after man. Most such people have never experienced intimacy, growth or true, selfless love. Their love is self-focused and they get off on this 'drug' that makes them high. Indeed, some say it is like a true addiction, and it is. Like all addictions it can't be dealt with without insight and a sincere desire to change. And many women I see with this addiction don't want to change. They are determined to prove me, and everybody else, wrong by searching for the perfect romantic relationship that will prove the Hollywood theory right – if only for them! Alas, such a search can last a lifetime and many such women feel alone, if not lonely, unable to experience intimacy, and suffer a permanent yearning for completeness. Eventually they give up on men as a lost cause.

This is primitive psychological stuff and is usually an unconscious retreat from intimacy and connectedness. Many such people tell of remote parents (especially mothers) as they search in adult life for a 'perfect' relationship to make up for the original, idealized, one they never experienced in childhood. Needless to say no real-life man can ever match up to their unconscious shopping list of requirements, so he gets dumped. Such women appear so loving, so needy and so desirable that many men fall for them, only to realize that the woman is on a self-destructive search that can end only in tears.

Of course, true love can also die. If our partner has an affair, or betrays our trust in some other serious way, it can be hard to keep love alive. Apart from extremely serious or criminal issues, though, most such hurts and betrayals are possible to be coped with if true love can be expressed through forgiveness. For more on forgiveness, see page 163.

ASK YOURSELF

▶ What, in your view, is the link between love and romantic love?
▶ What are your experiences of people's love for you dying?
▶ How do you think you contribute(d) to this happening?
▶ Do you think you choose partners who are incapable of true love? If yes, why do you think you do this?
▶ What are your experiences of your love for people dying?
▶ What do you think about the lasting nature of love?

YOUR ACTION PLAN

How well do you love your partner? Make a list of the five things that are most important to your partner. Describe to yourself how, on a daily basis, you help your partner feel loved, fulfilled, and joyful in these areas. Tell yourself how you feel about the effort you put into doing this. Discuss all this with your partner.

How well does your partner love you? How does your partner actively encourage your growth, further your interests and values, and show their love for you each day? Does your partner involve you in his or her activities, or do you feel somewhat of a burden in their lives? Does your partner tend to make their decisions with your needs in mind? Think all this through and then discuss it together.

When you've done this you'll be ready for some more searching stuff to work on. How do you feel most loved by your partner? What behaviour from him or her makes you feel most loved? In what ways would you want to be more loving to your partner? How does he or she prevent you from doing this? How do you prevent yourself from doing this? There's many an hour of great material here to work on.

How well do you understand one another's 'love languages'? One of the interesting things about being a relationship therapist is seeing how differently people 'show' love to one another. Most couples have never thought how they differ in these matters yet to an outsider it can be so obvious. There are basically three main patterns: seeing; hearing; and touching. Go through this section and see how it can get you talking about things. It should help you see why you miss one another in your very real and well-meaning expressions of love. The secret is not to express your love in *your* way (that you'd like it expressed to you) but in the way that your lover needs and wants (that is meaningful to him or her).

Visual love language people say: '*Show* me you love me.' They want to receive cards with meaningful words and messages in them. Love receiving flowers, and other visual demonstrations of love. Like to get presents beautifully wrapped, and meal tables that are a delight to look at. Are turned on by visual stimuli such as good clothes, great lingerie, and so on. Use lots of visual phrases and metaphors such as 'If you see my point'; 'I can see right through him'; 'I've seen the light'; and so on. Learn best and get sexually turned on by watching. Like sexy videos and pictures. Have an active fantasy life. Like movies. Like things to be neat and tidy.

Hearing love language people say: '*Tell* me you love me.' They need to hear the words 'I love you'. Talk a lot and have loads of opinions. Feel that everything can be sorted out by talking about it. Use auditory phrases and metaphors such as 'Hear me out'; 'Just listen to me'; 'We need to talk about this', and so on. Use the telephone a lot (especially their mobile phone). Work off the model 'if you love me you'll talk to me'. Love music and poetry. Listen to the radio a lot. Are sensitive to the tone of voice of other people. Talk to themselves. Get turned on by romantic/sexy talk. Go on and on when arguing, not knowing when to stop. Talk when stressed. Try to have the last word.

Touch love language people feel loved only if they're being touched. They cannot imagine a loving relationship without lots of touch (sexual or not). Like the notion of 'being in touch' with one another's souls, not just bodies. Have gut reactions to situations and people. Feel things in their bodies. Dress for comfort rather than to impress. Hug and touch people whenever possible. Feel that talking about relationships is largely unnecessary. Respond to stress by working on their bodies. Enjoy sports and other physical activities. Like action movies. Learn by doing. Are spontaneous. Look for physical reassurance in times of stress.

It's fairly obvious that if we don't read our partner's love language accurately we're in trouble. Look at these lists and discuss where you both fit and how you could modify your loving life to better answer your partner's needs.

It's not the end of the world. Just because your love for one another has died, there's lots of living left to be done. You can show your love for others, or become more aware of their love for you. Your partner doesn't have to be the only person in the world who relates to you in a loving way. Many people never even expect their one-to-one relationship to meet all their needs for love. If you decide to stay together for other reasons you can get these needs met elsewhere. This doesn't mean having an affair, of course, because that could damage your relationship. Also, be warned that even though you think that love has died, it may not have. It's amazing how things can re-kindle with even the slightest provocation, personal effort, or professional help. This book is full of ideas that will help.

Work and No Work

We all like to feel fulfilled, wanted, stimulated, rewarded, and to have purpose and status. Work gives us the opportunity to obtain all these things – and to be paid for it!

The subject is vast so I'll look here at just some of the things that can go wrong in a couple's relationship.

There are three main issues, as I see it. Women going out to work if they have a family; either partner being out of work when they want to be employed; and retirement.

Most family women probably go out to work because they perceive the family needs the money. I say 'perceive' because it may only be a perception. Just how many women have to work to keep body and soul together for their family, I have no idea. What I do know is that most couples get used to having two incomes before they start a family and then find it hard, or unattractive, to settle for the sort of lifestyle that only one will afford them. Some women don't like to feel completely dependent financially on their partners and so work to be more self-sufficient. This in itself can be a source of friction if their man sees himself as 'the breadwinner'.

Today's younger woman doesn't usually see raising a family as 'enough' of a validation of her life skills, intelligence, or training, for example, and so looks to the workplace to increase her sense of self-worth. Being 'only' a mum carries with it little or no status today, so it's hardy surprising that most women want to return to the workplace once they have a family. The pros and cons of women working with a young family have been hugely debated and I won't go into them here. Suffice it to say that I believe, from clinical experience of dealing with people of all ages, that the best outcomes *for children* occur when they have their mother at home for the first few years. More than this I won't get drawn into!

But when you return to work it's not just your children that will have a view. Your man will have *his* life changed too. He may see your going back as a sign that you are dissatisfied, not just with your domestic set-up, but also with him. Many men tell me they fear their partner will find another man. It suits many men that their wives are out of the sex marketplace for many years. Some guys are jealous of their partner's new job. Some say she seems to have leap-frogged him, given the number of years she has been away from the workplace. Some fear the amount of domestic work they'll now be expected to do. Others see it as a definite curb on their free time, hobbies, and other interests. Others fear their partner will be so tired that they'll come even lower on her list of priorities than they already feel they do. Many men tell me they fear sex will suffer as her time and energy for it diminishes. Of course, some women go back to work for exactly this (largely unconscious) reason, The more absorbed or tired they are, the easier they can avoid sex, perhaps even the risk of more babies.

All this is a minefield for the average couple, even if they usually get on really well. The thing is that the fears both have are based in reality. Whatever the rewards for the woman, or her man, there are high prices to be paid for trying to run two careers and a family. There simply isn't enough time and energy to go round in an ever-demanding world.

Fights can now loom on the horizon, in even the best-regulated homes and loving partnerships. It is still a fact that working women do most of the housework and childcare, even if they are employed full-time and have outside help. This can quickly create resentment and their relationship suffers as a result. Many women find they become a 'mum' to the whole family, not just the kids. I once had a patient who, when I asked how many children she had, replied, without thinking, 'Four, including John' (her partner). And she was serious. Imagine how they dealt with one another as adults and lovers, given this view.

Being out of work is a serious blow to any relationship. The one who finds themselves unemployed, especially if it's the man, suffers loss, and even true bereavement. It is still possible for a woman who loses her job legitimately to become a 'wife and mother' in the eyes of society. It's as if she had another job and source of validation waiting for her in the background, whether or not she is employed in paid work or feels it is 'enough'.

As a result, many women say they don't feel quite so badly as their man does in a similar situation because to many men, work is what they *are*. The first thing anyone asks a man is what he does for a living.

But losing income is only one of the downsides to losing our job. Work gives us something to do, keeps us in the social marketplace, confers some status, however small, and gets us out of the home. Many people who lose their job lose confidence, not just in the context of their work but perhaps even in the whole of their lives. Many people fear not only that they'll be unable to get new work but also that all this will make their partner think less of them, or even not want them. No matter how much a man's partner reassures him he is still loved and valued, his own valuation of himself can be so poor he doesn't find this comforting, or even credible. He feels less of a man and this can reverberate in the bedroom. I see many men whose impotence dates from their redundancy or retirement.

Many men also rate their freedom very highly. (See also 'Children', page 96 and 'Commitment Problems', page 101.) Going out to work gives them a lot of freedom. Even if they love their wife and family they see staying at home as restricting their freedom, as indeed it does. If such a man finds himself contributing more to family life and household duties he can feel better about himself at some level but this in no way compensates for what he has lost. Also, some women see the home as their domain and resent their man muscling in on their 'workplace'. Some couples fight over domestic details, work methods, and so on for the first time when the man is at home a lot. A very few couples use the man's loss of work to reorganize their lives so the woman becomes the breadwinner and the guy looks after the home but this is still rare today.

As with any other serious setback in a couple's life, they find themselves facing difficult emotions at the same time. Both may feel sad, angry, or afraid, but each will experience these emotions in different ways, react to them differently, and find different significance in them. Talking all this through together gently can help but it calls for lots of empathic listening because the one who has lost their job almost always sees themselves as more deserving. If one of you feels the other brought their job loss on themselves, this can make it hard to be empathic and loving. After all, it has ruined your life too.

This life challenge can be seen either as a disaster or as a way of both of you learning how to listen and grow together so that you'll not only help the one who's out of work to find something, but also facilitate your whole relationship. Many couples say that, looking back, they grew from their experience and have worked together better as a couple ever since.

Retirement brings with it almost all of the feelings associated with losing one's job that I've touched on above, but in even bigger doses. This is now not just the loss of *a* job but the loss of the ability to work at all. Add to this the common story of the man who fears spending increased amounts of time with his partner in retirement and the dangers are very obvious. Most men about to retire, or soon after retirement, tell me they fear loss of status, loneliness, having to become something their partner wants, loss of freedom, relative poverty, the loss of their workmates and friends, loss of purpose, not having a life role that means anything to them, and much more. This can be a trying time for many couples, especially those in which the woman has been looking forward to her man retiring so they can have the sort of life together she has longed for. The trouble is that in many cases this is not at all the life the man himself has been longing for.

ASK YOURSELF

▶ Does your partner really understand how you feel about your work?

▶ Does he or she understand how you feel about their work?

▶ How do you make decisions about the balance between paid work outside the home and domestic work?

▶ How would you like this process to be different?

▶ What could you personally do to improve things on this?

▶ What are your views on retirement?

▶ How would you both spend the money if you won the Lotto?

▶ What does this say about your relationship?

YOUR ACTION PLAN

What work means. Make a list of all the things work means to you. Rate each item out of five. Now repeat this exercise for what you perceive your partner's view to be on the subject. Rate his list too.

Now get your partner to do their lists and exchange views on them. What do you agree on? What do you fundamentally disagree on? Look at ways in which your life together is harmed or helped by these views. Use the lists to talk about work for each of you and how family fits into this. Use this opportunity to reassess your positions on work and no work. Whatever age you are, think about what your ideal retirement would be. It's never to soon to start planning! Seriously, even if you are in your thirties it makes sense to have some sort of life plan. Society's notions of 'retirement' are changing almost every year. You can plan as a couple, though, for how you want to manage your life in your middle years and beyond. This can be really exciting and fun to do. Let your imagination run free. At the end of this session you might want to get a bit more serious about what seems possible and what doesn't. But you may not! I could never have foreseen what I'm about to do in my 'retirement' – even our wildest dreams didn't take account of it!

Index